Swinging '73

ALSO BY MATTHEW SILVERMAN

100 Things Mets Fans Should Know and Do Before They Die

Baseball Miscellany: Everything You Always Wanted to Know about Baseball

Best Mets: Fifty Years of Highs and Lows from New York's Most Agonizingly Amazin' Team

Cubs by the Numbers (with Al Yellon and Kasey Ignarski)

Mets by the Numbers (with Jon Springer)

Mets Essential: Everything You Need to Know to Be a Real Fan

New York Mets: The Complete Illustrated History

Red Sox by the Numbers (with Bill Nowlin)

Shea Goodbye (with Keith Hernandez)

Swinging '73

BASEBALL'S WILDEST SEASON

THE INCREDIBLE YEAR THAT BASEBALL GOT
THE DESIGNATED HITTER, WIFE-SWAPPING
PITCHERS, WORLD CHAMPION A'S, AND WILLIE
MAYS SAID GOODBYE TO AMERICA

Matthew Silverman

LYONS PRESS
Guilford, Connecticut

An imprint of Globe Pequot Press

Copyright © 2013 by Matthew Silverman

Lyons Press is an imprint of Globe Pequot Press.

Text design: Sheryl P. Kober
Layout artist: Justin Marciano
Project editor: Ellen Urban

Library of Congress Cataloging-in-Publication Data is available on file.

ISBN 978-0-7627-8060-0

Printed in the United States of America

10 9 8 7 6 5 4 3 2 1

For Jan Silverman

Forgive me. It's my night, but it's your night, too. I hope you go on to win the flag for the New York people. . . . There always comes a time for someone to get out, and I look at the kids over here, the way they're playing and the way they're fighting for themselves, and it tells me one thing: "Willie, say goodbye to America."

—*Willie Mays, Shea Stadium, September 25, 1973*

Contents

Rollie Fingers throwing out the first pitch to Gene Tenace in April 2012 AUTHOR PHOTO

Prologue

REUNION

Suddenly they appear from an elevator. It's difficult to tell who they are at first, though the small gathering of media knowingly eyes them. The dozen men who step into the otherwise empty East Side Club at the Oakland Coliseum look like three foursomes on Senior Day at the local golf course, their hair a little thin or gone, some still trim but others feeling gravity's pull on their midsections. In the time that it takes for an intern to hand each of them a yellow numbered jersey, name stitched on the back, these men have instantly transformed. They are A's again.

This group isn't your run-of-the-mill collection of former ballplayers; they're the first Bay Area team to win a world championship: three years before the neighboring Golden State Warriors won their lone National Basketball Association title, four years before the Oakland Raiders captured their first National Football League title, a decade before the San Francisco 49ers won their first Super Bowl, and 38 years ahead of the first of two World Series claimed by the San Francisco Giants. Here on a sultry Friday night in April 2012, with barely a puff of wind, a smattering of TV cameras, microphones, and writers greets the A's. Meanwhile, on the other side of the Coliseum, reporters tarry in the press area, eat dinner, pound out pregame notes for the opener of an Oakland-Cleveland series that even three weeks into the season seems mundane. But there are other reasons that the reunion isn't getting all the coverage it merits.

"You have to be at least 50 years old for the [1970s] A's to mean anything," says Art Spander, who covered these A's in their prime for the *San Francisco Chronicle* and still writes about them frequently on the web. "I think that this is one of the great problems . . . there's no sense of history anymore."

"I have tried to impart on our media that would cover us that [the 1972 A's] brought the first championship in any major sport in the Bay Area," explains Bob Rose, Oakland's current public relations director and a Bay

Area native. "Trying to have people think about what it must have been like, for a franchise that had only moved to the Bay Area four years previous in a newly christened stadium . . . That four years later they won the first world championship of any sport in the Bay Area and then three years later to have a certain core of this group win their third straight—that really puts them in rarefied air."

Yet a concession by Rose gets to the heart of the deal between then and now: "I understand 'what have you done for us lately.'" And at this point in 2012, lately didn't yet include the team's strong September finish, which vaulted them over the heavily favored Texas Rangers for the AL West title. The 2012 A's, with the lowest payroll in the American League, rallied to force a deciding fifth game against the Tigers in the Division Series, but Justin Verlander shut out Oakland in the finale. Yet many minutes after the 6–0 game was over and the Tigers took their celebration into the visiting clubhouse, the Coliseum reverberated with the fans yelling over and over: "Let's go Oakland!" A chant that also happens to be the name of a group trying to keep the A's in the city they have called home since 1968.

The relationship between the ballclub and Oakland is ever changing. Even the name of the team's maligned home requires explanation. The Oakland Coliseum officially became O.co Coliseum as part of a 2011 rebranding strategy by online retailer overstock.com, which bought the stadium naming rights. The company's name change was so poorly received by consumers that the retailer backed off the name, though O.co stuck to the Coliseum—baseball's fifth oldest stadium. Unlike its elders—Fenway Park, Wrigley Field, Dodger Stadium, and Angel Stadium—the Coliseum, by any name, invokes little nostalgia for either its tenants or its patrons. The Coliseum is a home that everyone involved wants to see replaced. The new address is where viewpoints skew.

Despite their recent success, the A's of the 21st century exist in market limbo. Even as the 1972 A's marshaled their forces for the 40th reunion in Oakland, that morning's newspapers, websites, TV sound bites, and tweets burst with news of the beloved 49ers breaking ground on a new stadium in Santa Clara. The A's can only look on in envy. With their Coliseum lease set to run out after 2013, they dream of Santa Clara County, specifically San Jose, the Bay Area's largest city by all metrics, just as Charlie Finley, who brought the A's to Oakland, long dreamed of other cities before the A's vacated Kansas City after the 1967 season.

The 2012 A's were the last remaining major league team sharing a stadium with an NFL club—and sharing it in name only. When the Raiders returned in 1995 after 13 years in the bright lights of Los Angeles, Oakland prostrated itself to welcome back the prodigal team. The A's opened the 1996 season playing "home" games in a minor league park in Las Vegas that held just 10,000 people. They returned to the Bay Area to find a new football edifice, a monolith of green seats above center field, left-center, and right-center; a mass of concrete crammed with seats and suites that the A's could never expect to fill replaced the majestic view of the Oakland hills. For baseball season, four dozen custom-sized tarps cover these seats, the concealment cutting stadium capacity to the smallest figure in the majors: approximately 35,000—about 5,000 fewer than the home of the Little League World Series in Williamsport, Pennsylvania.

On those custom tarps that hide the excess of seats, the team emblazons the five retired baseball numbers from team history (three of them 1970s A's), the four Oakland World Series titles, plus the five won by the A's in Philadelphia under Connie Mack. That the Bay Area has forgotten Mack is to be expected: His last World Series title came in Philadelphia in 1930. That the Bay Area largely treats the A's as an afterthought is an ongoing story as the team fences with the Giants over territorial rights. Those issues continue to keep the A's in gritty, blue collar Oakland rather than the greener pastures of a more attractive—and lucrative—pocket of Northern California.

But East Bay officials have put together plans and studies to keep the team in the city. A group of fans calling themselves Let's Go Oakland! ran a full-page ad in the *Oakland Tribune* less than a month after the 1972 A's reunion calling on ownership to commit to the city in which they are playing and to stop denigrating it. In the team's 45 years in Oakland, the letter points out, the A's have produced five Cy Young, seven MVP, and seven Rookie of the Year winners, along with four world championships, six American League pennants, and 15 AL West titles. The only team that has more world championships in that span is the New York Yankees—and with far more cash to burn.

Not posting a winning record the six years prior to their surprising 2012 turnaround and finishing in the bottom five in major league attendance every year since 2005—including fourth from last in 2012—isn't helping Oakland's argument. That the A's have rarely stood among the top-drawing teams in baseball, even in their 1970s heyday, remains a fact of life in the

East Bay. Until their 2012 surge, the biggest news associated with the A's in recent years was *Moneyball*, a vaunted 2011 film about their success a decade ago under general manager Billy Beane, which received Academy Award nominations for Best Actor and Best Picture. Unlike the 1970s A's, the film lost.

Now with the familiar faces from the 1970s back in the Coliseum for a couple of days, these men with yellow shirts and gray hair serve as a reminder of a remarkable achievement in remarkable times. Manager Bob Melvin, in his second year on the job, makes the unexpected and classy move of lining up the current team's players on the field at the same time that the '72 A's are being honored—a show of respect that 1960s and '70s A's broadcaster Monte Moore said, "Gave me chills."

The now vintage A's had chills to spare in their heyday; 1972 heralded a three-year celebration of the only team—other than the Yankees—ever to win three consecutive titles. The 1972–74 A's dynasty stood in stark opposition to the Yankees dynasties that came before and after Oakland's famous run. Charlie Finley wooed and signed most of those A's players, whom the farm system had nurtured. Comrades in arms against both the competition and their own megalomaniacal owner, they banded together in front of the entire sports world in the wake of Finley's most outrageous and cruel stunt: the "firing" of a player, Mike Andrews, following the worst game of his life in the middle of the '73 World Series. Undaunted, Oakland rallied to claim its second championship in the dynasty by beating the New York Mets in seven suspenseful—if not always graceful—contests.

The 1973 title, the middle crown between the '72 upset of the Cincinnati Reds and the '74 stomping of the Los Angeles Dodgers, marks the difference between a team that wins two titles in three years—as achieved by several other non-Yankees clubs, including Mack's Philadelphia A's, who did it twice—and a team for all time. Three in a row defines a dynasty. As children's TV program *Schoolhouse Rock*, which also debuted that year, said so simply and eloquently on Saturday mornings in 1973, "Three, that's a magic number."

Yet as our magical year dawned, no holy trinity held sway in baseball—just the usual balls, strikes, and outs on the still relatively simple scoreboards at stadiums built for multiple purposes. Practicality determined stadium design then. Kansas City, having rinsed its mouth of Finley and starting fresh with a 1969 expansion team, opened its jewel of a ballpark in April '73. Its fraternal concrete twin, Arrowhead, gleaming across the parking lot, had opened eight months earlier with only football in mind. Royals Stadium's bursting fountains, picturesque landscaping, and clipped decks foretold of an exciting future for ballparks . . . even if the artificial turf hit 120 degrees on Missouri's sweltering summer afternoons. You expected real grass? *C'mon*, this is the '70s we're talking about!

New York's two ballparks went up when grass was what people played on, not toked. Yet those two stadiums spun in orbits as different as the teams that called them home. The Mets, four years removed from an implausible world championship that stunned and captivated the city, featured one of the game's best young pitching staffs and could match any team in a series—if only their paltry offense could muster a few runs. Passengers in cars and planes could see Shea Stadium's orange and blue metal panels for miles around. Less than 15 miles away, the Yankees, with more championships than any team in baseball—an even 20 then—had sunk to unaccustomed irrelevancy. They had become New York's other team. Their last world championship had come a decade earlier, the team's longest drought since Yankee Stadium went up half a century earlier, and now the old ballpark was coming down.

Nineteen seventy-three marked the year that shook the basic understanding of the rules both for baseball and for the presidency; the year that Vietnam ended and George Steinbrenner began his empire; that TV cameras peered into the homes of other people and called it entertainment while everyone debated White House wiretapping; that the original House That Ruth Built began its final year in the Bronx, an expensive replica in the works as if those who'd been coming to the old ball yard for half a century wouldn't notice the difference between gaudy and grand.

Just as no ballplayer from 1972 could have imagined the reception he would get in the same city in 2012, you couldn't even look from '72 and see what was coming in '73. Imagine sitting on a fastball and then getting a two-strike curveball. You can't believe the pitch is coming at you until it crosses the plate.

Strike three—and that's a magic number.

Ron Blomberg, Major League Baseball's first designated hitter

One

A WALK INTO HISTORY

The bat wound up in the Hall of Fame, and the batter didn't even put a ball in play. On April 6, 1973, the bases were loaded, two were out, and from the on-deck circle stepped a man whose seemingly limitless skill had made him the first overall draft pick in baseball.

Sherm Feller, the gravelly, invisible voice of Fenway Park, a talk radio pioneer and Top 40 songwriter, had begun his broadcasting career in 1941 as a 20-year-old at WMUR by informing the listening public of Manchester, New Hampshire, that the Japanese had bombed Pearl Harbor. Some 30 years later, Feller prepared for another historic, though far less grave, announcement to more than 30,000 people still finding their seats in Boston.

"Number 12. Ron Blomberg, designated hitter. Blomberg."

Great things were expected of Ron Blomberg. A distinguished multi-sport athlete at Druid Hills High School in Atlanta, Blomberg was offered more than 100 scholarships to play college football and basketball. John Wooden personally recruited him to play at UCLA, which had just begun its record run of seven straight NCAA basketball titles, nine of them in ten years. But when the Yankees made Blomberg the first overall pick in the 1967 amateur draft—and offered a $75,000 bonus—it was clear that his future lay on the diamond. Repeatedly taunted as a child for his Jewish faith, the Georgia-bred Yankees fan was thrilled to head north.

"The times in '67 hadn't totally changed, but it was changing a little bit," Blomberg says of his first two years in the low minors in the South, where, despite then-recent legislation, segregation and populist governors still ruled. "Lester Maddox was the governor in Georgia. George Wallace was the governor of Alabama. You'd go out to South Carolina, [and] it says, 'Welcome to Klan Country.' I grew up with all that. I did see quite a bit of problems when I was in small cities in North Carolina, Virginia, places like that because unfortunately people did not know what a Jew was. At that particular time, the only really good Jewish ballplayer was Sandy Koufax."

Blomberg debuted with the Yankees in 1969 and left the minor leagues for good in 1971, batting .322 in 199 at-bats. He received 100 more at-bats the next year and doubled his home run output to 14. His spot on the roster seemed secure heading into the 1973 season opener. Late in spring training, however, Blomberg pulled a hamstring. He didn't think much about the injury, nor did he think much about being the designated hitter—the accepted term for the new position.

Blomberg hadn't served as DH at all in spring training as the Yankees racked up more wins than any club in the 1973 exhibition season (19). Veterans like Felipe Alou and Johnny Callison seemed better served for the new role. On the flight to Boston for the season opener, 24-year-old Blomberg didn't know what to expect when word came that the manager wanted to talk to him. He figured his roster spot was safe, given that he'd hit the ball hard all spring and was on the plane. When he sat down with manager Ralph Houk and coaches Dick Howser and Elston Howard, Houk asked what he thought about being a DH. Blomberg recalled being "a little dumbfounded."

"Skipper, I don't really know much about it," he told Houk. "What do I do?"

Houk's response still applies some four decades later: "You're basically pinch-hitting for the pitcher four times in the same game."

His hamstring wasn't bad enough to put him on the disabled list but not good enough to put him in the field—"full time" as Blomberg calls it—so they asked if he was fit enough to bat against Luis Tiant in Boston. "I said absolutely because back then when you were on the disabled list you could be like a Wally Pipp and never play again."

At the Fenway Park press box back in 1973, cigar-chomping scribes talked about the new rule, whether it might work, and what it could do to the game. But the pressing thought among the writers and everyone else in Fenway wasn't so much the DH . . . it was the weather.

Dick Bresciani had left a public relations job at his alma mater, the University of Massachusetts at Amherst, to join the Red Sox as PR assistant in May 1972. The historic 1973 game was his first Opening Day in the press box. Now a vice president emeritus with the team, Bresciani quickly locates his scorecard from the 1973 opener, with the weather report he penciled in: "It was 55 degrees at game time with 20 to 25 miles an hour winds out of the northwest. It was probably colder than that as the afternoon went on. It was raw, swirling . . . it was a nasty day."

The Fenway press box had a roof but no window, leaving the overcoated reporters to gird themselves against the frigid wind. The team had just come from balmy Florida, so the contrast made it feel like midwinter on the field as shadows increasingly stole what little warmth the sun could provide. The Sox wore their traditional home whites, the Yankees their new road uniforms with white piping around both "New York" on the front and the numbers on the back—with these new duds the Yankees became the final American League holdout to ditch flannels for polyester. But every player would have traded their double-knits that afternoon for fur-lined suede jackets, like in the Marlboro Man ads. Players wore wool caps pulled over their ears and hugged hot water bottles during batting practice as they waited to take aim at the 37-foot-high, tin-plated Green Monster in left field.

Blomberg picked up his mitt to field some balls in his normal pregame routine. Coach Elston Howard shooed him away. "You're not playing first base today," Howard said. "I don't want you to hurt your hamstring any more. Come back to the cage, and keep hitting."

A seemingly harmless flyball to center field by Matty Alou should have ended the top of the first inning, but Reggie Smith lost sight of the ball, and it fell untouched. "A gift double," proclaimed Yankees announcer Bill White. Tiant walked the next two batters, costing Orlando Cepeda—a 35-year-old former MVP signed by Boston specifically to fill this newly created job—the chance of becoming baseball's first professional batter.

Blomberg's landmark at-bat might have been historic, but it wasn't memorable. Like the previous two batters, Tiant fell behind. As Rogelio Moret started throwing in the Boston bullpen, Blomberg fouled off the second pitch. He watched three more balls, tossed aside the bat, and marched to first base. Alou crossed home plate with the first run of the season. Blomberg might as well have been called the designated walker.

Tiant allowed a double to his second Alou of the inning: Matty's brother Felipe. Two more runs put the score at 3–0. Tiant finally got out of the inning when Thurman Munson, batting eighth, popped up to Carl Yastrzemski. The Yankees picked up their gloves and hit the field, Blomberg remaining behind with the pitchers and reserves. Reporters asked Blomberg, who tended to get a little antsy sitting on the bench, what he'd do while his Yankees teammates were out in the field.

"I'll probably go back in the clubhouse and eat a sandwich."

It was at least healthier than White Sox DH Dick Allen's regimen between at-bats: "You smoke cigarette after cigarette, drink 19 cups of coffee. Get your heart beating again, hit again, sit back down."

Orlando Cepeda struck out in his first at-bat as DH (taking an 0-for-6 collar even as the Red Sox pounded out 20 hits). Blomberg became the first designated hitter to land a hit, singling in the top of the third. By then, the Red Sox had taken the lead against Mel Stottlemyre on their way to a 15–5 win, the most runs the Yankees have ever allowed on Opening Day.

History, however, remembers the Yankees and Blomberg. Yet if not for a high fly that dropped in on a blustery day, Cepeda, the future Hall of Famer known as the "Baby Bull," might also be known as the first DH. "It would have definitely had a different spin," considers Bresciani, official Red Sox historian. "Blomberg would have been more forgotten. In everything you read, Cepeda would have been the official, the first DH to ever bat. . . . He was the DH of the year while Blomberg kind of faded away as the DH."

The next day, Cepeda collected two sacrifice flies, but he was still hitless in his new position when he came to bat in the bottom of the ninth in the series finale on Sunday afternoon, minutes after the Red Sox had botched a potential game-ending double play that let the Yankees tie the score. Cepeda faced southpaw Sparky Lyle, a homegrown Red Sox reliever shipped to the Yankees in 1971 for Danny Cater, another lopsided trade in the ongoing appropriation of Boston property by the Yankees that dated back to Babe Ruth five decades earlier. But Cepeda cleared the Green Monster and won the game. For the Red Sox, denied a division title on the final weekend in 1972, sweeping the Yankees to open 1973 made for a fantastic start.

For New York, it made for an inauspicious beginning to the Steinbrenner regime.

⚾ ⚾ ⚾

The other American League openers that day followed the lead of the game in Boston: all one-sided. In Baltimore, the Orioles and Brewers lost out on making designated history due to a starting time 40 minutes behind the first pitch in Boston. Inaugural DH duties at Memorial Stadium arrived with little fanfare and little result: Milwaukee's Ollie Brown went hitless, and both hits by Baltimore DH Terry Crowley came after the Orioles had built a huge lead on the way to a 10–0 shutout by Dave McNally. Whitey Herzog's managing debut would have to wait since the Rangers and White Sox were washed out in Texas. Out in Anaheim, the Royals and Angels made uninspired inaugural DH selections with Ed Kirkpatrick and Tom McCraw respectively. Kirkpatrick could play all three outfield positions, catch, and man first base, yet his bat—.238 career average and only once driving in more than 50 runs over his first dozen seasons—wasn't why the new position had been created; he went 0 for 3 in his DH debut. Ironically, new Royals acquisition Hal McRae, later the first three-time winner of the Outstanding Designated Hitter Award, started Opening Day 1973 in right field for Kansas City.

The Royals-Angels game provided the first manipulation of the new rule. Angels manager Bobby Winkles, a stellar skipper at Arizona State with three national championships, became the first manager plucked directly from the collegiate ranks to the big leagues since Hugo Bezdek with the 1917 Pittsburgh Pirates. Winkles made an eighth-inning decision to remove left fielder Frank Robinson for pinch runner Rudy Meoli. Winkles then inserted McCraw into left field—meaning that by the new rules the Angels forfeited the DH spot. So Nolan Ryan had to be inserted into the lineup, batting cleanup, the first pitcher returned to the batting order in the designated hitter era. Since the Royals were retired to complete the Angels' 3–2 win, Ryan—a .134 career hitter at that point—didn't have to bat. Ten AL pitchers stepped to the plate in 1973, most by accident, batting a composite .200.

The flags were flying high up the coast in Oakland—not in honor of the DH, though owner Charlie O. Finley had long been a proponent of the concept. A massive green flag with gold lettering measuring 15 by 37 feet soared to honor the team's seven-game World Series victory over Cincinnati the previous October. Just five years after escaping Kansas City, the A's were playing in picturesque Northern California in a new stadium with expansive foul territory that turned should-be souvenirs into easy outs—a delight to Oakland's talented pitching staff. For the first time since 1930, two franchise moves ago, the A's were champions. So what could be wrong?

Johnny Carson, that's what.

Despite the colorful uniforms, wacky nicknames, facial hair, and find-a-way-to-win mentality, the team's triumph in a thrilling World Series had caused little more than a collective shrug in the national media. Gene Tenace, who'd won the starting catching job late in the 1972 season, hit five home runs all year—then collected four in the World Series. He had an unprecedented two homers in his first two World Series at-bats and drove in nine of Oakland's 16 runs in the World Series against the Reds. He also broke Babe Ruth's mark for slugging percentage in a series with a .913 mark and pulled off one of the great fakes in baseball history by putting out his arm for an intentional walk on a 3-2 pitch and then jumping back into his crouch for strike three against a stunned Johnny Bench. Tenace figured his phone would ring all winter.

"No one ever called," he lamented in March '73. "Not even in Oakland. And it wasn't just me who was left out. None of the A's got asked to do much of anything. Here we are the world champs, and no one pays attention. I don't know, maybe the people in Oakland don't deserve a champion. I know I expected more. Carson's only down there in Los Angeles. I would love to have been on his show."

The Tonight Show's guest list for that period includes everyone from clean-cut Pat Boone, funnyman Rodney Dangerfield, and giggly Charles Nelson Reilly to resonant-voiced Lorne Greene, sultry Suzanne Pleshette, and spooky Vincent Price. To salt the wound for Tenace, New York Jets quarterback Joe Namath made a guest host appearance a few weeks after the A's won the world championship—and taped in Los Angeles two days before Namath beat Archie Manning's Saints on the other side of the country. Johnny Carson's set was glaringly A-less.

Perhaps Carson and the media in general were skittish about inviting the young, long-haired, mustachioed A's into the national spotlight that was still considered the domain of the conservative older set. Maybe baseball players—especially lower-profile players from an outer burg like Oakland—weren't deemed worth bringing out compared to the Carson-approved Namath, boxers Muhammad Ali, George Foreman, and Joe Frazier, or motorcycle daredevil Evel Knievel. Whatever the booking agents' reasoning, they missed interesting guests like Oakland's colorfully named and phenomenally talented rotation front men, Catfish Hunter and Vida Blue; or third starter Ken Holtzman, who stood second all-time to Sandy Koufax for most wins by a Jewish pitcher (93 through '72). Left fielder Joe Rudi finished second to White Sox slugger Dick Allen for league MVP (the only Oakland team member to land in the top 10 for the award). Rudi's remarkable leaping ninth-inning catch against the wall in Cincinnati saved Game Two of the World Series, but no one cared when it came to national press or endorsements. Rudi admits that he and many A's made enough local "banquet circuit" appearances that winter to slow the team down a little the next spring.

Team captain Sal Bando, 29, got one of the few gigs—a regular 90-second sports commentary on San Francisco radio station KYA. Bando's ghostwriter was then–TV sportscaster Steve Somers, three years his junior. "He didn't want the humor," recalls Somers, a San Francisco native who became famous for his amusing monologues on WFAN in New York City. "I tried with the metaphors and the puns, like what you could get away with, and he would erase them. But he wanted it to be straight, like you're writing a newspaper article."

Rollie Fingers's Snidely Whiplash handlebar mustache—which he devilishly twisted and tugged as he retired 30 of 39 Reds whom he faced during the 1972 World Series—went unnoticed by the media once the series ended. Even gregarious slugger Reggie Jackson had trouble finding a microphone beyond the normal beat writers covering the team. As for Bert Campaneris, the A's All-Star shortstop, he wasn't even in the lineup when it came time to raise the championship flag in Oakland on Opening Day in 1973.

Campaneris began the '73 season serving a five-game suspension. In a career that saw him play all nine positions in one game, lead the league in steals six times, and collect more hits than any player in A's history, he will always be the player who threw a bat at an opponent on national TV during the 1972 playoffs.

With the A's up one game to none over Detroit in the best-of-five '72 American League Championship Series, and leading Game Two by a score of 5–0 in the seventh inning, Tigers reliever Lerrin LaGrow hit Campaneris in the left ankle. Campy, having a 3-for-3 day with 2 steals and 11 chances handled cleanly in the series, didn't pause. He got to his feet, reared back, and hurled the bat at LaGrow with the accuracy and speed of an All-Star shortstop. Luckily LaGrow ducked in time.

A beanball episode had taken place between the clubs earlier that summer, and, with all eyes trained on him in the ALCS, Campaneris simply snapped. "In that moment you don't think about it," he says four decades later. "It hit [me]. I throw the bat. It almost cost me going to the World Series." As Detroit's catcher tells it four decades later, Campy should have been infuriated.

"So the reality was, the perception, that we wanted Bert to know that we respected his legs," says Duke Sims, catcher for the Tigers that October afternoon in 1972. "The ball didn't actually get away from him. I called a breaking ball, but the plan was to actually hit him in the leg. It turned out that Lerrin was good at it—he hit him right in the ankle bone. That thing probably hurts the [worst], which is why Bert probably threw the bat. That's what needed to be done to get him out of the series. So it was premeditated, yeah. Then Bert knew it was. It wasn't one that actually got away. We were trying to go to the World Series. That was the plan at the time."

Both Campaneris and LaGrow were ejected from the game. Incensed Tigers manager Billy Martin, whose orders instigated the incident, tried to get at the A's shortstop three times in the wake of the bat throwing, without luck. Campaneris was fined $500 and suspended for the rest of the ALCS by American League president Joe Cronin.

The 1972 World Series began in Cincinnati with an odd sight: Campaneris in the batter's box. On October 13, 1972, one day after the ALCS ended and five days after Campaneris had thrown the bat, commissioner Bowie Kuhn announced that Campaneris would be allowed to play in the World Series. Kuhn cited the precedent of Yankees shortstop Frank Crosetti, suspended for 30 days because of an altercation with an umpire late in the 1942 season. Rather than suspend Crosetti through the World Series—and hurt his league's chances of winning the title—AL president Will Harridge had decided that the suspension would commence at the start of the 1943 season.

Kuhn initially told Cronin that he thought Campaneris should be suspended longer than just through the end of the ALCS. "Be my guest," the AL president replied. But Kuhn the lawyer sought precedent to appease himself as a judge. He suspended Campaneris for the first five games of the 1973 season but not a single inning in the '72 World Series—a slap on the wrist for launching a bat at a man's head.

Underlying reasons justified postponing Campy's punishment. Because Reggie Jackson tore his hamstring stealing home with the tying run in Game Five of the ALCS, baseball—and NBC—ran the risk of a potential World Series slaughter. The favored Big Red Machine with a legendary lineup featuring Pete Rose, Joe Morgan, Johnny Bench, and Tony Perez having home-field advantage against an Oakland club missing its catalyst at the top of the order *and* its cleanup hitter? Yeesh. Jackson's injury left Oakland no choice but to play second-year center fielder George Hendrick, a .182 hitter in '72. Now add Dal Maxvill, a .220 hitter with six home runs and seven steals in 1,232 career games, as the starting shortstop? In the World Series? Campy played.

The A's, who'd lost twice after the bat-throwing incident, were lucky to escape hostile Detroit with a 2–1 win in deciding Game Five of the ALCS. In the first World Series by the A's in 41 years, Campaneris had more plate appearances than any player on either team in the 1972 Fall Classic. Though he batted just .229, his presence proved crucial in the defense-minded World Series. His only run scored turned out to be the decisive run of Oakland's 3–2 win in Game Seven. Campy led the singing in the victorious locker room as the A's roared on.

Now as the 1973 season commenced, Campaneris said little about the suspension. Who would? Not owner Charlie Finley, manager Dick Williams, Campaneris's teammates, or the 38,000-plus fans who welcomed the team to Oakland Coliseum for the first time since the A's clinched Game Seven in Cincinnati. The only appropriate words from anyone in Oakland would have been a simple "thank you."

Taking Campy's place in the leadoff spot to open 1973 was new acquisition Bill North, the club's first designated hitter. With Matty Alou traded to the Yankees, North was a cheaper, faster, younger alternative. Rick Monday, sent from Oakland to the Cubs for Ken Holtzman a year earlier, had occupied North's preferred position of center field in Chicago, so the Cubs miscast North as a right fielder in 1972. In Oakland, you might say that the speedy North was equally out of place as a DH to begin 1973. The "position" was created seemingly for older, slower, more powerful hitters—big-name sluggers who couldn't run any more but still drew crowds. North was the first DH to bat in the leadoff spot.

North reached on an error in his first Oakland at-bat. By that time, however, Tony Oliva—a perfect fit for designated hitter given his three batting titles and repeated leg injuries—had become the first DH to hit a home run. His two-run shot in the first against Catfish Hunter put a damper on Oakland's flag-raising. The Twins cruised to an 8–3 win and swept the world champs to open the 1973 season. By the time the reinstated Campaneris had a game under his belt, the A's were 1–5 and in last place. The mighty were falling.

⚾ ⚾ ⚾

The temperature in New York didn't get out of the 40s all day. The clear, cold afternoon kept the Opening Day Mets-Phillies crowd to just 27,326. The weather could have been worse—and soon was. The game two days later was called due to snow.

Among the dignitaries on hand at Shea Stadium for the Friday afternoon opener were 11 recently released American prisoners of war from Vietnam. Each man had spent at least six years in captivity, but they livened up what could have been a downer moment by pelting catcher Duffy Dyer with 11 baseballs simultaneously. He used a bucket instead of a glove.

In the first row, next to the home dugout, sat New York Mayor John Lindsay. It was the final year of his second term in office. He'd all but been counted out of the mayoral race in 1969, yet he won the election as a third-party candidate. Treading on the coattails of the unlikely Mets championship euphoria of '69 (Mets Jerry Grote and Rod Gaspar dousing hizzoner with locker room champagne in front of eager cameras), Lindsay pulled off a political miracle. While the middle class tuned him out, the wealthier precincts liked him. But it was the minority vote that had played the deciding role in the 1969 election. NBC estimated that 85 percent of blacks and 63 percent of Puerto Ricans voted for him in 1969. The off-putting conservatism of Democratic opponent Mario Procaccino resulted in a third-place finish, but Procaccino siphoned enough support (20 percent) to doom Republican John Marchi, who had beaten Lindsay in the Republican primary. Lindsay's predecessor, Robert F. Wagner, who'd lost the '69 Democratic primary to Procaccino, summed up the voting options: "Lindsay is the least of three evils. You have to vote for somebody." Lindsay won by a larger margin than he had four years earlier.

Sitting in a faded yellow wooden seat at Shea in April 1973, the mayor couldn't hope for another reprieve from voters, and not even another Mets miracle could save his foundering career. The Republican turned Liberal turned Democrat (the latter switch in 1971) had sought the presidential nomination in '72 but dropped out after a dreadful showing in the Florida primary. It had taken a special preview of the new Stephen Sondheim musical *A Little Night Music* to retire his $200,000 debt from the failed presidential run. The $2 to $13 preview tickets at the Schubert Theater were resold to Lindsay's remaining well-heeled friends at prices ranging from $20 to $500. *A Little Night Music* racked up 601 Broadway performances and won the Tony Award for best musical—a far better showing than Lindsay had in 1973. Fewer than three weeks after he'd bought out the theater, Lindsay threw in the towel and announced he wouldn't seek a third term as mayor.

Lindsay's career had sputtered and crashed amid ineffectual leadership and divisive scenes such as the 1970 Hard Hat Riot involving World Trade Center construction workers, students, police, and even bankers in a demonstration following the shooting of protesting students at Kent State University in Ohio. With no support from either major party in the city council, with an acrimonious relationship with the state legislature in Albany, and a recurring diatribe between the mayor and Governor Nelson Rockefeller, Lindsay's second term was doomed. His goals, not to mention his legacy, grew tarnished from the severe social and economic problems the city encountered during, in Rockefeller's words, Lindsay's "inept and extravagant administration." Like a pitcher who can't get anyone out yet retains his spot in the rotation, the mayor declined to be introduced at Shea for his last Opening Day in office. He endured the jeers from those among the crowd inclined to boo him on sight. Then he watched the ballgame—and a good one at that.

Tom Seaver, who had started every Mets opener since 1968, faced Steve Carlton, who'd stepped out of Bob Gibson's shadow in St. Louis and become a star in Philadelphia. Seaver and Carlton were the best righty and lefty pitchers in the National League, respectively, over the next decade. The pair of aces combined for seven Cy Young Awards, 640 wins, and 7,776 strikeouts in their careers. Both men easily walked into the Hall of Fame on the first try. But all anyone could really know about these two on April 6, 1973, was that they were both just 28 years old (Seaver five weeks younger than Carlton), both coming off 20-win seasons, and each owned a World Series ring as well as a Cy Young plaque.

Carlton had become one of the league's top pitchers seemingly overnight, going 27-10 with a 1.97 ERA and 310 strikeouts in 1972, stats made even more remarkable given that he did it for the 97-loss Phillies following a straight-up trade for Rick Wise the previous winter with the Cardinals. Seaver's star, on the other hand, had climbed steadily since winning 16 games for the last-place Mets in his first year in 1967. Even as a rookie it was clear that Seaver belonged in the locker room at that year's All-Star Game in Anaheim, a feeling not shared by past Mets All-Stars—they of the "every team needs a representative" variety. Seaver became close friends with Jerry Koosman, the club's rookie sensation of 1968. Seaver also befriended another raw, rocket-throwing Mets rookie named Nolan Ryan. Then in 1969, with the building blocks of a legendary pitching staff in place, Seaver won 25 games, a World Series, and a Cy Young while still just 24. He transcended the sport, his face instantly appearing everywhere and on everything. "The Comfort Shirt from Sears," claimed an advertisement for a polyester blend short-sleeved shirt, "keeps Tom Seaver as comfortable off the diamond as he is on."

By 1972, Seaver had maintained his high level of personal achievement, but his team had become, well, just another team. On April 2, 1972, the Mets endured the tragic and sudden passing of manager Gil Hodges. Not only was Hodges the team's stern, silent, successful manager, but he served as a father figure to many players on the young club. Yogi Berra, a longtime Mets coach and one of the most familiar faces and names in New York sports, took over the reins. After the best start in team history, the Mets sank to third place in August 1972 and stayed there, the same place they'd finished each year since their 1969 world championship.

The Mets wanted a clean start in 1973, with the expectations that come every Opening Day. Starting Seaver on the mound never hurt those expectations. He held the Phillies hitless into the fourth inning of the opener. After Willie Montanez got Philly's first hit, Duffy Dyer promptly threw him out stealing. Felix Millan, acquired from Atlanta over the winter, collected his first hit as a Met, a double to start the home fourth. After the next two batters failed to budge the runner, Cleon Jones homered.

The Phillies got the tying run on base four times, but Seaver held firm. Jones hit his second home run off Carlton, making it 3–0 in the seventh. (Carlton went the other way in '73, following his 27-win breakout with a 20-loss breakdown for the 71–91 Phillies.)

With two on and two out in the top of the eighth, and with a left-handed hitter scheduled up, Berra made his first of 194 calls to the bullpen that year, summoning workhorse Tug McGraw. Converted to a reliever by Gil Hodges in 1969, the left-handed McGraw had amassed 162 appearances over the past three seasons, saving a club-record 27 games in '72. Yogi's move prompted a counter move in the Phillies dugout.

Danny Ozark had never made the majors as a player but spent eight years as a manager in the Dodgers' minor league chain. Finally reaching the big leagues as part of Walter Alston's coaching staff in Los Angeles in 1965, Ozark gained a reputation as a solid baseball man known for getting crossed up when trying to be glib—the best example: "Even Napoleon had his Watergate." Yogi certainly had his share of malapropisms, but Berra—never considered a great tactician—managed to force the 50-year-old rookie skipper (two years Berra's senior) into a difficult decision on his first day as a major league manager. Should Ozark stick with left-handed Montanez, his third-place hitter and arguably best bat? Or should Ozark go with an experienced righty-swinging pinch hitter against southpaw McGraw? Montanez had gone 2 for 10 to that point in his career against McGraw, including a double-play grounder in the first game of a September 1972 doubleheader, and then flying out with two on to end the second game that day.

Ozark went straight to "The Book," an imaginary tome of stratagems apparently delivered from Mount Olympus to Connie Mack in the mists of the 19th century. "The Book" said that, when in doubt, go with your best righty pinch hitter when facing a tough lefty—so he did. Deron Johnson, seven years Montanez's senior, his last 30-homer year in 1965 (whereas Montanez had reached 30 home runs as a rookie in 1971), stepped out of the Philadelphia dugout. In a fast-moving game barely 90 minutes old, here came the moment of intrigue.

No manager save Baltimore's Earl Weaver had any kind of reports available on pitcher-batter matchups in 1973, and most managers wouldn't have known what to do with such information. Nor, more important, did they want any part of such numbers—even if a notebook filled with statistics for this *exact* situation had sat open on a stool next to the bat rack. Managers went by feel, the old gut instinct. So Berra's gut wouldn't have known that Montanez—despite a hit and a walk in this game—was only 4 for 22 (.182) in his career against Seaver to that point. Or maybe Ozark should have realized that McGraw's patented screwball bored down and in on righties, making them easier prey for the southpaw than left-handed swingers by almost a 2-to-1 margin (.169 batting average for righties against .323 for lefties versus McGraw in 1972). But the dice hung in mid-air. The result? Pop up to third base, three Phillies righties retired by McGraw in the ninth, game over, the house won.

There's something to be said for having a man in your dugout with 27 years of winning major league experience, who called almost 1,700 games behind the plate, who communicated flawlessly in Stengelese with the great Casey Stengel, and who now made his own calls in his own language. Seat of the pants was the official style at Shea Stadium, and it served Berra's club all year, a roller coaster ready to ride the manager out of town one minute and then deliver him deep into October the next. Maybe the guy operating the Shea scoreboard knew something, too. As the club prepared for the season's opening pitch, the big board in right-center read: "Welcome home, Yogi. We hope you've got a pocketful of 1969 miracles for the Mets' fans in 1973."

Fritz Peterson lets a ball fly. NATIONAL BASEBALL HALL OF FAME LIBRARY, COOPERSTOWN, NY

Two

"Matter of Fact, It's All Dark"

*I*t didn't matter if you found yourself in a hippie commune getting high or in the California Governor's Mansion turning over cards with Nancy Reagan—in 1973, astrology was in. People looked to the skies to make sense of it all, and the first thing a neophyte astrologer or buzzed teenager generally spotted in the clear night sky was the moon.

Just four years had passed since Neil Armstrong had set his bootprint into it, but five more manned moon landings had occurred, the last taking place on December 11, 1972. The novelty of a man stepping foot—or even swinging a golf club—on the moon had worn off for some. Elvis Presley, in his own orbit, circled the globe in his 1973 "Aloha from Hawaii" concert via the earth-shattering phenomenon of satellite TV. The broadcast was reportedly watched by more people than Armstrong's historic first steps on the moon four years earlier—that report emanating from Presley promoter Colonel Tom Parker. Yet even as white-jumpsuited Elvis hit the Honolulu stage to the same instrumental that opened Stanley Kubrick's *2001: A Space Odyssey*, the Richard Strauss classical composition *Also sprach Zarathustra*, lunar allusions persisted on earth.

Paper Moon, the Peter Bogdanovich comedy starring father-and-daughter tandem Ryan and Tatum O'Neal, ranked among 1973's biggest screen hits. A tale of a flimflam family selling Bibles door to door in the Midwest during the Depression, *Paper Moon* earned Tatum O'Neal an Academy Award for best supporting actress at the ripe old age of 10, making her the youngest actor ever to win an Oscar (a distinction she still holds).

The best-selling concept album of all time, *The Dark Side of the Moon*, also appeared in spring 1973, rocketing Pink Floyd from acquired taste to musical gods overnight. The tour that followed included a first set with meandering early songs like the sinister "Careful with That Axe, Eugene" and a 23-minute psychedelic excursion called "Echoes." The second set featured an album that remained on *Billboard* magazine's top 200 for an unprecedented 591 consecutive weeks—or 11 years and four months. *The*

Dark Side of the Moon LP, with its now iconic cover image of light refracting through a prism, included stickers as well as posters that became de rigueur for teen room decoration for a decade and beyond. One poster featured members of the band in concert, the other an infrared image of the pyramids at Giza. All the better to behold while pondering the societal perils of time, money, war, isolation, and insanity—or simply contemplating one's navel.

The album begins with a faint heartbeat growing louder, its songs bridged with instrumentals and stereophonic sound effects and voices. After 43 minutes of cutting edge synthesizers, percussion, and guitar, fueled by the despairing yet captivating lyrics of bassist Roger Waters and the languid voice of David Gilmour, the album ends with the same heartbeat from which it began. As the pulse grows fainter, the Floydian trance concludes with two lines culled from interviews taped during the recording sessions at Abbey Road Studios in London, spoken in the timbered brogue of the building's Irish doorman, Jerry Driscoll: "There is no dark side of the moon, really. . . . Matter of fact, it's all dark."

While *The Dark Side of the Moon* was blowing kids' minds at home and in auditoriums around the world, many parents feared Korean industrialist turned evangelist Reverend Sun Myung Moon far more than the hypnotic tunes gliding over the waves on recently christened FM radio stations, hi-fi turntables, or eight-track players. The Unification Church, started by Moon in Korea in the late 1950s, had spread to all 50 states by 1973. That year the "Moonies" opened their international headquarters in Tarrytown, New York, near iconic 19th-century author Washington Irving's home and not far from a corridor of corporate headquarters in Westchester County known as the Platinum Mile, which hosted several of the country's largest corporations, including IBM, Pepsi, and General Foods—all of which had fled Manhattan in recent years. The Moonies had hit mainstream America.

Stories of the rapidly growing religion's mind-control techniques on impressionable young followers frightened parents, who believed that cults were coming for their children. Mass marriages at sports stadiums and international proselytizing still stood a couple of years away, but the Moonies took politics very seriously. The vehemently anti-Communist Reverend Moon supported Richard Nixon and ordered his followers to attend anti-Nixon rallies as counterdemonstrators. Plenty of opportunities to show that kind of support presented themselves.

A Moon less frightening—save for hotel managers—also rolled up on American shores in 1973. At age 27, Keith Moon, The Who's drummer, already had a reputation for destroying musical equipment onstage and hotel rooms after hours that matched his status as the premier percussionist of the stadium rock era. Transformed from a hard-working if underappreciated British band into megastars with the 1969 release of the album *Tommy*, The Who hit the States in 1973 to tour in support of *Quadrophenia*, another conceptual double LP, this one more autobiographical, focusing on the band's early roots in Mod-mad Brighton of the early 1960s. On the first night of the American leg of the *Quadrophenia* tour, Moon drank brandy spiked with animal tranquilizers just as the warm-up band, Lynyrd Skynyrd, finished their set at the Cow Palace in San Francisco—or so the story goes. Whatever was in his system and however it got there, Moon lasted barely an hour onstage before collapsing midway through "Won't Get Fooled Again." Roadies carried him backstage.

"He's out cold," guitarist Pete Townshend confessed to the crowd, adding that the band would try to revive him by punching him in the stomach and giving him an enema. After a 15-minute break, roadies dragged Moon back on stage, where he took up the drumsticks to start "Magic Bus." But he passed out a minute later, prompting Townshend to address the audience in search of a replacement. "Can anybody play the drums?—I mean somebody good." Nineteen-year-old Scot Halpin of Muscatine, Iowa, who had recently moved to Monterey, California, stepped out of the audience and into history. He played three numbers—all simulcast on the radio in San Jose, San Francisco, and Sacramento. The three still upright members of the band ditched the Cow Palace shortly after the impromptu jam session ended. Halpin was left with a tour jacket, which was promptly stolen, and all the post-gig buffet food he could eat. Moon lay passed out for 10 hours straight at his suite at the St. Francis Hotel—the establishment safe, for a night, from the untamed drummer.

Far from the revolutionary revelry and irreverence of movies, music, and religion came the square who would save New York sports. He certainly didn't seem like a savior at first, publicly playing down the coup he had been planning for most of his adult life, but George Steinbrenner III stood ready when the spotlight beckoned.

Born into a shipping dynasty, Steinbrenner dreamed of running a sporting empire. But before he became the omnipotent team owner in New York, he learned in his Ohio hometown that sports could be cruel. In 1961, the then 31-year-old Steinbrenner headed the owners group of the Cleveland Pipers from the long-forgotten American Basketball League. The ABL brought the wider free-throw lane and the three-point shot to basketball, and Steinbrenner himself innovated as well, hiring whom many consider the first black head coach in any major professional sport (though he never hired a black manager during his more than three decades running the Yankees). John McLendon, who developed the fast break while mentoring under the game's founder, James Naismith, at the University of Kansas, became the first coach to bristle at Steinbrenner's interference and intimidation. McLendon resigned as Pipers coach midway through the 1961–62 season as the owner defended himself in the press, saying, "The players don't hate me, as he would have everyone believe." Steinbrenner hoped to rebound with a big splash, signing former Boston Celtics star Bill Sharman as coach.

But the splash made barely a ripple in the puddle, and Steinbrenner soon was drowning in debt. Even after Sharman led the Pipers to what would be the only ABL title, the club's foundering finances short-circuited a deal that could have landed Steinbrenner as an owner in the established National Basketball Association. He asked his father to loan him the money for the $400,000 NBA expansion fee. Henry Steinbrenner, despite having been a world-class hurdler in the 1920s, thought professional sports distracted his son from the family shipping business and refused to lend him the money. George Steinbrenner had been a graduate assistant to legendary football coach Woody Hayes while studying at Ohio State and then served as an assistant coach at both Northwestern and Purdue in the 1950s, but he now put basketball on the shelf, working diligently not only to expand his family's business but also to work off his debts for his Pipers dream.

He purchased a controlling interest in Kinsman Marine, the Great Lakes shipping company that his family had owned since the turn of the century, expanding the business. He arranged to purchase American Shipping Company and took over as chairman and chief operating officer. Yet Steinbrenner, now past 40, still had his eyes on the sports world. In 1971, just a year before the Yankees became available, Steinbrenner thought he had purchased his hometown Cleveland Indians . . . only to be turned away at the 11th hour by a drunk frozen-food mogul, who changed his mind after word of the sale leaked to the press. Steinbrenner thought the handshake on the $8.6 million purchase sealed the deal, the press on its way to AmShip's offices in Cleveland, but the biting, slurred words of Vernon Stouffer ended Steinbrenner's dream of owning his hometown team. "I won't be pressured," Stouffer said. "I'm not selling to you."

On January 3, 1973, the first Wednesday of the new year, the man who would be Boss made his move. Though, to be clear, this George Steinbrenner stood a far cry from the man whom the sports world came to know and love—and hate. This fifth-generation shipping magnate stood at the podium and introduced himself to people who neither knew nor cared about the Great Lakes shipping business. The 42-year-old son of Cleveland now owned the New York Yankees, one of the most significant yet underutilized brands in American sports at the time.

⚾ ⚾ ⚾

The end of the tumultuous 1960s had turned the establishment on its ear, forcing those who long had been calling the shots to take serious note of the new competition. Like many other businesses, the sports scene had changed significantly. The biggest pro team in the country at the time, the unde-feated Super Bowl–bound Miami Dolphins, hadn't even existed seven years earlier. Expansion had changed the sports landscape, bringing new teams to cities longing for a taste of the big-time while also adding competition to cities with established franchises. The New York Mets and Joe Namath's Jets played in a stadium built for the space age, bringing championship trophies to Shea Stadium during 1969. The Yankees won their last World Series title in 1962, the year the Mets were born. The Yankees won two more successive pennants, but 1963 marked the last time the Yankees would outdraw the Mets for 13 years.

The Yankees were black and white compared to the Technicolor Mets. Perhaps at no time since 1923—the Yankees' first world championship in the inaugural year of Yankee Stadium—had the team's history made *less* of an impression. In 1973, for the Yanks, history wasn't what it used to be.

And CBS knew it. The network had bought high in 1964, purchasing the team just as the Yankees dynasty was drawing to a close—a surprise to everyone involved. William S. Paley, legendary chairman of CBS, had agreed to the $13.2 million purchase as a way of extending the network's holdings not just of a team but a brand and not just any brand: the top brand in the top market. It made perfect sense . . . if the Yankees had still been the Yankees. They looked like Yankees and dressed like Yankees and played in the same stadium as Ruth, Gehrig, and DiMaggio, but the CBS Yankees were hollow. Mickey Mantle was still productive, but he had become a shell of the former Triple Crown slugger and national idol. The team's farm sys-tem had gone bone dry. The kids they promoted as next in the great line of succession didn't live up to their own billing. The advent of the major league draft in 1965 had prevented the Yankees from signing players simply impressed by the team's crisp pinstriped uniforms appearing on television every October.

The constant, Ralph Houk, was breaking in as a major league manager with the M&M Boys as Roger Maris and Mantle lit up the Bronx sky with a barrage of homers, not to mention another world championship, in 1961. They beat San Francisco for the series title in 1962, and, after a surprising sweep by the Koufax Dodgers in 1963, Houk had left the dugout to take control as general manager. But Houk failed to see the change coming. When Houk began his second tour of duty as manager in 1966, he had to live with this lack of foresight. So did CBS.

By September 12, 1972, the Yankees had pulled to within half a game of first place. But a lot of it was window dressing. The Orioles, who still had the league's best pitching staff, had a down year after three straight pennants, and the Tigers and Red Sox took the race to the wire while the Yankees, who'd been just half a game out on Labor Day, watched the finish from too respectable a distance, embarrassingly dropping the last five games of the year at home to bottom feeders Cleveland and Milwaukee. Fans were not amused. The Yankees drew under one million fans for the first time since World War II. Due to the team's third straight winning season and their respectable final standing of 6 ½ games behind the Tigers, however, the CBS brain trust felt the network could sell the team and still maintain dignity. They almost pulled it off, too.

When Vernon Stouffer had changed his mind about selling the Indians in 1971, Steinbrenner called the man who had tried to make the deal happen, longtime Cleveland GM Gabe Paul, to tell him to be in touch if he heard of another team up for sale. Less than a year later, they were discussing Steinbrenner purchasing the Yankees. He was not alone. Among the more than a dozen investors, heavy hitters included John DeLorean, the future eponymous stainless steel car maker but then vice president of General Motors; Henry Bunker Hunt, horse breeder and brother of American Football League founder and Kansas City Chiefs owner Lamar Hunt; and James M. Nederlander, famed Broadway producer and owner of nine theaters. Steinbrenner's controlling 11 percent stake personally cost him a reported $168,000. It wasn't exactly the Dutch buying Manhattan from the Lenape for 60 guilders in 1626, but by 1970s standards buying the Yankees for $10 million—or $8.8 million after the city bought back the parking garages that CBS had included in the deal—was an absolute steal.

Or in the words of Steinbrenner himself: "The best buy in sports today. I think it's a bargain."

Part of the reason Paley had assented to the sale was that Michael Burke, a loyal CBS employee going his own way by staying with the Yankees, was part of the package. As president of the Yankees, Burke had put together the deal to renovate Yankee Stadium, to commence after the '73 season. With Steinbrenner purchasing a storied team with a stadium renovation deal already in place *and* the previous owner selling at a loss, the one word that proud Paley didn't want to hear was "bargain." Which, of course, is exactly what Steinbrenner called it. Burke later wrote that "Paley held me responsible for Steinbrenner's boast and felt I had not been faithful to his request."

More admired, debonair, and modern than Steinbrenner—despite being 14 years older than the brash new owner—Burke became the first of many Yankees officials tossed under the wheels because of something Steinbrenner said. Yet disrespecting CBS and Burke wasn't the most memorable utterance from the new owner's opening press conference. Three sentences came out again and again, living on long after Steinbrenner, Burke, Paley, and even the reconstructed Yankee Stadium had all been laid to rest: "We plan absentee ownership as far as running the Yankees. We're not going to pretend we're something we aren't. I'll stick to building ships."

Steinbrenner had to wait until June to be approved by the other major league owners officially, and he did spend his first winter as owner somewhat removed from his prized possession. But his first week of spring training made him feel about as comfortable as if Keith Moon—or even Sun Myung Moon—had just checked into the hotel room next door for spring break in Fort Lauderdale.

⚾ ⚾ ⚾

Fritz Peterson was the Yanks' class clown. The prototypical flaky lefty, Peterson sent teammates letters from Gulden's Mustard saying that they were wanted for a big-time commercial, then got the whole clubhouse to watch as the ballplayer—in this case, light-hitting, forever-yapping infielder Jerry Kenney—strutted around thinking he'd hit it big. Even the players in on one practical joke weren't immune from other Peterson pranks. He had a stewardess hand out a clipboard with a form about Yankees being paid to take their wives on a tour of Japan—in this case, longtime teammates Roy White and Horace Clarke were the dupes. Peterson especially enjoyed tormenting his catcher, Thurman Munson, sending him things he didn't order and changing orders he'd actually made.

When southpaw Mike Kekich came up to the Yankees in 1969, he gravitated to the Yankees' "Nursery," a baseball version of the Merry Pranksters. Kekich took the spot held by Jim Bouton, the former phenom chosen in the previous fall's expansion draft by the Seattle Pilots, the nouveau baseball locale where Bouton forever opened the door to the locker room with his revolutionary book *Ball Four*.

Change crept slowly into pre–free agency clubhouses, and an angry front office really could keep a ballplayer from earning a living. *Ball Four* shot across the bow of baseball culture when it appeared in 1970. The locker room—especially the Yankees locker room that Bouton had occupied for most of the 1960s—was exposed as a frat house, where players often seemed more worried about chasing women than running down the first division clubs in the league. Managers and coaches whom fans liked to think of as watchful or entertaining uncles were characterized as looking to save their own skins. The game's establishment and most players resented the unwelcome intrusion of *Ball Four*, not to mention the revelation to the public that ballplayers weren't heroes and certainly not choirboys. Off the field, players weren't that much different from many fans who watched them; they just had more unsupervised time on the road, where women could check them out on cards, in print, or on television before eyeing them in the flesh, perhaps entering a bar with several of their comely young friends.

Fritz Peterson and Mike Kekich were family men. That's where the trouble began.

The former friends remain mostly mum on what exactly happened— Kekich still reportedly "desperate to block" an oft-rumored Ben Affleck–Matt Damon movie with a working title of *The Trade*. Peterson is a consultant on that Warner Bros. project, which, as of 2012, was still in the rumor stage of production with Affleck as Peterson and Damon as Kekich. Peterson became involved when it appeared that the film would be based on the writing of late *New York Post* columnist Maury Allen. A party he threw played a minor role in the swap saga, but the writer didn't get all of his facts right, according to Peterson. "I encouraged Mike to be involved in it [the film] as well," he says. "Mike can't stop the movie. Nobody can. Warner Bros. builds litigation money into most of the films they produce. They have more money than we all do."

Until the first week of March 1973, however, very few people knew of or even believed the story. "Nobody knew," says Peterson. "The only player that knew anything was Mel Stottlemyre since Marilyn and Mike stopped out to see them during the offseason just before spring training in 1973. Mel and his wife Jean thought it was a joke and waited for me and Susanne to show up. It wasn't a joke. We never showed up. I hoped it would have worked out for all of us."

In Peterson's 2009 memoir, *Mickey Mantle Is Going to Heaven*, he explained that, before the Fort Lauderdale media blitz in spring training, there was a midsummer Fort Lee supper. The subject of changing partners first came up in July 1972 in a diner in the New Jersey suburb, following a cookout at Allen's home in Dobbs Ferry, New York. The couples and their families, who lived near each other in Jersey, had spent a lot of time together since Kekich's trade from the Dodgers to the Yankees in 1969. The two left-ies were roommates on road trips, but it was at home where the southpaws made news.

In the six months after Maury Allen's party, the two families essentially changed households: the two Kekich children went with Susanne Kekich to live with Fritz Peterson while Marilyn Peterson and her two children joined Mike Kekich. The deal included houses, furniture, even dogs. It caught the Yankees completely off guard. Marty Appel, Yankees public relations assistant at the time—who has gone on to a long career in the field of spin—said he was never caught so unaware in his life. Appel was 24 then and knew the players and the habits of young men of the day better than just about anybody in the front office. For the old guard at the Yankees, the development was even more shocking. Trouble was, they tried a 1940s solution to a 1970s problem: treating it as a private matter. Yankees president Michael Burke, general manager Lee MacPhail, manager Ralph Houk, and the PR staff met with beat reporters to tell them the story at once to diffuse the situation.

In the pre–*Ball Four* days, the Yankees' plan to keep a lid on it might have worked. Mickey Mantle's years of carousing and drinking had never bled into the press adulation of the clean-cut hero with the alliterative name and the tape-measure bombs. But in a few short years the line demarcating private from public had blurred—and scandal sells, even on the sports page.

"Back then the writers were almost like part of the family," says Appel, who was in the room when the bomb dropped on the press. "That's why we thought that we could get away with that." Except not everyone was in on it. Milton Richman at United Press International had gotten the scoop; his call for confirmation alerted the Yankees that the story was going to run. The *New York Post* had sent Sheila Moran to get a new angle for what seemed, from the copy desk, an otherwise dull spring training in Fort Lauderdale.

"Foolishly she was excluded from that meeting in Ralph Houk's office because she wasn't part of the family—she was very much new on the scene," Appel recalls. "We naively thought that we would just keep this among ourselves and it won't get out: 'Sheila Moran will never find out.'" Oh, but word got out, and those who flocked to Fort Lauderdale in early March 1973 weren't the usual spring break crowd.

WABC-TV sportscaster Sal Marchiano arrived in Mets camp in St. Petersburg a little after 7:00 a.m. on Monday, March 5. He had been in New York at Madison Square Garden the previous night, calling Rangers hockey with Bill Chadwick on WOR-TV (Channel 9), which at the time carried games for the Mets, Nets, Knicks, Islanders, and Rangers, plus professional wrestling. Marchiano spent most of that Monday morning at Mets camp doing interviews about the upcoming season. Nothing too strenuous or earth-shattering, but after spending most of the night in airports and on airplanes, Marchiano went to the hotel that afternoon for a needed nap. When the phone rang at 6:30 p.m., his station's assistant news director told him to drive across the state to Fort Lauderdale because two Yankees had swapped wives.

"I hung up on him because I thought it was a cruel joke," says Marchiano. "He called me back and said he was serious. So we got our stuff together, checked out, and drove to Fort Lauderdale from St. Pete, taking Alligator Alley to make sure we got there in plenty of time. Alligator Alley was a two-lane road. I remarked to my cameraman that it would be fitting to die in a head-on crash chasing a story that we had no business chasing."

Peterson—on top of everything else, a contract holdout—met with Marchiano on the lawn of the house he was renting. Peterson's former teammate and Nursery-fellow Jim Bouton, who worked the 11 o'clock sports desk at WABC-TV in New York, had set up the exclusive interview. Despite the attention and the headlines all over the country that morning, Marchiano recalls that the kid from Illinois was interested mostly in tuning in the radio to find out if he had landed on the radar of Paul Harvey, he of the distinctive voice elocution, syndicated editorials, and tales ending with "The Rest of the Story," which originated out of Chicago. "Sure enough Paul Harvey had an item," Marchiano said. "Peterson was thrilled. He thought it was big time to be on Paul Harvey's newscast."

When his interview with Peterson ended, Marchiano went into the house and saw Susanne Kekich and her two children. "Nowadays my boss would want footage of Susanne in the kitchen with the kids," says Marchiano, "but the kids were crying because their father wasn't there and they were in a different house."

The simpler time also meant that physically delivering the film itself was half the battle. It wasn't the same as journalists using diplomats to smuggle photos and copy back to the United States to circumvent the maniacal South Vietnamese government in the 1960s, but the technology for transporting news hadn't much improved. With simple satellite hookups and digital uploads still years away, Marchiano drove the film of the Peterson interview to the airport, shipped it to New York, and it ran on *Eyewitness News* that night.

"When I got back I was told by my news director that the 6:00 p.m. audience that night had quadrupled."

So much for nothing happening in Yankees camp.

With more women taking birth control and divorces easier to get for those who wanted out, a new freedom had entered the sexual revolution. What happened with these two pitchers on the New York Yankees, the long-time bastion of the straight-laced and square—at least to those who hadn't read *Ball Four*—was a real-life version of *Bob & Carol & Ted & Alice*, the acclaimed 1969 Paul Mazursky film about two couples considering a foursome. (ABC even produced a short-lived 1973 TV show based on the movie, starring Robert Urich, Anne Archer, and 11-year-old Jodie Foster, who was graduating from cartoon voices and *The ABC Afterschool Special* to more complex roles. The show aired opposite the World Series that year.)

"I was astounded when I first started to work [in TV], the first few years, how much the ballplayers played around, especially on the road—certainly with the press it was a wink and a smile," recalls Marchiano, who in the late 1960s hit the same watering holes as ballplayers in Manhattan, most notably a place on First Avenue called Mr. Laffs, owned by former Yankee Phil Linz. "Married guys walked out of there with stewardesses and hookers and whatever, but no one ever knew about it. . . . *Ball Four* changed everything. All of a sudden the public knew for sure that ballplayers screwed around. That's why the book was so popular."

The growing obsession of people both titillated and repelled by a situation that the Yankees considered a private matter wasn't lost on Major League Baseball. This was the family game, the affordable sport, the daily obsession. Baseball needed modernizing, sure, but this was moving much too fast for the tradition-bound pastime. Commissioner Kuhn, who had few qualms reversing trades he found unfavorable during his tenure, was at a loss how to deal with this particular transaction. After receiving more mail about the Peterson-Kekich affair than he had about the designated hitter rule, Kuhn finally spoke two weeks after the story had broken. He said he was "appalled" and that the situation "does no good for sports in general."

Caught off guard once more, the Yankees were furious. The situation, which they had hoped was dying down, flared up all over again following Kuhn's comments. "I thought it was a closed issue," barked general manager Lee MacPhail. "What would you expect him to say to them: Don't do it again?" Manager Ralph Houk, the gruff World War II hero who had attended every Yankees spring training since the 1940s, didn't mince any words in his assessment of the commissioner's stance: "I don't think it's any of his business."

Peterson tried his best to stay close-mouthed but couldn't help but blast Bowie. "We're not gambling or murdering people," Peterson said. "What's he going to do about all the other players who are getting divorced, suspend them, too?"

There would be no suspension, though Steinbrenner certainly suspended his belief in the staid old Yankees he'd bought, the same team, he'd said, that was part of a "wave of nostalgia sweeping the country." He tried to support Peterson and Kekich publicly, but the Yankees ditched both pitchers over the next year. By then, the wife swap—or as Mike Kekich had deemed it, "life swap"—had gone the way of many memorable baseball trades: one side made out fine while the other suffered.

Three

RING OF TRUTH

The rings were dazzling—the 1972 World Series rings, that is. Even four decades later, A's players still insist on that clarification.

Oakland's Chicago-based owner made a special trip in March 1973 to spartan Rendezvous Park in Mesa, Arizona, where he personally distributed the rings celebrating the previous year's title. Finley boasted that each player's ring cost him $1,500. Sal Bando later noted the rings were deemed worth $3,500 when players had them appraised for insurance. Finley's own ring, along with the much-less valuable 10-karat gold 1974 World Series ring that belonged to his ex-wife, sold for $14,100 at auction in 2009.

In all caps, the words "WORLD CHAMPIONS 1972" encircle a full carat diamond. One side of the ring features the player's last name along with the team's name. In small letters inside the team logo runs the ALCS triumph over Detroit: "A's 3, Tigers 2." The other side of the ring hails the verdict of the seven-game World Series against the Reds in much larger letters, along with the engraved signature of Charles O. Finley and his coded motto: "S + S = S," meaning: Sweat plus sacrifice equals success. Oakland's 1972 World Series rings were the most lavish in history, which thoroughly annoyed the other owners in Major League Baseball. Finley liked that most of all.

Charles Oscar Finley lived by, and talked at length about, his "S + S = S" motto. The sweat originated in a steel mill. He had been born poor in Birmingham, Alabama, in 1918, son of a first-generation Irish-American steel mill worker. His father, Oscar, lost his longtime job—as did many others during the Depression—when Finley was 15. The family moved north to Gary, Indiana, Charlie joining his father in the stifling mills when he graduated high school. There he might have remained, but Charlie Finley never sat still for a single predictable outcome.

Southern boy turned Midwestern man, Finley started a family, attended college (never finishing), and rose to division head at an ordnance plant during World War II while also selling insurance on the side. The Marines

Reggie Jackson, left, and Gene Tenace, right, get their 1972 World Series rings from Charlie Finley in Mesa, Arizona. RON RIESTERER

judged him unfit for service because of an ulcer, but the biggest break that may have come his way, strange as it sounds, was contracting tuberculosis. Though the disease caused him to lose almost 100 pounds and put his family into financial peril, it was during his 27-month stay at a sanatorium that Finley came up with his greatest idea: selling affordable group disability insurance to doctors. A born salesman with an innate ability to charm, Finley took his idea national and soon had the wealth to pursue one of his favorite hobbies: baseball.

But infiltrating the old boys' network to own a major league team in the 1950s was no easy feat—no matter how much money a man suddenly had. Finley's first attempt to buy the A's for $3 million in 1953 came to naught; the team instead went to insider Arnold Johnson, who owned both Yankee Stadium and that organization's minor league ballpark in Kansas City. Though relocating major league franchises was a relatively novel idea, the A's desperately needed to flee Philadelphia after wilting for decades as the once proud ownership of legendary Connie Mack came to a sad end. The A's moved to Kansas City—Johnson unloading both stadiums when he acquired the team—and fared far better at the gate than the club had in Philadelphia if not on the field.

Never one to be deterred, Finley tried to buy the Chicago White Sox and Detroit Tigers before attempting to get involved with an expansion team in Southern California. In March 1960, however, Arnold Johnson died suddenly, creating a void in Kansas City. The American League, in the midst of unprecedented change, let down its guard long enough to let Charlie Finley into their exclusive club by allowing him to purchase what was clearly the league's weakest link.

Yet it was only after Finley lost his expansion bid to singing cowboy–turned–business impresario Gene Autry that he turned back to Kansas City. In the style forever after associated with Finley, he came in late, pushed others aside, and slapped the winning bid on the table. Knowing that the probate court handling the Johnson estate would look for the highest bid, he pledged $1.85 million to buy the A's. The sum came in just $50,000 more than the bid submitted by a group of Kansas City leaders and businessmen who believed they'd won the bidding. When the group scrambled together more money, Finley increased his bid, telling Byron Spencer, the bidder representing Kansas City, "I don't care how high you go. I'm prepared to go higher." Finley ultimately bought controlling interest of the A's for a shade under $2 million, but no sooner had the new owner pledged that the Kansas City A's were "here to stay" than the new owner began scheming to find a new location for the club.

Granted, the team was truly a mess. Wins seemed to occur more by accident than by design. Johnson had created a veritable shuttle that sent Kansas City's best prospects to New York—Roger Maris, Ralph Terry, and Clete Boyer among others—in exchange for the fading or extinguished stars of the 1950s Yankees dynasty. Finley trumped the club's past history with stunts like burning a bus representing the New York shuttle and attempting to move the right-field fence in to correspond with Yankee Stadium (which the league forbade). He also poured $411,000 of his own money into

Kansas City's Municipal Stadium, fired managers and front office employees at whim, and continued deceiving the public about his intentions of relocating the franchise. When the Dallas Texans of the American Football League moved to Kansas City in 1963 and received a lease at Municipal Stadium for $1 for each of their first two years as the renamed Chiefs, Finley raged. He managed to sweet talk the outgoing city council into agreeing to fund a new baseball stadium, but the new council immediately voided the contract. Finding a new home became an even greater obsession, but, even as the franchise's future home remained in flux, the championship club he proposed to build was slowly coming to fruition.

Finley couldn't compete with the Yankees and Dodgers, but the major league draft of high school and college players, instituted in 1965, allowed the best young amateur talent to fall right into any ballclub's hands if the team chose wisely—and the A's did. Because the team had been so bad and draft order reversed the order of finish in the standings from the previous year, the Kansas City A's could funnel the nation's best amateurs into a farm system already brimming with talent. The A's had the first pick in the first draft and chose Rick Monday, a slugging outfielder from Arizona State. Sun Devils teammate Sal Bando (sixth round) and Ohio high school standout Gene Tenace (20th round) were also taken by the A's in that first draft. Reggie Jackson, another Arizona State slugger, was taken with the second overall pick in 1966 after the Mets famously bumbled and spent the first overall pick on high school catcher Steve Chilcott, who never spent a day in the majors. The A's took Vida Blue in the second round in 1968. These high draft picks joined an army of up-and-coming players like Catfish Hunter, Blue Moon Odom, Joe Rudi, and Rollie Fingers, all of whom were signed the year before the first draft. Finley signed most of these players, having become the de facto general manager after adopting the minor league development philosophy of Hank Peters, a man whom Finley fired—twice.

One of the incentives for signing with the A's was upward mobility. Joe Rudi grew up loving Mickey Mantle and the Yankees, broadcast frequently in his home in Modesto, California, but he turned down a better offer from the Yankees to sign with the A's out of Thomas Downey High School in 1964. Scout Don "Ducky" Pries, who had long had his eye on the angular shortstop with the sweet swing, told Rudi that he had a much better chance of reaching the majors quickly with the A's than the Yankees, who at the time were on their way to the World Series for the fifth straight year. A decade later, the Yankees hadn't seen an October showdown since; the A's, meanwhile, reached the postseason for five straight years with Rudi as an All-Star and Gold Glove left fielder. "Most of those years the Yankees hadn't kept up the team," Rudi says. "It was just a great move. . . . All that they said [when I signed] came true."

Another incentive for signing with the A's, believe it or not, was money. Though famously tight-fisted later on in Oakland, Finley was doing so well in his insurance business in the mid-1960s that he wanted to avoid paying more taxes. So he spent far more freely on bonuses for his newly signed ballplayers than the enduring Finley legend would lead you to believe. Biographers C. Michael Green and Roger D. Launius estimated the amount that Finley spent between 1962 and 1967 on bonuses for approximately 250 amateur players exceeded $1.5 million, a princely sum at the time but an absolute bargain for what those players achieved at the big-league level.

"You had to give credit to the scouting staff he had," says Sal Bando, Oakland's third baseman and captain and later general manager of the Milwaukee Brewers. "He was willing to spend the money for the Catfish Hunters and the Blue Moon Odoms. They were nondrafted players, signed before the draft [began], so he went out and overpaid for them. Not overpaid, but paid big bonuses for them. He had good scouts, and he listened to them. He drafted Reggie, myself, and Rick Monday. He made the trades for Ken Holtzman and Bill North, who became great assets. He [signed] Rollie Fingers and drafted Vida Blue, so you have to give him credit for that. It's a lot easier being the GM when you're the owner. You don't have to check with the budget. You know what you're going to spend and you spend it."

While stockpiling young talent in the mid-1960s, Finley was also acquiring all the shares of the team. As he toured the country looking to relocate, he used his own peculiar methods to lure fans to Kansas City with animal-themed gimmicks: a mechanical rabbit that rose from the ground to hand the umpire new baseballs, sheep and goats that grazed on a hill beyond Kansas City's outfield fence, and, most famously, a mule named after himself as team mascot. Many claimed—and not without warrant—that Charlie O., the mule, received better treatment than many players. That mule traveled in high style: his own uniform, hotel room, and press conferences. But the Missouri mule moved to California along with everyone else.

Oakland came as a bit of an afterthought. By the time Finley got around to Northern California, he had looked into relocating the team to Atlanta, Dallas, Louisville, Milwaukee, New Orleans, and Seattle. With the end of his Municipal Stadium lease—the other owners had forced him to sign an extension in 1964 or else face "termination of Charles O. Finley & Co. from the American League"—the league finally granted his wish to relocate but only because baseball was ready to expand again. The AL placated Kansas City with a new expansion franchise, known as the Royals; Seattle got a new AL team as well, the ill-fated Pilots, who became the Milwaukee Brewers.

What Finley got in Oakland was a ready-for-baseball stadium less than two years old plus a five-year TV and radio deal worth more than $1 million a year—almost 10 times what he'd had in Kansas City—yet Finley overestimated his new city's size and enthusiasm about baseball. Half the size of San Francisco, Oakland and its big brother across the Bay created the smallest two-team market in the majors, well behind New York, Los Angeles, Chicago, or Baltimore-Washington. The addition of the A's to the region did no favors for the Giants as the National League club's already slipping finances fell into even steeper decline. The 20-year lease at the Oakland Coliseum wasn't finalized until shortly before the 1968 season began, and as a result the A's sold just 1,500 season tickets at Oakland–Alameda County Coliseum.

After 50,000 came out on Opening Day, the crowds dwindled to the consistent four-digit attendance level that the A's experienced far too frequently over the decades to come. Catfish Hunter's Wednesday night perfect game on May 8, 1968—the first perfecto in an American League regular-season game since 1922—drew just 6,298 fans during the team's second-ever Oakland homestand. The night after Hunter's gem the team somehow drew an even smaller crowd. But while market support appeared poor from the start, the team was becoming a winner.

The 1968 A's improved by 20 games from their last year in Kansas City. The following year, Reggie Jackson had 30 home runs by the start of July, threatening Roger Maris's record 61 home run pace of 1961 and earning a personal note from President Nixon after a well-timed blast at Washington's RFK Stadium. In 1971, it was Vida Blue's turn to come out of nowhere and spur talk, much of it from Finley himself, about the 21-year-old becoming a 30-game winner. In the case of Jackson in 1969 and Blue two years later, the young star faded down the stretch but still had an outstanding season. Each player also partook in acrimonious contract talks with Finley that spoiled much of the joy of the achievement and permanently soured the player on the owner. Reggie and Vida by no means stood alone in their sentiments.

That's why the 1972 World Series rings came as such a shock. Well known for his stinginess as well as for mistreating those who got in his way, Finley was still giddy months after winning his first championship. In the winning locker room, players had asked for miniature replicas of the World Series trophy given to the owner. Finley made better on his champagne-soaked locker room promise and handed out full-size trophy replicas of the two-foot-tall trophy. Finley distributed rings to many non-uniformed personnel, even giving rings (sans diamond) to select members of the press. The players' wives received attractive charm bracelets with their last names on them.

Finley also tried to lavish bonuses on his players during the 1972 World Series, but Commissioner Kuhn jumped on him for that. While such practices certainly weren't unheard of, the climate of labor unrest created by the first play stoppage in 1972 resulted in disallowing the bonuses and a fine of $2,500 for breaking the rules. When it came time to sign new contracts the following year, all the A's regulars received raises, with Catfish Hunter and Reggie Jackson both peaking above the $70,000 mark. Though the players felt they deserved more, six-figure players were still pretty rare in 1973. Though Bobby Murcer had controversially crossed that pay threshold for the Yankees, most of the other members of that exclusive club were perennial All-Stars late in their careers, like Bob Gibson, Carl Yastrzemski, Willie Mays, and Hank Aaron. At a time when the average American worker was earning $7,580 and the average major league salary was $36,556 (about $21,000 over the new league minimum), the A's were underpaid but not completely out of line with the rest of baseball. Yet with their new status as the game's best team, some players still felt slighted, even as their flashy new jewelry, courtesy of Charles O. Finley, gleamed in the Arizona sun.

Blue fumed that Finley wanted to renew the star southpaw at $51,000 for 1973. With an MVP, Cy Young, and World Series ring in his trophy case at the age of 23, Blue showed up to spring training on time, but he didn't sign his contract. Instead, he told a United Press International reporter that he might inquire to Players Association head Marvin Miller about being a test case for free agency. (Dodger Andy Messersmith and Expo Dave McNally ultimately undertook that test case a couple of years later.)

Catcher Dave Duncan, unhappy with Finley's $40,000 offer for his '73 contract, joined Blue in not signing. Even George Hendrick, with just 100 career games at the major league level, wanted out of Oakland. Finley told Hendrick to expect to spend the summer in Tucson, the club's Triple-A affiliate. When Hendrick publicly requested a trade, he spent the summer in Cleveland instead.

Finley had an eye for talent as good as any owner's—and probably better than most. He had, after all, chosen Hendrick as the first overall draft pick in 1968. In his first full season in the majors in 1972, Hendrick had started five times in the World Series as fill-in for Reggie Jackson, who had injured his knee in the last game of the ALCS. Hendrick went on to be an All-Star four times, collect almost 2,000 hits, and drive in exactly 1,111 runs. But in spring training 1973, all Finley could see was that his starting outfield was already filled following his offseason acquisition of Bill North from the Cubs—trading 34-year-old reliever Bob Locker and getting a fleet-footed, 24-year-old center fielder from Chicago to replace Rick Monday, the slugging center fielder whom Finley had sent to the Cubs a year earlier for starting pitcher Ken Holtzman. Hendrick essentially served as a fourth member of the Oakland outfield in the spring of '73, and Finley wasn't going to let a spare part keep him from upgrading a catcher while also getting rid of a headache in Duncan. Discussing the subject of his unsigned players in March 1973, Finley said, "A Vida Blue or a Dave Duncan aren't going to stand in my way." Neither was a George Hendrick.

Hendrick and Duncan went off to the Indians in late March for catcher Ray Fosse and utility infielder Jack Heidemann. Though Fosse's memorable 1970 All-Star Game collision with Pete Rose began a series of injuries that prevented him from becoming a feared hitter like Boston backstop Carlton Fisk or Yankees catcher Thurman Munson, Fosse was a far superior hitter to Duncan as well as a two-time Gold Glove winner. Cleveland hurler Gaylord Perry, the 1972 Cy Young winner, recoiled at the Fosse trade. "You've got to be kidding. . . . I don't believe it. But why would we want to trade our quarterback?" With Charlie Finley, anything was possible, and whatever was possible often worked out for the A's—at least on the field.

"It was an artfully constructed club," said John Thorn, Major League Baseball's official historian, working on the first of the 70 books to his credit in 1973. "The A's had a lot of good, seemingly spare parts. We don't think of synergy as counting for much in baseball. In baseball it's always one man against nine. It's not five on five or eleven on eleven, but that intangible of camaraderie and clubhouse effectiveness really came in for that club."

The flashy new rings that got the goat of the other owners spoke even louder than Charlie Finley. As the A's kept winning, the jewelry handed out would be far simpler—and cheaper. (Catfish Hunter called the rings for Oakland's second title "a dime-store creation.") As the A's finished up spring training in 1973, however, Finley wanted the world to know that he owned the best team in the sport, and it was clear that he would do whatever it took to win again: $S \times S = S^2$.

Finley's A's stood on top of the world as the 1973 season got underway, but so did Finley's adopted hometown of Chicago—just not on the baseball field. A month after the 110-story World Trade Center officially opened in April 1973, the Second City pushed it to second place. The Sears Tower rose 88 feet taller when completed on May 3, 1973. Chicago had unseated New York City.

The largest retailer in the world at the dawn of the 1970s, Sears Roebuck and Company employed some 350,000 people worldwide. The operations end of the business took place in Chicago, and the company hoped to consolidate as many people as possible into one building, a really big building. Architect Bruce Graham designed a 1,450-foot-tall "bundled tube" construction, forming nine separate 75-by-75-foot square steel frame buildings. Graham, whose 100-story Hancock Center opened in Chicago in 1970, demonstrated the Sears Tower concept to engineer Fazlur Khan at dinner by holding nine cigarettes in his hand. Others didn't wonder so much about the technology but fixated instead on what might happen if those demo butts all caught fire at once. Two best-selling novels—*The Tower* by Richard Martin Stern in 1973 and *The Glass Inferno* by Thomas N. Scortia and Frank M. Robinson a year later—fed off the hysteria of what might occur if fire and skyscraper met. The two books inspired the following year's top-grossing film: *The Towering Inferno*, a star-studded blockbuster from *Poseidon Adventure* producer Irwin Allen, out just in time for Christmas.

The real disaster that occurred didn't take place in Sears's building but its business. Competition pushed the company from its lofty perch, and Sears didn't need anywhere near the space offered by the world's tallest building. The company vacated the landmark tower it had built for $150 million two decades after the grand opening. The official name of the structure eventually changed to Willis Tower, after the British insurance broker. The Midwestern monolith remains functional, offering a view of four states on a clear day and an ideal perch for TV and radio station antennas—even if it never came close to fulfilling its original purpose. The Freedom Tower of the new World Trade Center stands 325 feet taller than Chicago's tower.

Bigger isn't necessarily better when it comes to baseball, either. Two rounds of expansion, creating eight new teams in the dozen years leading to 1973, led to growing pains for the game and many more players on major league payrolls. But the system that controlled those players still favored the people that signed the checks, just as it had since 1880, when major league owners first enacted the reserve clause. Upheld by the Supreme Court in a challenge by former outfielder Curt Flood in 1972, the reserve clause ensured that players remained in a team's control for as long as ownership wished. Realizing that baseball's longstanding antitrust exemption was coming increasingly under fire despite the court victory over Flood, owners and players concluded a three-week spring lockout with an agreement to salary arbitration as a way of diffusing free agency.

Finley warned that putting salary determination into the hands of someone not in the owner's box was opening a Pandora's box, but as far as the 1973 season went it was business as usual, especially in Oakland. Whereas the reserve system offered stability to major league rosters on most teams from year to year, 10 A's who had been on the major league roster when the 1972 season ended were no longer members of the team when Oakland broke camp in 1973. The list of the missing included former MVP Orlando Cepeda, whose legs kept him from playing the field without pain, and whose absence left the A's short at a position that hadn't existed a year earlier: the designated hitter.

Finley had long pushed for the designated hitter in baseball—as well as orange baseballs, three-ball walks, and designated pinch runners—but several other owners came to see things his way about the extra hitter. By 1973 the American League was almost desperate for the DH (or DPH, for Designated Pinch Hitter, as the position was known in some newspapers until Opening Day). The American League certainly needed something to help it out of the older league's shadow, not a place the AL was used to.

Since its founding in 1901, the American League had held its own with the National League, its senior by 25 years. The AL was well organized and well positioned from the start. When the National League eliminated four teams after the 1899 season—kissing off and pissing off fans in Cleveland, Washington, Baltimore, and Louisville—they inadvertently opened the door for the formation of the rebel league. The American League fed the appetite of three disaffected cities abandoned by the National League, reclaimed Detroit and Milwaukee as major league cities, and also offered competition in current NL strongholds Chicago, Philadelphia, and Boston.

Only in baseball's archaic vernacular could the 72-year-old American League still be known as the "Junior Circuit," yet by 1973 the AL looked as outdated as any league in professional sports. The National League had a faster, more modern style of player and play. The crowds bore that out. The American League hadn't surpassed the National League in attendance since 1961, the year the AL jumpstarted expansion by adding two extra teams. The

NL waited another year to add its pair. Even given another round of expansion in 1969, American League average attendance stood at 953,321 per franchise in 1972. NL teams averaged 1,294,144, almost 27 percent more.

But the shortened '72 season hurt every team's bottom line. With half a dozen games stricken from the 162-game schedule due to the first stoppage in sports history, only three of the AL's dozen teams surpassed one million fans. Recently opened AL outposts in Milwaukee (for the relocated Pilots-turned-Brewers) and suburban Dallas (for the uprooted Senators-turned-Rangers) barely drew 600,000 apiece in '72. Also take into consideration that the American League counted tickets *sold* in its attendance figures while the National League counted tickets *used*, and the disparity between the leagues proves even more glaring.

So why were fewer people attending games in the American League? Some preferred the argument that the AL's older, outmoded stadiums in inner cities were to blame. The figures show, however, that Boston's Fenway Park, Tiger Stadium in Detroit, and Comiskey Park on Chicago's South Side, the three oldest stadiums in the league, had the highest attendance in the AL in 1972 (though Fenway had slipped some 237,000 from '71). Another lingering and less discussed reason for the declining interest in the American League went back a quarter century to the integration of baseball.

The National League maintained an advantage that had begun in 1947 when Jackie Robinson became the first black player in the major leagues in the 20th century. The groundbreaking event happened in the National League, in Brooklyn, despite threats from owners, managers, players, and even the stands in some cities. "Baseball's Noble Experiment" turned out to be in everyone's best interest, whether they liked it or not, and many did not.

The Brooklyn Dodgers stayed ahead of the competition when it came to signing players of color and became the National League's preeminent team, capturing six pennants in a decade after winning just three in the previous 45 years. The most dominant team in either league, however, the New York Yankees, didn't integrate until 1955. The far less successful Red Sox were the last major league team to put a black player on the field, fabricating reasons not to sign either Jackie Robinson or Willie Mays in the 1940s and ignoring the obvious on-field benefits of integration until 1959. Come the 1970s, the American League on the whole looked like a decrepit cruise ship in an age of supersonic jets.

A look at the rosters from the 1972 All-Star Game, a cross section of the most popular and successful players in the game, shows 24 blacks and Latinos among the 62 players named to the two teams: 14 from the NL and 10 from the AL. The only black or Latino ballplayers to represent the American League in that All-Star Game who were later enshrined in the National Baseball Hall of Fame were Rod Carew and Reggie Jackson. (Hall of Famer Luis Aparicio was named to the team but missed the game due to injury.) The NL dugout featured eight future Hall of Famers classified as minorities: Hank Aaron, Lou Brock, Bob Gibson, Ferguson Jenkins, Willie Mays, Joe Morgan, Willie Stargell, and Billy Williams. (Roberto Clemente was chosen to start but didn't play due to injury.) The National League won the '72 contest in Atlanta, marking the league's ninth win in 10 years. Most unaffiliated, or honest, fans believed that the National League was just more interesting.

The commissioner, for one, felt that a change was needed to try to bridge the gap in interest in the two leagues. When Bowie Kuhn addressed owners of both leagues in Chicago on January 11, 1973, he shared three potential ideas with the press:

1. Interleague play. Kuhn's version would only affect cities with multiple teams in one geographic area.

2. Designated Pinch Runner. An idea espoused by Charlie Finley, it allowed for speedy runners to enter the game without a substitution.

3. Designated Pinch Hitter. The proposal that Kuhn thought had the best chance of passing ran counter to the "everybody bats" concept followed even in the game's earliest forms.

Kuhn wasn't the first to champion the idea of a regular hitter to take the pitcher's spot in the lineup. The idea had arisen periodically for 80 years. National League president William Temple put it to a vote in 1892, where it lost by a slim 7–5 margin. In 1906, Connie Mack also suggested taking the bat out of the pitcher's hands. Mack's proposal was pooh-poohed, but the idea came up yet again in 1928. National League president John Heydler floated it, though the American League voted it down. At the time, it took approval of both the AL and NL for either league to enact a major rule change. If that had still been the case 45 years later, there may have never been a designated hitter. But an 8–4 vote by AL owners in 1973 changed the basic structure of the baseball lineup.

"Whenever the game had been in trouble in previous decades, the answer was always: more hitting," said John Thorn, MLB's official historian.

"People liked 14–11 games. They don't like 1–0, or 2–1. It's only for the purist, and the purists are going to come anyway. So you need the casual fans, who have to have more action."

The owners admonished Kuhn behind closed doors in Chicago for publicly airing the game's dirty laundry, but the commissioner had pressed the issue and forced action on a growing problem. Owners had previously moved to boost offense after the Year of the Pitcher in 1968 by lowering the mound and shrinking the strike zone; designated hitters had even been tried, in limited doses, in spring training. Offense did perk up in '69—adding four expansion staffs loaded with discarded pitchers certainly helped—but the public's interest had waned since then, especially in the AL.

Now, four years later, the DH was in, though owners only authorized a three-year trial. The designated hitter, like arbitration, became a part of the baseball equation in 1973. While arbitration would surprise many owners by altering the game's salary structure over time, the DH did what the American League hoped—and did so immediately. The league's hitting spiked by 20 points to .259, the highest average in the AL since 1956. And '73 marked the first time in a decade that the AL outhit the NL. The new rule also won over many of the people it displaced in the batter's box. Oakland's Ken Holtzman, a good-hitting pitcher who proved as much in October '73, says he always liked the DH "because it enables the starting pitcher to remain in the game longer and I wanted to be in control of the game for the longest possible time." Holtzman and his fellow AL pitchers tossed 614 complete games—112 more than in 1972 and the most in either league since 1928. In 1973, AL relievers didn't have to worry about getting an at-bat, they were concerned about getting in a game. As ever, managers would iron out the strategy in time.

The face of Willie Mays says it all. NATIONAL BASEBALL HALL OF FAME LIBRARY, COOPERSTOWN, NY

Four

THE PLAYERS' MARCH

The Paris Peace Accords, signed on January 27, 1973, marked the end of American involvement in Vietnam. The United States hadn't seen anything like it since the Civil War more than a century earlier—a war that didn't unite the country but divided it instead. Unlike past wars, during which newspaper dispatches or newsreels showed edited images from days or weeks earlier, footage from across the Pacific came home nightly, in color, served alongside a Swanson's TV dinner. ABC, CBS, and NBC all had Saigon bureaus that rivaled only their New York and Washington departments in size. Though rarely graphic, the footage was raw and less censored than anything shown during World War II or Korea, and it fed many Americans' open opposition to the war. Disquieting news about US soldiers or what they were doing—setting Zippo lighters to thatched roofs in Cam Ne, for instance—fueled the growing exhaustion with the war.

Walter Cronkite, the most beloved television newsman of the day, perhaps any day, went to Vietnam during the Viet Cong's Tet Offensive and reported from the front lines as he had done as a newspaper reporter during World War II, filing reports from the Normandy beaches and hitching a ride on a bombing raid over Germany. Following his 1968 tour of the action in Vietnam, he realized that the war was unwinnable, and he did not mince words about it. At the end of his February 27 special report, Cronkite looked America in the eye and said it straight:

> For it seems now more certain than ever, that the bloody experience of Vietnam is to end in a stalemate. To say that we are closer to victory today is to believe in the face of the evidence, the optimists who have been wrong in the past. To say that we are mired in stalemate seems the only realistic, if unsatisfactory conclusion. On the off chance that military and political analysts are right, in the next few months we must test the enemy's intentions, in case this is indeed his last big gasp before negotiations. But it is increasingly

clear to this reporter that the only rational way out then will be to negotiate, not as victors, but as an honorable people who lived up to their pledge to defend democracy, and did the best they could.

President Lyndon Johnson reportedly told a White House aide: "If I've lost Walter Cronkite, I've lost America." The Democrats also lost the election. A month after Cronkite's report, LBJ announced he wouldn't run for a second full term. After Sirhan Sirhan assassinated antiwar candidate Robert F. Kennedy, hawk Hubert Humphrey won the Democratic nomination . . . before decidedly losing to Richard Nixon, who claimed to have a "secret plan" to extricate America from Vietnam. It took until the week after his *second* inauguration to get there.

Despite thousands of protests at home and millions of bombs dropped in Vietnam, Laos, and Cambodia, the Viet Cong showed little sign of relenting. Many said the peace treaty came eight years too late, but, pro or con, by the end of 1972 most Americans took solace in the prospect of America letting North and South Vietnam settle a conflict themselves that had started under French colonial rule in 1945. More than 58,000 Americans died in Vietnam, plus 153,000 wounded requiring hospitalization, and 2,300 missing in action.

The end of hostilities also brought an end to the draft. The Selective Service System had inducted almost two million men between 1963 and 1972. Many joined the military willingly, while many others fled the country to avoid the draft. Stopping the spread of Communism didn't resonate as a rallying cry with American youth like "Remember Pearl Harbor!" or "This is our war!" had a quarter century earlier with their parents. Kitchen tables, college campuses, and neighborhood meeting places throughout the country hosted debates about just and unjust war during the 1960s. Ballplayers were torn, just like anyone else, and regardless of whether they believed in the justification for the war, military commitment could directly affect their chances of reaching the major leagues.

Joining the National Guard and Army Reserve units fulfilled military obligations while generally avoiding overseas combat, an especially attractive option for athletes with a short window of opportunity in their chosen field and for those whose health was paramount for their careers. They were the lucky ones.

Many players did see combat in Vietnam. Before becoming the 1973 American League Rookie of the Year with the Orioles, outfielder Al Bumbry served as a lieutenant and led a platoon in Vietnam, earning the Bronze Star without losing a single man under his command in combat. Jim Bibby spent two years of dangerous duty driving trucks in-country and threw a no-hitter for the Texas Rangers against the A's in 1973, his first full season in the majors at age 29. San Francisco's 1973 Opening Day center fielder Garry Maddox, an eight-time Gold Glove winner, spent 1969 and 1970 in Vietnam, where a reaction to unknown chemicals left his skin permanently hypersensitive to touch. (The forthcoming return of facial hair to the majors allowed him the welcome relief of no more shaving.)

But just because a player didn't see combat didn't mean he was out of danger. White Sox rookie outfielder Carlos May was enjoying an All-Star season in 1969 interrupted by the call to duty at Camp Pendleton in California. While he was swabbing a mortar, the weapon misfired and sliced off part of the thumb on his throwing hand. Fearing the loss of his finger—and presumably his career—May received a series of skin grafts that restored the use of his right thumb. In 1973, he hit a career-high 20 home runs and knocked in 96.

But the war didn't spell all bad news for the game. Jerry Koosman, one of the stalwarts of the 1973 Mets rotation, was discovered while doing his hitch. A Minnesota farmboy, Koosman was drafted into the Army at age 19 in 1962. He had hoped to be able to play ball while in the service, but his base in Illinois didn't have the facilities. So Koosman took the officer's candidate test and was working toward becoming a helicopter pilot, which virtually assured an overseas combat posting near the action. Fortunately for Kooz, his dentist intervened. The commanding general of the Minnesota National Guard, who also knew a thing or two about the lefty's molars, extracted Koosman from his predicament and arranged for a transfer to Fort Bliss in El Paso, Texas, where Koosman instantly became the base's starting pitcher. His catcher was John Luchese, son of an usher at Shea Stadium. Word reached the front office, and the Mets sent area scout Red Murff to see Koosman. The futures of the bungling expansion team and would-be chopper pilot both changed for the better.

The war reached its peak when Koosman's future teammate Jon Matlack turned 18 in 1968, the year he was selected in the first round of the amateur player draft by the Mets. The phenom from West Chester, Pennsylvania, where Matlack had thrown eight high school no-hitters, worried more about his draft status with the USA than MLB.

"I did have to worry about it [the draft], and it was a huge issue," Matlack says. "I think my draft number was 54. I was married, I did have kids, or one kid at that point, I had been in school. Because of that combination of things I was unable to not be in school and get a marriage deferment. The school thing was out because I hadn't been in school long enough, so it was the appeal process at the draft board to kill time and get into a Reserve unit. [This] was about all that was left to me." He got as far as going to sign up for an Army Reserve unit when he overheard others in line talking about meetings twice a week.

"Wait a minute," Matlack recalls telling a guy in line, "this is supposed to be one weekend a month." The guy responded that the unit met Thursdays and Saturdays. "I'm thinking, 'I can't do this and play,'" Matlack says, "so I ended up walking out."

About the same time he started the process at another Army Reserve unit, he wound up at an awards dinner with Arlen Specter, future senator from Pennsylvania, then the Philadelphia district attorney, who had served as assistant counsel on the Warren Commission, which issued the 888-page report that Lee Harvey Oswald had acted alone in the assassination of President John F. Kennedy. Even at this stage of his career, Specter, a Korean War veteran, had connections. "Just on the side, he [Specter] asked me about my draft situation," Matlack says. "I briefly told him that I was appealing to the state draft board to kill time because I was trying to get into a Reserve unit. I explained to him why and all the troubles I was having. That was it. Nothing was said about it. When my appeal came back . . . it was overturned by the state board. They gave me my deferment, and that was that."

Matlack never found out if Specter or anyone else had something to do with his sudden and welcome change of status, but he knows that "it was unheard of in that time for an appeal to be overturned based on the reason that I submitted . . . to kill time to try to get into a Reserve unit. . . . He didn't say he would do anything. . . . It just came back overturned—I got my deferment, and that was all there was to it."

For Matlack, a high major league draft pick for a previously moribund franchise that suddenly had one of the most talented pitching staffs in the game, it was crucial to be able to concentrate on developing his skills without interruption or worry. "It worked out in a very, very favorable way," Matlack says. "Looking back on it, probably in large part, allowed me to become whatever class player you want to put me in."

It was, of course, a far more perilous lot to end up in a frontline unit on the Mekong Delta than with a Reserve unit near your hometown. Yet for a teenaged athlete, whose lifelong goal of signing with a major league club just came true, it was torment to defer that dream or, worse, to risk losing it. A very real threat existed, that careers could be compromised and end before they began, that if a player missed a single meeting, wound up with the wrong unit, or angered the wrong commanding officer, he might still end up in Vietnam.

"We lost a lot of friends that I went to high school with that got killed over there and bad injuries where they never recovered from serving in Vietnam," explains 1973 A's outfielder Joe Rudi, signed to his first pro contract the year before the major league draft began, but who turned 18 when the military draft was very much in effect. "It was just part of the times that we had to deal with."

Rudi's situation was even trickier because he was with another organization. Under the rules of the day, players like Rudi who received bonuses over $5,000 had to stay on the major league roster all season or be claimed by another team. In a prearranged, hush-hush deal, the Indians took Rudi and the A's took Cleveland prospect Jim Rittwage. The "first-year player draft" ended after the 1965 season, thanks to the arrival of the amateur player draft. Now young players who received handsome bonuses for the era wouldn't have to rot for a year on a major league bench; they could be where they should: playing every day in the minor leagues. So hand it to Charlie Finley to beat this arcane system, sending Rittwage and Rudi back where they came from after the '65 season as throw-ins in a deal involving established major leaguers: Phil Roof (coming to the A's with Rudi) for Jim Landis (heading to Cleveland with Rittwage). Though Rudi was hidden in the minor leagues for a year in this illegal deal, there was no way around the US government. Rudi received his draft notice after the season.

The only Reserve unit he could get into was the Marines, which kept him on active duty for six months, ending that year's commitment after the 1966 baseball season began. Fortunately, Rudi was playing in his backyard for Modesto on a team filled with future major leaguers. The A-ball team full of future A's dominated the California League with the likes of Rudi, Reggie Jackson, Rollie Fingers, and Skip Lockwood, plus the pairing of Tony LaRussa and Dave Duncan, a legendary manager–pitching coach tandem for 29 years in the majors. At a time when the military draft status of a roster was as important as who was on it, even this powerhouse of a minor league club had to make sure everyone's military status was up to date.

"The A's put me in the Marine Corps Reserves because at that time they had a Class-3 Reservist," Rudi explains. "Those were people serving [who] had jobs which interfered with their doing multi drills, so all of '66 and all of '67 I was in Class-3 Reserves. When I got out in '66 I was OK for the rest of that year. In January of '67 I did 30 days duty. That's what most of the guys did—Duncan, Rick Monday, and myself. There were a whole bunch of us baseball players—Mike Torrez; Mickey Lolich's cousin, Ron Lolich, who played in the big leagues for awhile, was in there with us—over a dozen guys. We all went in because we thought we could go in between January 15 and February 15, for 30 days of duties and we were good for the whole year; we didn't have to go do it. That worked out in '66 and '67."

Then everything changed.

"Vietnam got heated up so much they thought they were calling up the Reserves, so they [the A's] closed that out and made us all join the Reserve unit. That's when Monday, Duncan, and I joined the Reserve unit in Oakland. That's where we spent the rest of our military time, but you couldn't miss a drill. If you screwed up or didn't show, they would activate you and send you off. So we couldn't miss a drill.

"We got through it, thank God," Rudi says. "All of us that went in during that same period of time were all done in 1971." That's when the A's embarked on their run of five straight AL West titles, the only team to win that many consecutive division titles during the era of four-division baseball. In Rudi's case, the timing worked out, but not everyone was so fortunate.

Bud Harrelson's military obligation was agonizing. One of the National League's best-fielding shortstops sat in a barracks while the team he'd come up with as the perennial punching bag of the league was now handing out the punishment and packing them in at Shea Stadium in the summer of 1969. The switch-hitting Harrelson, part of the minority of '69 Mets who played against both right- and left-handed pitchers in the strict Gil Hodges platoon system, missed the first two important series in team history in July that year, both against the Cubs—including roommate Tom Seaver's Imperfect Game—because of military commitments.

"I was one of the few guys [on the team] that had to go to meetings," Harrelson recalls. "I was in an Army Reserves unit in New York. Some guys skated that. I skated for the first three years when they put you in a control group, almost like when you go in the Army and they put you on a baseball team, because of your season. But I was away at summer camp a lot. . . . The Mets were worried about the Vietnam War, so they told guys to go into the Reserves. I actually went into the National Guard [unit] that got converted."

Mets infielder Wayne Garrett caught a break when a 1970 New York postal strike resulted in Reservists sorting and delivering mail. Garrett didn't actually end up handling the mail, but he was on the waiting list for the duty and as a result had a year cut off his service time, from six to five. That came as little consolation the next year when he was called to active duty for six months, just before 1971 spring training started. When he returned that July, the Mets had another third baseman, Bob Aspromonte, and Garrett agreed to a temporary demotion to the minors. He spent two weeks in Triple-A to get into game shape and returned to the majors. He batted just .213 in half a season for New York; Aspromonte fared slightly better at .225. After the season, the Mets, blinded by their desire to upgrade the third base position, thought they had made a good deal by trading Nolan Ryan and three prospects for Angels infielder Jim Fregosi. That was the first real stroke of luck in Ryan's previously stalled career. His military status hadn't helped.

Ryan's Army Reserve unit was in Houston, near his hometown of Alvin, so there was no sneaking back to New York to pitch on a 24-hour furlough, as some players could. His unit constructed landing strips, so he had sound concerns about being activated and sent to Vietnam—though that possibility became remote after the Tet Offensive. Ryan's military commitment, combined with the pioneer use of the five-man rotation by Mets manager Gil Hodges and pitching coach Rube Walker, resulted in Ryan not getting as many chances to start and develop as other pitchers who came up in the minor league system with him. Pitching every four days in Anaheim—and having also fulfilled his military commitments—the Ryan Express finally got on track at age 25.

Detroit's Mickey Lolich, one of the game's top left-handers through the early '70s, headed downstate from his Michigan National Guard unit to pitch occasionally for the Tigers. Proximity cut both ways, however. During the 1967 Detroit riots, Lolich had to patrol the streets not far from Tiger Stadium, armed with a National Guard rifle.

"It was a very stressful, trying time due to Vietnam," Matlack says of being draftable in the late 1960s and early '70s. "There were guys I went to school with [who were] sent over, and a lot of them didn't come back."

⚾ ⚾ ⚾

After the tumultuous spring of 1972, with the game's first strike and the death of beloved manager Gil Hodges on Easter Sunday, it seemed like 1973 spring training would be a breeze by comparison, and the Mets officially became old news on March 5, when the Peterson-Kekich wife swap story broke. Every sportswriter previously crowding the Mets camp descended on Fort Lauderdale Field as if gold had been found behind second base.

Then, as now, most teams that held spring training in Florida concentrated on the west coast of the state. The Mets, who had shared the St. Petersburg complex with the St. Louis Cardinals since 1962, had no shortage of nearby opponents to play. Nor were teams afraid to bus across the state to get a look at their rivals. The first game Fritz Peterson pitched following the big news came at Al Lang Field in St. Petersburg against the Mets. Onlookers booed him unmercifully. It wasn't the last nor the harshest booing he encountered in 1973.

The Peterson appearance was about as wild as it got at Mets camp for most of March 1973. Tom Seaver gave his usual pithy quotes for the sportswriters who stuck around dreary old St. Petersburg; Tug McGraw was good for a laugh; and the next Yogism was never far away from the manager's mouth. It was all pretty tame. But one of the biggest stars in the game going AWOL and disappearing almost 3,000 miles away? That was news.

Willie Mays had become a Met on Mother's Day, 1972. Owner Joan Payson, a diehard New York Giants fan and a former minority owner of that club, had cast the lone vote against the move to San Francisco and spent a decade trying to bring Mays to the Mets. Now she brought Willie back where he belonged, Shea Stadium standing in for the long-demolished Polo Grounds. Unfortunately for Giants owner Horace Stoneham, he had waited too long to part with the Say Hey Kid—because he couldn't imagine ever parting with him. Mays was a perennial All-Star who wasn't just the face of the team; he had helped the Giants win the National League West title in 1971.

But the wear and tear of the race with Cincinnati had left him dead tired. In a crucial moment in a tied Championship Series in Pittsburgh, the great Mays laid down a bunt in the sixth inning, not only giving up his bat but failing to get the job done. The runner couldn't advance on the little trickle in front of the plate. The Giants did tie the game—Mays singling and stealing a base later in the game—but the Pirates won, 2–1, and took the pennant the next day as Mays went hitless and the Giants let an early 5–2 lead disappear. He flew home separately from the rest of the team.

He had signed a two-year, $330,000 contract after the financially struggling Stoneham had turned down a 10-year contract request that would have kept Willie in the team's employ into the 1980s. It soon became apparent that the Giants couldn't even afford the two-year deal. Mays learned from a reporter that the Giants were trying to trade him to the Mets.

Pushed by the Oakland A's, Giants attendance had fallen by nearly half in 1972. The Giants had left New York 15 years earlier for a fresh start as no longer the poor kid in town. But it had happened again. Stoneham hoped to get at least one of New York's top prospects and a chunk of Payson's money, but he got only Charlie Williams, a minor league relief pitcher, and a reported $100,000, though Stoneham later admitted he received no money.

A few years earlier, Payson had offered $1 million for the Giants great, but Mays, unlike Hank Aaron, had slowed considerably. Owner of Van Goghs, Picassos, and champion thoroughbreds, plus a valuable baseball team with a world championship trophy in the same market the Giants had vacated, Payson wanted Mays in her stable. He represented not just a piece of the game but a piece of herself—something from the past no longer there, someone she still treasured. Stoneham also realized that Payson was the only other owner he could trust to take care of Mays when he finally retired. The outfielder had fallen into financial trouble and was slowly pulling himself out, but Stoneham as well as Payson understood that he needed to continue to be paid—even if it was just for being Willie Mays.

Mays gave a Mother's Day bouquet to Payson in his first game with the Mets, May 14, 1972, wearing his familiar number 24. (Bench player Jim Beauchamp switched from 24 to 5, no questions asked.) His home run landed the deciding run in a 5–4 victory in front of the owner at Shea—and against the Giants, no less. Mays, who had led the league in walks in 1971, continued to be an on-base machine as a Met, even if his speed, power, and—most shockingly to New Yorkers—outfield play had slipped to pedestrian standards. His .375 batting average in his first weeks as a Met pushed longtime fan favorite Tommie Agee, a 1969 World Series hero for his Mays-like catches, to the bench and eventually out of town altogether. But injuries slowed Willie, who said goodbye to the National League home run record he had held for seven years when Aaron surpassed him for good in June of '72. Mays was one of several Mets who limped to the finish after a promising start that year, the team tumbling from a 6½-game lead in late May to a 17½-game deficit four months later. The Mets finished 13½ games behind Pittsburgh and in third place at season's end, but it did nothing to wash the sour taste from a season remembered more for Gil Hodges's tragic death than for Mays's long-awaited return to New York. His swan song at Shea Stadium was ultimately "an unhappy experience," says Stan Isaacs, who grew up a New York Giants fan and later covered both the Yankees and Mets before becoming sports editor at *Newsday*. "He was not the vibrant Say Hey Kid who was here with the New York Giants."

He was also newly married to a second wife who had taken the alliterative, rhyme-y name, Mae Mays. He adored her. When she became ill during 1973 spring training, he flew home to see her. But getting back from his cross-country odyssey was another matter.

Mays hadn't been to spring training outside of Arizona since his rookie year of 1951. He took the long flight from St. Petersburg to SFO on an off day. Weather delayed his return flight, and he didn't get to camp until the team had finished for the day. Berra, never much of a disciplinarian, fined him $1,000, saying, "I can't let him get away with it or every player in camp would start taking the day off when he feels like it." Syndicated columnist Shirley Povich, who retired from a long career as sports editor of the *Washington Post* in 1973, blamed Payson for putting Berra in the position of dealing with "a teacher's pet" on the team. Povich had covered legends Walter Johnson and Babe Ruth in the final years of their careers and didn't like what he saw with Mays. "There can't be one rule for Mr. Wonderful No. 24 and another set of rules for the other 24 on the roster," he wrote. Povich also related that other players complained about Mays cutting workouts short—the same complaints heard in his later seasons in San Francisco.

Joan Payson would hear none of it. She lavished a contract on Mays in which he could be either the game's highest-paid player ($165,000) or highest-paid coach ($50,000). Willie's old friend, confidant, and manager Herman Franks, who helped orchestrate Leo Durocher's sign-stealing scheme at the Polo Grounds in Mays's rookie year to snatch the '51 pennant from the Brooklyn Dodgers, observed Mays in March 1973. Despite Mays playing with two knee braces and a slow bat, Franks declared him fit for a 23rd major league season. The munificent coach's salary had to wait.

To top it off, the Mets had no legitimate center fielder besides the limping legend. Rich Chiles, who came to the team from Houston in the trade for Agee, quickly proved not the answer. George Theodore was a good story but not a great center fielder. Don Hahn, trying to prove that he could hit at the big league level, was dispatched to the minors. How the Mets could have used former farmhand Amos Otis, ready to begin another All-Star season in

Kansas City after being traded away after the '69 season. The Mets wound up using their first pick in that spring's draft on a local center fielder: Lee Mazzilli from Abraham Lincoln High School in Brooklyn. He was a few years away but a good pick. In the 35 rounds of the amateur draft that followed, the faltering front office signed exactly two players who ever played for the team—neither spending more than a few months in New York City.

Whether Yogi liked it or not, the 1973 Mets had no real choice but to start Mays in center field for old times' sake. It looked like they were in for a long year.

The ever suave Yankees president, Michael Burke

Five

THE CUTTING

*M*arty Appel mistook the Yankees' purebred dynasty for a scruffy under-dog. On October 4, 1955, with his native Brooklyn in the throes of unparalleled joy after the Dodgers beat the Yankees in the World Series on their sixth try, Marty cast his lot with the downtrodden Yanks. At age seven, Marty didn't know that the Yankees had vanquished "dem Bums" in 1941, 1947, 1949, and 1952–53, not to mention the World Series the Bronx Bombers had won against other teams in 1923, 1927, 1928, 1932–33, 1936–39, 1943, and 1950. Sixteen world championships in 32 years. Downtrodden indeed.

Seven-year-olds are not generally keen students of history, but what they put their hearts into at that age can stick for life. So the kid from Brooklyn became a Yankees fan because of his pang of sympathy for this rare moment of suffering. Two years later, when the Dodgers played their final game in New York before relocating to California, taking the Giants with them in the bargain, Marty looked like a prescient young man whose favorite team was yet again in the World Series and would be staying put in a nearby borough.

Ten years later, home for the summer after his freshman year at SUNY Oneonta, Appel put a sheet of paper into his Royal typewriter and wrote a letter to these same Yankees asking about the possibility of joining their rank as an employee in the public relations department. This missive to public relations director Bob Fishel resembled nothing so much as a member of the chess club asking the homecoming queen to the prom. The queen said yes. It was 1967, after all, the Summer of Love.

Appel began with the Yankees answering Mickey Mantle's fan mail. He progressed from summer employee to full-time PR flak by midway through his senior year in Oneonta, restructuring his final semester to independent study courses so he could work at Yankee Stadium. It was the Yankees, it was 1970, and it seemed about as exciting to most of his fellow students as work-ing in an office building when so much was going on in the world. So much injustice, so much prejudice, a war to stop—and weren't the Mets the more interesting New York team now anyway? Regardless of public sentiment, but very much aware of history, Marty's path was chosen. He had joined a winning team. It just wasn't the Yankees.

The owner of the ballclub, the Central Broadcasting System, was a programming juggernaut. Some of the decade's top programming, both in terms of ratings and critical reception, aired on CBS. During the 1972–73 TV season, all the pieces lay in place to dominate the airwaves. Over the next year, the network added to an already impressive array of crime shows—*Hawaii Five-O, Mannix,* and *Cannon*—by adding new programs with familiar faces: aging Buddy Ebsen in *Barnaby Jones* and smooth-headed Telly Sevalas in *Kojak.* The network's touch was so good that they even brought back the bland game show *Match Game* with more ribald questions, transforming it into a daytime hit that ran another dozen years and remained a TV staple, off and on, through the end of the century.

Dick Clark, known to audiences for his Saturday daytime dance show on ABC, *American Bandstand,* helped contestants scale *The $10,000 Pyramid* on CBS (the show moving to ABC in 1974 before returning to CBS in the 1980s). CBS had hits with such varied programming as *The Waltons, Mission Impossible,* and *The Sonny & Cher Comedy Hour.* Even when the network rolled out movies in prime time, as the other networks did on nights they ceded to CBS, they still beat NBC and perennial third-place finisher ABC. But CBS truly shone on Saturday night. Five comedies, each in the top 30 ratings rank, dominated Saturday, making for appointment television before video recorders, cable, or satellite TV had even entered the scene.

The juggernaut began promptly at 8:00 p.m. with the country's top-rated show, *All in the Family,* followed by the fourth-rated *M*A*S*H,* then ninth-ranked *The Mary Tyler Moore Show,* and number 12 *The Bob Newhart Show.* At 10:00 p.m. came *The Carol Burnett Show,* the last in a long line of hour-long variety shows, but with a signature twist: the host, Harvey Korman, Tim Conway, Vicki Lawrence, or other assorted cast members and guest stars cracking up mid-sketch as the audience howled with them. She wrapped up the hour of laughs with a poignant farewell song and a tug on her ear, a message to her grandmother who raised her. CBS was already dominating Saturday night when they moved *Carol Burnett* from Wednesday to Saturday and *M*A*S*H* from Sunday, replacing *Bridget Loves Bernie.* The top-five comedy about the tensions of a young, Irish-Jewish couple became a hit in real life, with David Birney and Meredith Baxter falling in love on the set and later marrying. But CBS canceled the show in March 1973 because it wanted stronger programming on Saturday night. It wasn't the Tiffany Network's first rough judgment.

CBS president Robert Wood had decided in 1970 to retire the stalwarts of the 1960s, like *The Ed Sullivan Show* and *The Beverly Hillbillies*, in favor of shows that catered to younger viewers, the demographic preferred by advertisers. In less than four years, the network had completed the makeover and hit the jackpot demographically, critically, and culturally. Norman Lear's *All in the Family* became the first TV show in history to hit number one for five consecutive seasons (1971–76). In nine years *All in the Family* inspired no fewer than four different spinoffs before changing its name and focus to *Archie Bunker's Place* for four more years through 1983. One of those spinoffs, *Maude*, spawned three spinoffs of its own. Bea Arthur played Maude Findlay, Edith Bunker's "limousine liberal" cousin from the New York suburb of Tuckahoe, the polar opposite of Carroll O'Connor's Queens row house–dwelling, meathead-hating, "stifle-yourself" screaming, über-bigot Archie Bunker. Both shows unabashedly took on race, sex, religion, Vietnam, and other subjects taboo in decades past on network television.

Maude came out ahead of the curve with a show about abortion two months prior to the landmark Supreme Court *Roe v. Wade* ruling that legalized abortion nationally in January 1973. Just nine episodes into the show's first season, the two-part episode "Maude's Dilemma" entered television history as the first program to deal with the subject. For Maude's character, age 47, four times married, with a grandchild already living under her stately suburban roof—and with none of the pressures of young, unmarried, impoverished couples whom this controversial law seemed most aimed at assisting—the plot resolved with far less scrutiny than would have been the case had a network dared deal with the polarizing subject in the same manner four decades later. "It's like going to the dentist," Maude's daughter, played by Adrienne Barbeau, says. She also repeatedly mentions that it's legal in New York, one of four states pre–*Roe v. Wade* to allow abortions upon request and without statutes or stipulations (Alaska, Hawaii, and Washington being the others).

Regardless of which side viewers favored, the issues being explored on network television—and on comedies, no less—had lifted the experience of watching TV from passing time to something viscerally important. Mary Tyler Moore played a liberated Minneapolis career woman with no plans to marry. Bob Newhart examined the life of a Chicago psychiatrist when most thought anyone going to a "shrink" did so because of mental imbalance. Another landmark program, *60 Minutes,* investigated current issues in segments that ran longer, dug deeper, and were more confrontational than the evening news, but the TV news magazine was a long way from the ratings powerhouse it later became. The program spent the first half of 1973 on Friday nights before going off the air entirely in the fall and landing back on Sundays at 6:00 p.m. after football season ended. With the kind of run CBS was having, its coverage of the more established National Football Conference provided higher ratings than NBC's American Football Conference, though ABC's *Monday Night Football,* beginning in 1971, presented one of the few time-slot setbacks for the powerful CBS lineup.

CBS proved it could take on the world's thornier problems and still entertain the viewer, but the network couldn't turn the most successful team in sports history back into winners—even with their best man on it.

⚾ ⚾ ⚾

Connecticut-born, prep school–educated, Ivy League football star, and 1970s renaissance man Edmund Michael Burke had succeeded at every turn. While working as a cargo inspector after college, a chance meeting with William J. Donovan, commander of the newly formed Office of Strategic Services (predecessor of the CIA), led to Burke becoming an agent in occupied Europe during World War II.

He uncovered information about Axis weapons, smuggled out an Italian vice admiral who possessed desperately needed technological information, and parachuted into France to help organize the Resistance. He earned a Bronze Star, Silver Star, and France's Médaille de la Résistance. He served as technical adviser for the 1946 Gary Cooper espionage film *Cloak and Dagger,* based on his own wartime exploits. He joined the CIA—under the front of scouting European locations for Warner Bros.—and took part in operations in Albania, Poland, and Italy. He also served as assistant to John J. McCloy, US high commissioner of Germany, when West Germany was created.

Burke transitioned from the Cold War to "The Greatest Show on Earth," as general manager of Ringling Brothers Barnum & Bailey Circus. His knowledge of Europe brought him back there to develop programming for CBS, and he rose to the presidency of CBS Europe. Returning to the US, Burke became CBS vice president in charge of diversification, one aspect of which was expanding network holdings in the entertainment field beyond television.

Burke had spoken casually with CBS president Frank Stanton about buying a football team, but one day in 1964 Stanton took a different tack.

"What about the New York Yankees?" he asked.

"Terrific idea," Burke replied.

The well-connected Burke knew one of the owners of the Yankees, Dan Topping, and arranged for a lunch with CBS CEO William S. Paley. Burke led the difficult negotiations, and the $14 million deal for an 80 percent stake in the team solidified shortly after the Yankees lost to the Cardinals in the '64 World Series. Former co-owner Del Webb sold his remaining 10 percent to CBS for another $1 million, but Topping stayed on as president. Burke traveled with the team to spring training and went to Yankee Stadium on weekends and at night after he finished poring over price-earning ratios, balance sheets, and other business matters at CBS's Manhattan offices. By the time the Yankees tumbled into the basement in 1966, Topping's interest in the team had faded, and he wanted out. The natural choice to succeed him, Burke was elected chairman and president of the Yankees at a board meeting that September. Stanton insisted he take the dual titles, "So there won't be any question of who is in charge." There was little question of who was in charge for the next six years.

Not a clueless corporate suit presiding over the most fallow period in the history of the original Yankee Stadium, Burke tried to maintain tradition and change what no longer worked while slowly rebuilding a player development system that had run dry. His fellow team executives saw enough in him to push him toward the commissioner's chair in 1969, but Bowie Kuhn became the compromise candidate following a stalemate between Burke's supporters and National League favorite Chub Feeney.

Which was fine by Burke, who had already fulfilled his biggest ambition in baseball. He referred to running the New York Yankees as "a long lilting holiday," but it was filled with hard work and had no shortage of critics— Steinbrenner the biggest.

The animosity between the two men began early. Though Steinbrenner had called Burke "Mr. Yankee" in front of Paley at the initial meeting with CBS about buying the team in December 1972, by spring training Steinbrenner was heard harrumphing to his Cleveland cronies by the pool at the team hotel in Fort Lauderdale, "I'll make that long-haired Irish sonofabitch dance to my tune." Burke's long, flowing white hair belonged to the early 1970s, but it was beyond comprehension in Steinbrenner's button-down version of how things should be done. Steinbrenner was irate that Yankees employees received fresh-cut flowers on their desks every day; furious that Burke had authorized a 15 percent raise for outfielder Bobby Murcer—the '73 yearbook cover boy—for $100,000 per year; and livid that the picture of the managing general partners in the 1973 yearbook, his first yearbook as owner, should feature the uncombed Burke in a ratty denim shirt, unbuttoned, with white chest hair visible, his hands stuffed into the back pockets of white flannels gone yellow with age. To his left stood Steinbrenner in a jacket, his sport shirt buttoned to his neck—frowning. Burke described the scene in *Outrageous Good Fortune*, saying that Steinbrenner looked "altogether well scrubbed and fit to pass a spit-and-polish inspection. His unspoken displeasure at my impromptu attire screwed his face into a sour glare."

Burke made friends easily and made an impression wherever he went. The former spy and circus leader was a ladies man, a bon vivant, a man about town, and a little vain. "Burke, at that time, was very popular," recalls Steve Jacobson, who covered the sale of the Yankees for *Newsday*. "He was urbane, witty, an elegant man. He presented a much more agreeable face to the franchise. CBS wouldn't put any money into him and into the Yankees at that time. He was a friendly image of the Yankees, but they weren't getting better."

Burke was uncharacteristically unaware when it came to dealing with his new partner. Yankees VP of administration Howard Berk, whose wife had overheard Steinbrenner's poolside comments about Burke in Fort Lauderdale during spring training, told *New York Daily News* writer Bill Madden years later: "I couldn't believe Mike still didn't get it. He was a very bright and incisive guy, but in many ways he was also very naive."

The purchase arrangement had awarded 5 percent of the team to Burke, less than half of Steinbrenner's share as chief operating officer. The two had agreed that Burke would be president of the club, with Steinbrenner telling William S. Paley as much when they met at the CBS offices the previous December. By March, Steinbrenner and Burke were still working out the formal agreement on Burke's position with the team. Nothing was a given, not after the January breakfast among Steinbrenner, Burke, and Gabe Paul.

Paul, who had informed Steinbrenner the Yankees were available, figured he would get a prominent position with the team, even sending a presale gift of third baseman Graig Nettles, a future home run champion in the Bronx, Gold Glove third baseman, and Yankees co-captain, from the Indians a month before the public knew the Yankees were being sold. In return, Cleveland received four touted young players who never amounted to much in the majors. After the initial sale press conference on January 3, the Yankees scheduled a second conference a week later at a private upstairs banquet room at the swanky 21 Club to announce the other limited partners. Only hours earlier had Paul been able to extricate himself as Indians general manager officially. That morning at the Carlyle Hotel, Burke learned that Paul expected to be introduced as president of the Yankees. Steinbrenner had promised him the post. But it was taken—by Burke; so was the general manager's position, by Lee MacPhail. Burke later wrote that, when Paul and Burke learned that they were both sitting on the same musical chair, "Steinbrenner withdrew to his bedroom to comb his hair, leaving Paul and me in the sitting room to 'sort it out.' We did quickly, if temporarily."

Burke knew at least that Paul was coming aboard and would buy a 5 percent stake, the same size as Burke's, if Paul could sell his shares in the Indians. Steinbrenner had told Burke: "Gabe is 63, you know. He has a home in Florida, and he and Mary will retire there in a couple of years. An association with the Yankees will be a good way for him to end his career." Now Burke came face to face with Paul, the grizzled baseball veteran, who had gotten into the baseball business with the Cincinnati Reds in the 1930s under Larry MacPhail, father of the current Yankees GM. But Paul wasn't working on his exit from the game. Burke was—courtesy of Steinbrenner.

At the January 10 press conference at the 21 Club, Burke told the press the Paul retirement story, with the veteran exec taking the title of administrative partner for the time being. Yet when Burke's arrangement was put to paper in March, matters became messier still. Steinbrenner retained George Martin from Mudge Rose, the Wall Street law firm that had served as the legal launching pad for Nixon, soon to start his infamously brief second term as president.

The papers seemed to be in order; Steinbrenner and Burke even shook on the deal. But the next day, after Burke had flown back to New York, he received a call from his lawyer, Bruce Haims: "Steinbrenner has repudiated the deal." Burke and his lawyer both felt that the agreement had reflected the terms discussed by the two general partners. Burke quickly made a decision: "I am going to disengage." He told his lawyer that he planned—or at least spun it that way in his memoirs—to go out his own way. He would get the season started, with Steinbrenner growing "more and more agitated, more and more paranoid by my presence. By the time I tell him I've decided to withdraw, he'll kiss me."

Agitated? Yes. Paranoid? Yes. A kiss goodbye? Well, let's just say that no cut flowers were sent to anyone's desk.

The last Opening Day at the original Yankee Stadium was supposed to be special. It wasn't.

On April 9, six Mondays after the Peterson-Kekich affair had exploded in print and across airwaves, the Yankees took the field at Yankee Stadium for the first time under the watchful eyes of George Steinbrenner and for the last home opener at the old ball yard that had crammed in 72,000 on day one in 1923. Fifty years later, facing Steinbrenner's hometown Indians, the home opener drew just 17,028. Later in the week fans coming to the park received a more festive birthday offering with cake—a Hostess cupcake wrapped in a special 50th-anniversary logo, the same as the Yankees wore on their left sleeves.

Cleveland's lineup for the Yankee Stadium home opener featured three players whom the Tribe had acquired from the Yankees for Nettles: right fielder Rusty Torres leading off, left fielder Charlie Spikes in the cleanup spot, and John Ellis as designated hitter. The Tribe also had two players from Charlie Finley's doghouse: center fielder George Hendrick and catcher Dave Duncan. While the Tribe would miss Nettles, his replacement at the hot corner was Buddy Bell, son of former All-Star outfielder Gus Bell. Buddy made his own way in the game as a five-time All-Star, six-time Gold Glove third baseman, amassing 2,514 hits over 18 years. The new faces led the Indians to a 3–1 victory over the Yankees, with rookie Brent Strom, another new member of the Tribe (acquired from the Mets), earning his first major league victory. The loser? Fritz Peterson.

Strom had his toughest moment in the eighth inning. With Bobby Murcer representing the tying run, the Cleveland lefty caught Murcer looking for the third out. Strom finished the Yankees in the ninth, and the smallish Opening Day crowd disbursed. When Steinbrenner came across Burke in the narrow hallway between their offices, Cleveland cronies surrounding the two men, George was still fuming over the Murcer strikeout.

"There's your goddamned hundred-thousand-dollar-a-year ballplayer," the new owner snarled.

Burke growled back, "Bobby Murcer will strike out again, knock in runs again, hit home runs again."

When he wrote his memoirs later and reflected on the confrontation, Burke noted how Murcer finished the '73 season—22 home runs, 95 RBI, .304 average. "Baseball people will tell you," in an obvious dig at the novice owner, "that's very good indeed." Just don't mention that Strom, whose strikeout of the Yankees' cleanup hitter had led to the confrontation, went just 1-10 the rest of the year.

The next day the players were in for a surprise. Ralph Houk had a list of uniform numbers of those players judged by the new owner to have hair whose length was "unacceptable." Though the team had yet to win a game, the first edict of the new boss—quickly morphing into Boss with a capital "B"—was for the Yankees to get a haircut. Steinbrenner had noticed the offending players while the team lined up on the first-base line and had doffed their caps for "The Star Spangled Banner."

Manager Ralph Houk, running the club his own way through two previous ownership groups, tried to keep a straight face as he read the numbers in the clubhouse. It was as if he were telling front-line troops holding out at the Battle of the Bulge—where "The Major" had been decorated for repelling a massed German assault and then crossing enemy lines in a jeep to deliver crucial orders to besieged Bastogne, returning two days later with two holes in his helmet—that the commanding general wanted the men to put their rifles in the snow so they could shave off that three-day stubble.

"I was on the list," says Fritz Peterson, who recalls seeing Steinbrenner's hair-razing roll posted in the locker room. "I said to the guys, 'Learn the players' names, George.'"

Despite not being able to tell who was who on his first day—or bothering to look at a program to find out—Steinbrenner didn't make it easy for other visitors to the stadium to learn who was on the team either. He never put players' names either on home or road uniforms, even after every other team did so on road jerseys and all but two other clubs (Red Sox and Giants) on home uniforms.

"In college football, there's a whole subculture of coaches who refuse to put names on the back unless the team 'earns' it by going to a bowl game, or improving on last year's record, or whatever," says Paul Lukas, an expert on this and other uniform related subjects at the web site Uni Watch, regarding the no-name jerseys for the Yankees. "It's used as a motivator. I don't think this is done so much in baseball, but the underlying principle—the team versus the individual—is the same." But wouldn't it be like an old Big Ten football coach like Steinbrenner to bring that mentality to baseball; just like the military school graduate brought the attitude of his own Battle of the Bulge hero, "Blood and Guts" Gen. George S. Patton, to the owner's box: "Do your duty as you see it, and damn the consequences."

The Yankees finally won their first game of the year following the haircut edict, a two-hit shutout by Mel Stottlemyre, his hair always closely cropped. Burke of course didn't cut his hair; he cut ties with the organization. It wasn't about hair, it wasn't about the team—which spent all of April under .500— it was about quality of life. The time had come to disengage. Howard Berk, VP of administration, left the Yankees the same week. Absentee ownership was piling up victims already.

"It made no sense for us to try work together," Burke later wrote of Steinbrenner. "We came at the world from two different poles, and Yankee Stadium was too confined a space to contain us. . . . He [Steinbrenner] shouted and blustered for lack of fundamental self-assurance, terrible tempered for reasons perhaps as unclear to himself as to others." Burke's letter of resignation was even more succinct:

> The scope of responsibilities and authority proposed to be assigned to me are so limited as to be incompatible with even the narrowest definition of "chief operating officer" and I must conclude that you do not want me to operate the Yankees. Slowly and sadly, I have come to this conclusion. It represents a stunning, personal setback.

When the players heard of the resignation on April 29, Graig Nettles quipped, "Was his hair too long?" For the Yankees, it was the beginning of the "Bronx Zoo" period. Those who had options started to weigh them.

"Any time ownership changes, you're nervous about that," Marty Appel says. "When we had the press conference in January to announce the owner and a week later to introduce all the partners, he [Steinbrenner] was reading over all of our press material and the little bios of all of the partners. He would say something like, 'This is well done. This is a good job.' Bob [Fishel] and I both had a sigh of relief that he liked it. I remember that very well. We didn't have much exchange with him until mid-April when Mike Burke resigned. Suddenly George was the principal owner all by himself. Then he very much became a daily presence in our lives." Appel chose to hold onto his dream job with the Yankees and moved up in the firing line as head of the PR department after the '73 season when Fishel jumped ship to the American League office with Lee MacPhail, who got to see Steinbrenner's tirades from the other side as AL president.

Burke took over as president of Madison Square Garden in July 1973, assuming dual roles to head both the New York Knicks and Rangers. It wasn't the same as his years with the Yankees, which he called "idyllic; nothing would be quite like them again." Competition from other venues, especially the emerging sports complex in New Jersey, was changing the landscape.

Even as Burke took over two New York teams riding high on success in 1973, the city itself was decaying. Many who worked in New York hustled home to the suburbs or the safety of dwellings high above the increasingly perilous streets. The city was still *the* city, but it would take a long time before many felt safe walking in certain parts of it or taking the graffiti-strewn subway after dark. To outsiders, New York more and more conjured images of *Death Wish*, the 1972 crime novel by Brian Garfield that became a Charles Bronson movie filmed in New York in 1973. Bronson played a law-abiding businessman turned vigilante because of what the streets had done to his family and the city he called home. It was the first of his five *Death Wish* movies.

Burke left New York and the Garden in 1981 at age 63. He retired to a farm in County Galway, Ireland, land of his forebears, taking with him his memories and mementos. Among these was a photograph from his final weeks with the Yankees, the yearbook picture with Steinbrenner from spring training 1973, the free-spirited and unbuttoned Burke next to the owner who got what he most desired and looked as miserable as ever.

"I still have the picture," he wrote in 1984, "framed and hanging on a wall, and it makes me smile every time my eye catches it. It tells the story of the time and the difference between us. George is tight, angry, and uncertain. I am relaxed and content, a man with a secret, certain of where I am going and how it will come out in the end. He is still plotting my undoing, and I know that he can't win; I have already left."

Joe Rudi coming home on a walkoff homer, greeted by Sal Bando among others RON RIESTERER

Six

NOT YOUR AVERAGE JOE

One of the first moves Charlie Finley made after relocating the A's to Oakland in 1968 was hiring the man officially designated by Major League Baseball with the sobriquet he thought he owned all along: greatest living ballplayer.

Joe DiMaggio relished the title and could back up the claim. He had knocked in runs at a staggering rate even for the high-powered 1930s, established the longest hitting streak in major league history at 56 (after owning the Pacific Coast League record of 61), won three American League MVP Awards, had his own song as the best of the three DiMaggio brothers manning center field in the big leagues, was an All-Star in each of his 13 seasons, sat on the losing end just once in 10 World Series as a Yankee, and did all this while spending three full seasons in the military and retiring at 36. Joltin' Joe had even married the girl of everyone's dreams, Marilyn Monroe. He was the crown prince of baseball: valiant, stately, aloof. The world had only seen him in three outfits in his life: a Yankees home uniform, a Yankees road uniform, and a tailored suit. Yet somehow Finley got the great DiMaggio to don the flamboyant green and gold A's uniform and smile while wearing it.

DiMaggio had retired in 1951, quitting while still among the best in the game. Admirable, certainly, but it left him two years shy of accruing the maximum pension for a major leaguer. The son of an immigrant fisherman in San Francisco, Joe D. returned to the Bay Area after he retired. He put in the required time with the A's and began receiving the pension in 1974, which, in the words of his thorough but less than laudatory biographer, Richard Ben Cramer, "He never touched but piled up in a satisfying stack." In the bright hue of an A's uniform—the 1960s duds accentuating the Kelly green more than the Fort Knox gold—Joe D. took to the role of mentor. His two years with the A's not only forged the legend's full pension, they also helped create the best Oakland left fielder this side of Rickey Henderson.

Joe Rudi was a shortstop in high school and shifted to third base in the minors. He wound up in the outfield, but Rudi was far from a finished product when he arrived in Oakland in May 1968. He had been with the team in Kansas City the year before and recalls playing left field in Yankee Stadium, where "the hitter looks like he's nine miles away." Rudi struggled enough in the outfield that he shifted to first base after being sent back to the minors, but the A's had a need in left field.

For a 21-year-old who grew up an hour away in Modesto, the Oakland Coliseum was intimidating—even more so when, in Rudi's first game there after his '68 call-up, Catfish Hunter set down Twin after Twin. "I was scared to death," Rudi admits of playing in Hunter's perfect game. He made three putouts in the game, but manager Bob Kennedy took Rudi out for a defensive replacement in the ninth. Kennedy helped see to it that Rudi became the kind of outfielder whom managers would make sure to have in the field in the ninth inning of pressure games—and Kennedy saw to it the kid learned from the greatest ballplayer alive.

Kennedy fungoed balls to Rudi for half an hour before every game, Joe DiMaggio right there with him, teaching him all he knew about defensive positioning along with a few hitting tips as well. As hitting coach, DiMaggio helped many of the young A's hitters overcome bad habits at the plate, including Reggie Jackson and Sal Bando. Rudi, however, focused on the long hours DiMaggio spent with him on "footwork, how to follow the ball while you are turning, getting in position to throw." Yogi Berra said of his former Yankee teammate: "He never did anything wrong on the field," and DiMaggio's star pupil helped the A's hum defensively and offensively.

Despite a reputation as one of the game's most underrated players, Rudi earned his share of acclaim. He twice finished as runner-up in the MVP voting, was named to three All-Star teams, and won three Gold Gloves. "They sent me down at one point thinking I would never make it as an outfielder," Rudi says. "The thing I'm most proud of is winning three Gold Gloves as an outfielder. I worked my butt off to get those."

Many of the young A's saw a different DiMaggio than everyone else and benefited from the experience. In 1973, DiMaggio started making commercials for Mr. Coffee, helping move one million units in just a few months. Though he fought with Finley over making personal appearances in the East Bay to try to sell tickets, DiMaggio remained with the A's after Kennedy was abruptly fired on the last day of the '68 season. "He was such a great guy," Rudi says of DiMaggio. "Around people he doesn't know well or writers, fans, and everything else, he was always sort of . . . not standoffish, but he was protective of himself because he was inundated all the time. But around the players he was fantastic.

"He had a great sense of humor," Rudi says. "You had to watch out where you were sitting and stepping on things at times. He would put things in your shoes, light your shoes on fire—he was always playing practical jokes. . . . I loved him because he was a lot of fun with the players. So much different than when he was out in public. I had a great time with him."

The 1973 season didn't start out so great for the A's, however. The defending world champions didn't win their first series until their sixth try. Even that was somewhat aggravating since Darold Knowles blew the save in the ninth inning for what would have been Catfish Hunter's first win of the year. The A's did come up with a solution to their designated hitter problem after a month of floundering. While Oakland discard Orlando Cepeda was hitting .347 with six home runs and 17 knocked in during his first month as Boston's DH, six different A's combined to bat just .231 with two home runs and six RBI in the newly created position over the same span. So Finley found the best available ballplayer to fill that void.

Deron Johnson, who had spent parts of two years with the A's before being sold to Cincinnati in 1963, returned to the fold a decade later at the expense of low-level minor leaguer Jack Barnstable. Johnson, in a slump since faltering for the Phils as a pinch hitter on Opening Day at Shea Stadium, fit perfectly in Oakland. The A's stopped using speedsters like Bill North and Angel Mangual as DH and followed the path of other AL teams by going with a slow-footed slugger. "We changed our thinking on the DH," Dick Williams said. "Deron Johnson is the DH we've been looking for." Johnson, 34, who had never played in a postseason game in a major league career that stretched back to 1960, had three hits and knocked home four in his Oakland debut and barely missed a game until the last week of the season.

"In April and May all of us struggled except him," Rudi says of Johnson. "He smoked the ball. He was really the guy that carried us for the first couple of months until about June, when we all started coming around and playing better." The A's finally reached the .500 mark with a doubleheader sweep in Cleveland on May 6, the same weekend Johnson arrived. By the end of the month, however, the A's still stood at .500 and had slid to fifth place, six games behind the White Sox. That Chicago, a popular pick to claim the AL West crown before the season, had reached first place surprised no one. The second-place Royals were expected to contend, brimming as they were with talented young players, including Steve Busby, who on April 27 had thrown the first of the four major league no-hitters in 1973. But tied in the standings with the Royals in mid-April were the surprising Angels, a club that had been a distant fifth in 1972 after scoring the fewest runs in baseball.

The Angels' vexing pitching staff had made quick work of manager Del Rice after one year, allowing the fewest hits in the majors but making up for it by walking the most and wild pitching them up a base with league-high efficiency. Nolan Ryan was responsible for some of that wildness—157 of the 620 walks and 18 of the 49 wild pitches were his—but he had 329 of the club's 1,000 strikeouts in 1972. Less than six weeks into 1973, Ryan already had 82 strikeouts in 73 innings, 5 wins—all complete games—plus a save, as the defending world champions came to Anaheim to face the Angels for the first time on May 16.

The A's were lucky to have missed Ryan. The night before the A's arrived, Ryan had thrown the first of his seven career no-hitters. He had lasted just one-third of an inning in his previous start—such was the unpredictable Ryan the Mets had pulled the plug on. But the Angels reaped the reward of their patience.

Clyde Wright beat Oakland in the opener of the two-game set in Anaheim, 7–2. Bobby Valentine scored the go-ahead run, knocked in an insurance run, and caught both balls hit to him in center field for the Angels. On a challenged offensive club, Valentine was the shining hope. A heavily recruited schoolboy star from Stamford, Connecticut, Valentine had signed a letter of intent to play baseball and football at USC, where he inherited the running back position and number 32 of outgoing Heisman Trophy–winner O. J. Simpson.

The PAC-8 Conference was breaking new ground by allowing freshmen to play varsity sports, but Valentine, fifth overall pick in 1968 by the Dodgers, signed a pro contract instead when general manager Al Campanis convinced him to don the Dodger blue. Coming up through the system with a talented core of young hitters, Valentine was dispatched in a local blockbuster deal after the '72 season: a seven-player swap that sent Frank Robinson to Anaheim and Andy Messersmith to Los Angeles. The trade also opened up the roster so the Dodgers could regularly play an infield of Steve Garvey, Davey Lopes, Bill Russell, and Ron Cey, who began a record string of nine seasons as a quartet in 1973.

A shortstop by trade, the speedy Valentine had the tools to play anywhere. Dodgers manager Walter Alston used Valentine's athleticism to play six different positions in 1972; Angels skipper Bobby Winkles was intrigued as well. When Angels center fielder Ken Berry was injured in May 1973, Valentine took over in center, and rookie Rudy Meoli manned shortstop. Valentine was supposed to fill in for Berry just through the end of the road trip, but when Ryan ended the swing with the no-hitter in Kansas City, an exuberant Winkles told Valentine, "We can't switch a winner." When Wright beat the A's the next night with Valentine in center, the manager assured his third-place hitter that May 17 would be his last night in center field. It was.

Valentine lined a base hit in the first inning against Catfish Hunter, raising his average over .300 but getting gunned down in the process as he tried to stretch it to a double on center fielder Bill North. "I was the guy running around and hustling," Valentine described himself at 23 to Bob Costas in 2012. With two on and two out in a scoreless game the next inning, Dick Green lifted a Rudy May pitch to deep center and Valentine took off at full speed. "I thought I could catch anything, I thought I was invincible, I was a young player once, too, you know," Valentine relayed from the other side of 60. "I ran into the wall, my leg broke, and it did change." The "it" being his career.

Green's ball cleared the fence, but Valentine's right leg got caught in the wire, breaking two bones. He missed the rest of the year, but the new fiberglass casts just then coming into use allowed him to do more than he should have. "Instead of it healing straight, it healed at a bend," Valentine told Costas, "and there goes the speed and balance and all that good stuff."

From that game forward the California Angels went 61-70 in 1973 and weren't a factor in the AL West, even with Nolan Ryan throwing two no-hitters, winning 20 games for the first time, and breaking Sandy Koufax's record with 383 strikeouts. It's hard for a team to win when it loses both the shortstop and center fielder—even if it's just one man and even if that man is never the same again.

⚾ ⚾ ⚾

In 1973, Jack Nicklaus won the PGA Championship at Canterbury Golf Club in Cleveland. It was his 14th major victory, eclipsing the previous mark set by Bobby Jones. At 33, Nicklaus was five years older than Bobby Jones was when he retired after winning all four majors as they were known in 1930: the British and US Opens and the British and US Amateurs.

Golf, and life in general, had changed in those four decades, with two of the majors of 1973 different than in Jones's day. Nicklaus was a professional; at Ohio State in the early 1960s he briefly considered remaining an amateur and becoming a pharmacist, like his father. Jones, a lawyer, had stopped competing as an amateur to try his hand at other aspects of the game. He made instructional films, authored books, toured widely, and built what many consider his greatest legacy: Augusta National in his Georgia hometown. The annual tournament at that venue, the Masters, became a major tournament, as did the PGA Championship.

Like Bobby Jones, the legendary thoroughbred Man o' War hailed from the mists of the Golden Age of Sport. After the Great War and before the Depression, America threw itself into sports. Individual sports were tremendously popular, with Jones—as well as professional juggernaut Walter Hagen—on the golf course, Big Bill Tilden on the tennis court, and Jack Dempsey in the boxing ring. Despite all the great baseball players emerging during the decade, including Yankees slugger Lou Gehrig, Babe Ruth gave the twenties its roar. Yet even he was a relative babe when Man o' War commanded the field.

Due to antigambling legislation in New York, followed by World War I, horse racing had been down for a long time when Man o' War arrived on the scene in 1919. Before 1920 was over, the big red horse had galloped to 20 wins in 21 starts, won one race by 100 lengths, smashed the mark for a mile and three furlongs at the Belmont Stakes, and whipped every other horse in his path, save one (a thoroughbred at Saratoga fittingly named Upset). Then he sired a Triple Crown winner, War Admiral, and his descendents were so numerous and successful that in 1966 it was said that more than a third of the stakes winners descended from Man o' War.

Then came Secretariat.

Named after a stable secretary because the first 10 names submitted were already taken, Secretariat was one of a kind. The Virginia-born chestnut colt was the first two-year-old to be Horse of the Year and then took the honor again the next year. The horse even won the Man o' War Stakes at Belmont Park in October 1973 with a record time, but Secretariat's greatest moment had come four months earlier on June 9, also on Man o' War's home track.

With Secretariat attempting to become the first Triple Crown winner in 25 years, CBS again had a winner with track announcer Chic Anderson's famous call of the remarkable horse's crowning moment: "Secretariat is alone. He is moving like a tremendous machine!" The camera kept pulling back and panning to try to get another horse in the frame. When it was over and Secretariat had won by 31 lengths with the astonishing time of 2:24 flat to shatter the 1½-mile record by 2¾ seconds, Anderson declared: "That is a record that may stand forever." Forty years is hardly forever, but that time hasn't even been approached since.

Secretariat not only had to beat the other horses, he had to beat the hype. *Time, Newsweek*, and *Sports Illustrated* all featured the horse on the cover the week before the 1973 Belmont. Secretariat didn't read the clippings. He just blew the whole field, the whole crowd, and the whole country away. People rejoiced as owner Penny Chenery, a recently widowed housewife, waved her arms in jubilation while jockey Ron Turcotte tipped his hat gallantly to the roaring crowd of 70,000, as if in awe just like everyone else. "I was just along for the ride," said Turcotte, who famously peeked back at the other horses in the distance because Anderson's track call made him wonder if Secretariat really was that far ahead.

Halfway through a drag of a year on the national spirit, two record-setting sports performances had provided a jolt to a Watergate-weary, inflation-fatigued nation: The undefeated Miami Dolphins secured the Super Bowl, and the unsinkable Secretariat took the Triple Crown. So what exactly did a defending world champion ballclub have to do to get some attention?

⚾ ⚾ ⚾

Oakland's first trip to Detroit since the Bert Campaneris bat-throwing incident the previous October resulted in Campy sitting out another five games. The A's entered Motown the last weekend in May with the superior record, yet they were tied for third in the West while the 20-20 Tigers held first place in the East. Both teams' fortunes would change.

Booed lustily at Tiger Stadium every time he came up in the first game of the weekend series, Campy didn't face Lerrin LaGrow, but he did come face to face with Tigers catcher Bill Freehan. After Freehan singled as a pinch hitter in the 11th inning of a scoreless game, a groundball to first afforded a chance of retribution. As Campaneris took the throw at second base, Freehan slammed into the Oakland shortstop, resulting in an errant return throw as well as a pulled shoulder muscle. The A's lost the game and their shortstop for a week. Though Freehan had exacted revenge, manager Billy Martin, angrier than anyone when Campaneris threw the bat at LaGrow seven months earlier, put the matter in perspective by declaring: "It's history." History was a little different than it had been the previous fall, the home club winning twice in Detroit and then holding on for a one-run win in the third game to complete the sweep.

Without Campaneris, the A's seemed lifeless. They were just 2–11 in games he didn't start in 1973, and one of those wins came courtesy of Ken Holtzman retiring the first 20 batters at Yankee Stadium. Former A's teammate Matty Alou ended Holtzman's bid at a third career no-hitter, but his combined one-hitter with Rollie Fingers ended a five-game losing streak. It was Holtzman's 10th win, and it wasn't even June yet.

The rest of the team caught up with Holtzman, repaying the Tigers and Yankees by winning both series in Oakland. More important was winning both home and away series from divisional foes Chicago and Kansas City. The White Sox not only dropped six of nine to the A's in a 10-day span (two doubleheaders included), but they lost the previous year's MVP, Dick Allen.

Mike Epstein, the dispatched A's first baseman now with the Angels, collided with Allen and broke the slugger's leg on June 28, the same night Oakland climbed into sole possession of the top spot in the AL West for the first time in 1973. Allen, hitting .310 with 16 homers at the time of the injury, was done for the year save for five more wobbly at-bats. One game out of first place at the time of the injury, the White Sox finished the year 17 games back. With the Angels and White Sox done in by injuries, the Rangers well on their way to 100 losses, and the surprising first half by the rebuilding Twins about to enter an ugly phase, the only team really left in the AL West race was the Royals.

Kansas City had something to prove. They were where the A's had been a few years ago with a core of good young players who had come up at the same time. The Royals were playing in a beautiful, brand new stadium built just for them at taxpayer expense. Take that, Charlie Finley and your late Kansas City club, the patrons of brand-new Royals Stadium said with every lusty boo for all things Oakland at the 1973 All-Star Game.

Royals Stadium's massive crowned scoreboard, stylishly clipped upper deck, and signature fountains caught the oohs and ahs of everyone—and more people were invited than usual. Commissioner Kuhn, never afraid to butt into matters that others had already settled, added an extra slot to the team for Nolan Ryan after Dick Williams had already declared the Ryan Express wasn't making the cut. Williams preferred California's Jim Singer over the Angel who was the first pitcher since 1938 All-Star starter Johnny Vander Meer to have two no-hitters before the break, and in Ryan's last start he had come within six outs of matching Vander Meer's '38 feat of back-to-back no-hitters. The extra roster spot for each league was actually added to allow the National League to include 42-year-old Willie Mays, hitting a robust .214, who had last missed being invited to the All-Star Game during the Truman administration. While Ryan and Mays ended up on the team, Baltimore's Jim Palmer didn't. Despite a superb season that resulted in the first of his three Cy Young Awards, Palmer stayed home. The man making the picks for the AL roster almost didn't make it, either.

The Thursday before the All-Star Game, Dick Williams was rushed to the hospital for an emergency appendectomy. He awoke in the hospital in pain, missing all three games of Oakland's sweep of Cleveland to end the first half. Williams, who had an itinerant career as a player only to win a pennant as a rookie manager in Boston—earning his first All-Star managing assignment in 1968—understood how fortunate he was to have another chance to take part in the game. He gritted his teeth and got on a plane to Kansas City.

Finley had so enjoyed rubbing his world championship trophy in the faces of the old boy network of major league owners that there was no way he was going to miss a chance to show Kansas City that, like Mary Tyler Moore, he might just make it after all. Instead of throwing his hat in the air like Mary in the opening sequence, Charlie had the American League throw orange baseballs—another Finley innovation—during warmups. The fans rained cheers on Willie Mays and especially Hank Aaron, who was touched given the ambivalent and often angry reception he'd received in his home stadium as he got close to the Babe's home run mark.

But the spigot shot the other way for the A's throughout the night. Dick Williams, still in pain, had forgotten all about Finley's Kansas City past and was stunned by the crowd reaction. "So here I was, in one of the more heroic moments of my life, getting booed off the field," he said.

It was music to Finley's ears. This ill-treated and former tenant of Kansas City now sported the most luxurious World Series ring known to man. If critics couldn't get a chance to see what the rings looked like, you could spot the uniforms from Jupiter. While everyone else on the American League side wore white, the A's looked their colorful best. Six members of the first-place A's were All-Stars, so three donned the yellow uniform (Catfish Hunter, Bert Campaneris, and Reggie Jackson), and three were clad in green (Ken Holtzman, Sal Bando, and Rollie Fingers). Finley wore a huge smile—until the second inning, that is.

After not winning a game until the last day of April, Catfish Hunter had reeled off 10 straight wins and pulled into the All-Star break at 15–3 with the best winning percentage in either league. He started the All-Star Game, as did teammates Campy and Reggie, who came into the game as the AL leader in home runs (23), RBIs (81), and runs (69). Also in the starting lineup: six-figure Yankees slugger Bobby Murcer, hometown Royals Amos Otis and John Mayberry (picked by Williams to replace injured Dick Allen at first base), plus Rod Carew of the Twins, Carlton Fisk of the Red Sox, and Orioles legend Brooks Robinson, voted to start despite hitting just a shade better than Mays, at .216.

Hunter breezed through the first inning as did National League starter Rick Wise. When asked before the game about pitching to NL cleanup hit-ter Hank Aaron, who came in with 27 home runs for the season and an even 700 for his career, Hunter said, "I'm going to throw it down the middle; then I'm gonna duck." If only he'd followed that advice with the fifth-place hitter, Billy Williams. After Aaron popped up, the Cubs outfielder hit a line drive back through the box that Catfish instinctively lunged at with his pitching hand. Williams had an infield hit, and Hunter a broken thumb. The giddiness went right out of the big A's contingent. The pain was back for Dick Williams, and it had little to do with the 7–1 drubbing administered by the National League, their seventh win in eight years.

The A's returned home with serious concerns about the second half. But as bad as it looked with Oakland's ace knocked out—literally—in Kansas City, Hunter stayed positive. His last missed start had come in 1966 when he was out for a month with an emergency appendectomy, but he knew what it was to come back from injury.

While out hunting, his brother's gun accidentally discharged and blew off his little toe, threatening to end his career while he was still in high school in rural North Carolina. Hunter made his own rubber insole to keep the pellets from pressing against his foot when he pitched and came within one run of winning a second straight state title. The A's had continued their pursuit of Hunter after other teams backed off. That meant something to the farmer's son, the youngest of 10. Hunter signed with the Kansas City A's for $75,000 on June 8, 1964. Finley then sent him to the famed Mayo Clinic in Minnesota—two pieces of bone and 16 pellets removed from his right foot—and kept him working through his convalescence with a job in his company's mailroom. Finley even let the 18-year-old travel with the major league team while his foot continued to heal.

There was just one catch, though.

As negotiations were drawing to a close that June, Finley called up Hunter and asked, "Do you have a nickname?"

He did not.

"Well, to play baseball, you've got to have a nickname," said Charles Oscar Finley—nicknames apparently not required to sell insurance. "What do you like to do?"

He was a hunter both by name and passion. Jimmy also liked to fish.

"Fine," said Finley. "When you were six years old, you ran away from home and went fishing. Your mom and dad had been looking for you all day. When they finally found you about, ah, four o'clock in the afternoon, you'd caught two big fish . . . ahhh . . . catfish . . . and were reeling in the third. And that's how you got your nickname."

The young man said he understood.

"Good," Finley said. "Now repeat it back to me."

Catfish Hunter was all country boy and hardball. Charlie Finley was all showman and business. They were different, but there was a connection: Finley, the Alabama kid from the mills, didn't want to move north and ditched his accent after he got there, working his way up from the bottom; Hunter, a practical joker with deadpan delivery, was a North Carolina farmer with proverbial ice water in his veins.

Other than a few weeks of Instructional Ball in the fall of '64, Hunter never threw a pitch in a minor league game. He took his lumps in Kansas City. Everyone did. But almost a decade later, there was a very good team in Oakland with "A's" stitched on the pullover jersey in a variety of colors. (Finley briefly tried a green shirt and green pants combination for his club in June '73.) Even if Hunter had to miss four or five starts, if he healed quickly and properly, this team might yet win another world championship.

"Heck, it might help me," the 27-year-old pitcher told the press, his thumb in a splint. "I need the rest. I'll be strong for August and September."

Good. Now repeat it back.

Jon Matlack in mid-windup NATIONAL BASEBALL HALL OF FAME LIBRARY, COOPERSTOWN, NY

Seven

WOUNDED KNEE, FRACTURED SKULL

*T*he standoff finally ended after 10 weeks.

A shot fired during the 1890 disarming in Wounded Knee, South Dakota—the site of the last massacre of the Indian Wars—set off a fire-fight that left more than 150 Lakota Sioux dead, many of them women and children.

Eighty-three years later about 200 Oglala Lakota and members of the American Indian Movement arrived in the predawn hours of February 27, 1973, taking over the small hamlet in the Pine Ridge Indian Reservation near the South Dakota Badlands to protest the continuing mistreatment of Native Americans and corruption in the reservation system. Property was seized, US marshals were dispatched, supporters flooded in, and three people were killed in the 71-day standoff. Wounded Knee became a rallying point for Native Americans, though it remained a site of continued violence in the years that followed. In the mid-1970s in the tiny, stressful hamlet, the murder rate—many of them unsolved—ranked eight times higher than Detroit, then considered the murder capital of the country.

Alongside the violence and anger in South Dakota came Hollywood. The bizarre appearance of Sacheen Littlefeather in traditional Apache cloth-ing at the Academy Awards ceremony in April 1973, refusing the Best Actor Oscar for sympathizer Marlon Brando, star of the year's top picture, *The Godfather*, created popular support for the movement. The Academy never again allowed proxies and also watched its presenters more closely. The Hollywood ending to the tale is that Roger Moore, who took over the James Bond franchise in 1973 with *Live and Let Die*, took home the statuette that he was supposed to present to Littlefeather until a representative sent by the Academy removed it from his home.

Back in 1973 there were more urgent issues in the American Indian Movement than sports teams' misrepresentations of Native Americans as caricatures, but even as the siege at Wounded Knee ended on May 8, the grinning visage of Chief Wahoo hung on the exterior of Municipal Stadium in Cleveland as a scant 1,437 filed in to watch Gaylord Perry and the Tribe blank the Angels, 2–0—and the Braves had come to New York City.

The Braves weren't anyone's idea of a big draw, not even in Atlanta. Though the Mets and Braves had clashed in the first National League Championship Series in history in 1969—swept by the Miracle Mets— there wasn't much of a rivalry between North and South, NL East and NL West. The Braves, the top-hitting club in the National League, could thank Atlanta's launching pad, known as Fulton-County Stadium, just one in a coming generation of more hitter-friendly ballparks. By the end of '73, the launching pad created the first trio of 40-homer sluggers by any team: Davey Johnson, Darrell Evans, and Hammerin' Hank Aaron.

Aaron began 1973 needing 41 home runs to tie the Bambino. Having hit 25 or more home runs in 17 of the last 18 years, Aaron's longevity and remarkable consistency made it likely that he would achieve the feat. The Babe was an icon—and he was white. So Aaron was facing not only the pressure of scaling the vaunted Ruthian total of 714 that had stood for nearly four decades but also the unrelenting strain of doing it as a black man in the Deep South. Hate mail started to pile up along with the losses.

After dropping the May 7 series opener to the Mets, 7–2, the Braves stood at 9-17, last in their division and second only to the 5-19 Cardinals for the worst start in baseball. The next night looked to be a rerun, with the Mets holding a 3–1 lead in the seventh with Jon Matlack, one of the game's top young lefties, on the mound. Atlanta's lineup had firepower, but Marty Perez wasn't one of the big guns. In 310 career games to that point, he was a .230 hitter with a slugging percentage of just .294. Batting in front of the legendary Aaron in manager Eddie Mathews's lineup, no one was going to pitch around Perez, especially with the bases full, two outs, and Matlack holding that two-run lead with a light rain falling. Perez worked the count to two balls, two strikes, and Matlack threw a curve that he thought the batter went around on. The umpires said no. Here comes the payoff pitch . . .

"I'm trying to nail down this game," Matlack recalls. "I overthrew the next pitch. It was a fastball, and I landed really hard when I threw it. I lost sight of the ball to the plate. I could see him swing and hear the bat crack, but I don't pick up the baseball until it's right on top of me. I barely got the fingers of my left hand in front of my face. It hit my fingers [on the mitt], hit my cap, and it hit me just over the left eye. They tell me—I don't know because I couldn't see it—but it went from my forehead into the dugout. It cost me two runs and ultimately cost me the ballgame."

The sudden tie fell to secondary importance during this frightening moment at Shea Stadium. Right fielder Rusty Staub, shaking his head at the memory of it years later, summed up his teammates' reaction: "We were just all thrilled that he wasn't dead." Dee Matlack wasn't even sure of that as the trainer came out and pulled a tarp over her prone husband's body as the rain fell.

"They're messing with me, and it's raining," he thought as catcher Jerry Grote and his teammates gathered around him. "My wife thinks I'm dead because they cover me up with a tarp." Still conscious and bleeding from his head, the dazed pitcher thought he'd been struck in the mouth until things came into sharp, painful focus. "I can see my forehead at this point. I can see it literally swollen up to where I can *see* it. I had a whale of a headache and felt very weak."

First baseman Ed Kranepool stood over Matlack as he was attended to at Shea. "You think about Herb Score," he said, recalling the sensational Indians southpaw hit in the face with a line drive against the Yankees in 1957. "It changed his whole career. Matlack was very fortunate."

Like Score at the time of the injury, Matlack was a 23-year-old southpaw and recent Rookie of the Year winner with seemingly unlimited potential. Matlack had been the lone ray of sunshine to emerge in the wake of the Nolan Ryan trade. As a rookie taking Ryan's place in the rotation in 1972, he won 15 games, threw 4 shutouts, and compiled an ERA (2.32) more than half a run per game better than ace Tom Seaver's. Matlack also had better luck than Score, who came back a year after being hit but left baseball by age 28.

"That's the first I hear his name," says Matlack of Score. "I was reading the paper the next day in the hospital—there's my picture and this guy I don't recognize. It tells me about how Herb Score got hit and never came back and all this kind of stuff. I can't say I wasn't apprehensive about the whole thing, but I was of the belief that the only reason I got hit was because I was unable to track the ball. Had I been able to see the ball, one of two things would have happened—I would have defended myself, caught it, or otherwise would have been able to get out of the way. Through lack of seeing it was what caused me to get hit. That's what kept me moving forward, thinking that when I got back everything would be fine because I was going to see the ball. I wasn't going to overthrow fastballs, so I was going to be OK."

Matlack was going to be OK, but he sustained a fractured skull—and that was how it went for most of 1973 for the Mets: peculiar bounces, painful injuries, bad luck. With Matlack on his way to the hospital, the Braves scored five more runs in the inning, saddling the southpaw with a 10–6 loss as well as a throbbing, swollen head. The Mets found all kinds of ways to lose both games and players for most of 1973.

Though the Mets won four straight immediately after Matlack went down, the team stumbled to a 34-51 mark over the next three months that saw the manager nearly lose his job while players continued to go down with bizarre injuries. Eight trips to the disabled list by the Mets in 1973—the most in franchise history to that point—and that figure didn't even include Matlack, who didn't go on the DL after getting hit. He missed just two starts, fractured skull and all.

Name	Position	DL stint	Ailment
John Milner	first baseman	April 28–May 3	pulled right hamstring
Jerry Grote	catcher	May 12–August 11	fractured right arm
Willie Mays	outfielder	May 13–June 3	right shoulder
Cleon Jones	outfielder	June 1–July 7	right wrist/forearm in cast
Bud Harrelson	shortstop	June 5–July 8 August 3–18	fractured left hand fractured sternum
Jerry May	catcher	June 9–July 10	left forearm tendonitis
George Theodore	outfielder	July 8–September 5	dislocated right hip

The injuries frustrated the team and the fans, but they presented opportunities to players otherwise on the bench or in the minors. Ron Hodges and Buzz Capra saw extended time in the majors. Don Hahn started the year in Triple-A but made more starts in center field than any Met in 1973. Jim Gosger, briefly a '69 Met but stuck in the minors at age 30, returned to the big leagues to fortify the '73 bench. The most memorable Mets fill-in, though, was a man called the Stork—until he too wound up wounded.

A 31st-round draft pick by the Mets in 1969 during his senior year at the University of Utah, George Theodore was expected to fill out a minor league roster and maybe move a couple of rungs up the ladder before embarking on another line of work. But Theodore hit .331 in his first four stops in the minor leagues, picking up a lasting nickname in 1972 at Tidewater, the Mets' top minor league affiliate in Norfolk, Virginia. Nicknames come easily, bandied among athletes and peers since the first locker room was built. "There's the Krane," offered Theodore, referring to the resonant connection between the bird and Met Ed Kranepool. "Jim Gosger nicknamed me the Stork, and it just seemed to stick." With his seemingly unathletic gait, lanky frame, hunched shoulders, curly hair, large nose, and ever-present spectacles, he looked more destined to sit in the stands than launch balls into them. It didn't hurt that he was well educated—psychology major and a minor in English—as well as a plain speaker in an era when yessir drones with buzz cuts were giving way to players unafraid to speak their minds.

Popular with the press and fans alike, Theodore found himself in an epistolary battle with Mets farm director Joe McDonald over his next minor league contract, "dickering over $25 a month." Theodore accepted the team's salary figure, but he made a few demands in return. "I am imbedded in boredom, stagnation, and regression, and I am thinking about returning to Mexico, where I played winter ball for vacation and cultural investigation," he wrote to McDonald. Theodore asked for athletic glasses, Mets stickers, six bats, and an introduction to Yogi Berra. "They got a kick out of things like that," he said. The Stork got everything he asked for, tore up the Dominican Winter League, and arrived in St. Petersburg where he impressed a manager known for being a little quirky himself.

Yogi Berra and the Mets hierarchy agreed that the perennially punchless Mets offense would benefit by taking Theodore north in the spring of '73. His promotion also marked Theodore's first visit to New York. It was understood that he would stay only for a few weeks, until the Mets replaced him with a pitcher from the minors. His first major league appearance came in Philadelphia, taking over for legend Willie Mays in center field on a frigid April day at empty Veterans Stadium. Theodore, who had already spent several days freezing on the Mets bench, wore heavy long underwear beneath his uniform that made it difficult to move. "Wouldn't you know it, the first batter, Greg Luzinski, hits a long, towering drive to center field and somehow I went back and caught it," he recalled. Theodore struck out later in the game against Steve Carlton. His first major league hit occurred a few days later at Shea Stadium, sans long johns, but he was immediately doubled off on a line drive.

The injuries started to mount, and Theodore's playing time and popularity grew. Living in nearby Jackson Heights, he didn't look much different than the people around him and his everyman manner made him a crowd favorite among fans who grew up rooting for the underdog Mets. He eventually met his wife, Sabrina, a native of the area, but Theodore remembered others who wrote to him and of him. "There were some young girls from Brooklyn who wrote to me: 'Can we have a fan club for you?' What do I care? That would be great." So the Storkettes were born, and their namesake gave them a lot of front page material.

Playing regularly in left field because of injuries to Willie Mays and then Cleon Jones, Theodore reached base in eight of nine games in his most sustained stretch, including a three-hit game in a 19-inning win in Los Angeles on May 24. Tied for second on the team in hitting, at .284, he was hit near the left eye with a pitch in San Diego on June 3, shattering his glasses. The Stork was the sixth Met injured after being hit by a pitch in the first two months of the season. Embodying the eye-for-an-eye code of the day, Mets batters sustained hits by pitches 23 times in 1973, and Mets pitchers drilled the same number of opponents.

Theodore survived the San Diego beaning and returned to the lineup after missing two games, but during the West Coast trip he had a premonition of a more painful fate. "I woke up in a cold sweat, like a bad dream," he recalled, describing the nightmare. "Somebody was carrying me off the field, and I could see Tug McGraw and Jerry Koosman while I'm on the stretcher. It was just one of those anxiety dreams or something."

A month later on a Saturday afternoon against the Braves at Shea, Theodore was hitting .261 and a couple of days removed from his first major league home run. Hank Aaron, now just 20 homers shy of breaking Ruth's career home run mark, was sitting out the game. The Braves, though still struggling in the standings, were rallying. Theodore was playing left field and had just committed an error as the go-ahead run scored in the top of the seventh inning. The next batter, Ralph Garr, lifted a high fly to left-center with the sluggish runner on third, Frank Tepedino, preparing to tag up and score. Theodore and center fielder Don Hahn both gave chase and came together in a frightening collision on the warning track, slamming into the wall in the process, and coming down in a heap.

Hahn rose to his knees to retrieve the ball but collapsed as Garr circled the bases. Theodore lay on the field for several minutes, dazed from the collision and immobilized by a dislocated hip. He was moved carefully onto a stretcher, looking skyward, gazing up at Tug McGraw holding him steady, just as he had foreseen. But this was no dream—and 1973 didn't seem like anyone's kind of a dream season. This was an ugly reality.

Willie Mays was older than a dozen participants in Mets Old-Timers Day on June 9—the day the Mets retired the number 14 of the deceased Gil

Hodges—and Mays played in the game afterward that counted, hit the go-ahead home run, and made a tumbling catch in front of a crowd of 47,800. Yet two days later—against the first-place Giants, no less—the great Mays hauled in a run-scoring hit near the wall in center and tossed it to left fielder George Theodore to throw it back to the infield. The Stork was so stunned by the move that he bobbled the ball. The runner went to third, and the error went to Mays in the 2–1 loss. New Yorkers had once been used to Mays doing all sorts of things in the outfield they had never seen before, but relaying a ball to an outfielder was a new one.

Tug McGraw was among the few Mets not hurt in 1973, but it seemed that for the better part of three months he hurt the team every time he took the ball. A bullpen hero for the 1969 Miracle Mets, the winning pitcher in the 1972 All-Star Game, and the owner of a minuscule 1.70 ERA over 216 innings of relief during the previous two seasons, McGraw was a major reason the Mets fell out of contention in 1973.

The season began promisingly for McGraw. After saving the opener, he reeled off four more saves in a row, but it all fell apart starting with Houston's arrival at Shea Stadium during the first week of May. It would be Houston. New York's fraternal expansion twin of 1962, the club changed its moniker from firearm to spacecraft after moving into the Astrodome in 1965, but the club still had its hold on the Mets. The Astros (born the Colt .45s) had a winning record against the Mets 10 times in their first dozen seasons of shared existence. Even in miraculous '69, the Astros had been the lone team the Mets had not managed at least a .500 record against—nor was it close. The Miracle Mets went 2-10 against the Astros, including Gil Hodges's infamous walk out to left field to remove Cleon Jones for jogging after a ball in the midst of a one-sided loss.

On May 4, 1973, against Houston at Shea, the relief assignment was challenging but not out of the ordinary for McGraw. In the 1970s, a reliever's mettle was tested by coming into games with everything in danger of exploding, regardless of inning, hence the positional nickname of "fireman." In 60 appearances in 1973, McGraw came into games with runners on base 23 times, and threw multiple innings on 38 occasions. They didn't call them firemen from a lack of work.

Against the Astros, McGraw relieved Jerry Koosman in the seventh with one out, bases full, and the Mets leading, 5–2. McGraw walked in a run before striking out dangerous Lee May. Then Tug fell apart. He surrendered the lead by walking Doug Rader and Larry Howard, a .147-hitting backup catcher the Astros would soon ship out. Matters grew worse for McGraw against the Astros two days later. This time the lead was four runs, and it disappeared even more quickly and frighteningly. With two on, two out, and the Mets leading by four, McGraw served up a two-run double to Cesar Cedeno, followed by a two-run home run by Bob Watson. The next inning, he put the first four batters on base, walking his last batter to break the tie. By the time Ray Sadecki came in and allowed those three runners to score, McGraw's ERA had gone from 1.32 to 5.14—and rising.

In *Ya Gotta Believe*, written three decades after Houston's sweep of the Mets that weekend in 1973, McGraw recalled the events against Houston vividly. "The performance rocked me. From there I overanalyzed every pitch. I started getting a little nervous entering a game. I even referred to my slump as 'a slump,' a defeatist attitude." His defeatism had company.

The Mets had traded from strength over the winter and were paying for it come summer. Reliever Danny Frisella, who had taken some of the burden off McGraw the past two seasons, went to Atlanta along with former 1969 hero Gary Gentry in exchange for second baseman Felix Millan and left-hander George Stone. It stood as one of the team's best trades of the decade, but, when McGraw lost his confidence and control, Frisella's replacement fizzled. Phil Hennigan, picked up from Cleveland the previous November for two promising pitchers (including 1970 first-round pick Brent Strom), proved unable to be the right-hand man that the Mets needed. Hennigan saved three games, blew three others, and lost all four of his decisions before the Mets sent him to Tidewater in July, never to return.

At the same time the Mets farmed out Hennigan, the team finally cut bait on the supposed answer to their perpetual third base dilemma. The Mets said goodbye to Jim Fregosi, whose arrival in December 1971 had cost the team three prospects as well as Nolan Ryan, the fire-throwing superman who that same week threw his second no-hitter in as many months. Detroit's Norm Cash felt so helpless that he came up to bat against Ryan in the ninth holding a piano leg. Cash was sent back to the dugout for more traditional lumber, which he used to pop out, but Fregosi couldn't seem to buy a hit in New York with the proverbial paddle.

Wayne Garrett, whom the Mets had hoped Fregosi would replace, replaced him instead. "That was their choice, the organization's choice," he says of the team trying to replace him—first with Joe Foy in 1970 and then with Fregosi two years later, giving away future stars Amos Otis and Nolan Ryan, respectively. "I would just go out and play. I'd play every game the same, as hard as I could. . . . I can't go out and make demands. They're the ones that make the choices as to who plays and who doesn't play. I'd just do the best that I could and if they wanted me to play third base, then I'd play third base." The Mets had traded for Fregosi, a six-time All-Star shortstop, to play third base—even though the man had never played the position. The first time Gil Hodges hit him a grounder at third in spring training in 1972, Fregosi broke his thumb.

"I can't speak for him, but it just seemed like Fregosi didn't really want to play there," Garrett says. "He would rather play shortstop and have somebody else play third. I knew that he knew that the only way that he was going to be in the lineup was to be at third base. I think he made an honest effort to try to play the position. It's just a little bit different than playing short." The Mets sold Fregosi to the abysmal Texas Rangers, pawning him off on rookie manager Whitey Herzog, who a year earlier, as soon-to-be-exiled Mets director of player development, cautioned the Mets not to trade Ryan.

Who was listening now? Mets fans, that's who.

With rumors rampant that the Mets might fire Yogi Berra, the *New York Post* ran a poll asking readers to choose the culprit for the dreadful first three months of the season: general manager Bob Scheffing, board chairman M. Donald Grant, or Berra. That was how the voting went, with Berra a distant third in terms of culpability. No one had forgotten that Scheffing had pulled off the Ryan fiasco, and Grant got into a shouting match with *Long Island Press* reporter Jack Lang during a game, claiming that Lang had "made us make that deal" during the 1971 winter meetings. Announcer Lindsey Nelson, who had to close the door to the broadcasting booth to keep the argument from going out over the airwaves, told Lang later that night, "Say, I have to start treating you with more respect, I didn't know you had the power on this club to make trades."

But the poll empowered Berra. Grant had said he wouldn't fire the manager "unless forced to by public opinion." Only 611 of the 4,000-plus voters in the *Post* poll thought Berra should be fired. Grant wasn't firing Scheffing, and he certainly wasn't getting rid of himself.

Berra looks philosophically at his close call that summer. "You never know when you're going to get fired," says Berra, who got the axe three times in a managing career that lasted a little over seven years. "Remember, I never thought I'd be fired in '64. Maybe if we didn't turn it around [in '73] there was a good chance I'd be gone."

The way things were going, it certainly appeared that Berra would be gone by season's end. That *Post* poll was one of the few victories Berra managed as July swallowed the Mets. The club dropped the last four games of the month—at home, no less—to give them an even .400 winning percentage for July . . . and that was their best month since April. On Independence Day the Mets sat 12½ games behind the Cubs. A month later the Cardinals had taken over first, but the Mets were still last, 11½ games out. The deficit was greater than the Mets had faced at any point during their miraculous 1969 comeback. Unlike the '69 club, 11 games over .500 when it stood 10 games out in August, the '73 team was 13 games under .500 at its nadir.

The Mets appeared destined for their first sub-.500 season since 1968, the year Gil Hodges had come to New York. Nothing had gone right since Gil Hodges's death, and, truth be told, little had gone the team's way since Cleon Jones came down with the final out of the 1969 World Series. The team was injured, inconsistent, and incapable of putting together a prolonged hot streak. Though Yogi Berra seemed safe from a mid-season firing, his club certainly looked dead.

Eight

THE WINNING DIET

Eat as much meat and as much fat as you want, skip the carbohydrates, and lose weight.

A beef shortage, caused by a reduction in feed for cows, drove up meat prices and made meat both scarce and expensive in 1973, fueling a rise in tuna casserole, spaghetti, and long faces at American dinner tables. For a country weaned on beef and hungry for it, Dr. Robert Atkins told the world what it wanted to hear: The food they most desired would help them lose weight. People ate it up—his book at least. *Dr. Atkins' Diet Revolution* reached number one on the *New York Times* bestseller list on February 18, 1973, and stayed on the list until November, selling more than one million copies. Over the years, the book sold 15 million copies and, according to its creator, resulted in 200 million pounds lost among those who followed the plan. The book had everything you could ask for in a best seller: a popular message, controversy, and a juicy topic—literally.

Dr. Atkins said the human body burned its own fat if it had no carbohydrates to burn first, so the good doctor got the fire going by prescribing meat, meat, and more meat, plus plenty of eggs, cheese, Jell-O for dessert, all washed down with coffee, tea, or sugar-free soda. Top everything with mayonnaise, cook with lard, and cram in two salads per day—if you aren't too full. Don't fret about the sugar cut from your diet, use all the artificial sweetener you can scoop, and never mind what it did to those lab rats. Oh, and *don't* count calories. No wonder this New York cardiologist became a best-selling author.

In a 1973 Gallup poll, some 46 percent of Americans claimed to be overweight or on a diet. So this high-protein, high-fat, low-carb way to lose weight should be great, right? Not exactly, said the American Medical Association. The Council of Foods and Nutrition of the AMA warned that "no weight-reducing diet . . . can be effective unless it provides for a decrease in energy intake or somehow increase energy losses." Without getting too

A's ball girl Debbie Sivyer, who went on to become Mrs. Fields of cookie fame, keeps an eye on the Oakland bullpen—and vice versa. RON RIESTERER

technical, the AMA said the doctor's claims of success were overstated and the diet was more likely to lead to fatigue than substantial weight loss. But Atkins, who tried the diet on himself first when he was overweight and sluggish in the early 1960s, dismissed naysayers and the occasional lawsuit from dissatisfied consumers. He made dieting more fun than it had ever been. Thirty years later, a competing version of the plan by another doctor, the South Beach Diet, sold millions more books and had dieters delighting in steaks smothered in bacon once more.

Of course, for some people it wasn't a new diet plan so much as just how they always ate. Ever the epicurean, Charlie Finley loved to eat, but he enjoyed cooking even more. He wasn't afraid to go into a restaurant, walk into the kitchen, and inspect the food. He sometimes brought his own meat with him to a restaurant and supervised its preparation. Bringing food to close a deal was a Finley specialty as well. In the days before the amateur draft, when bidding was open and unchecked, he used food to up the ante. A pickup truck crammed with food arrived at a family's house, and then Finley oversaw the cooking and frying and bonding, pouring on the southern charm as needed.

For John Odom's family in Macon, Georgia, Finley cooked up fried chicken, corn on the cob, collard greens, and black-eyed peas. Dr. Atkins may not have approved, but Odom's mother certainly did. By the time Finley left the Odom home, the A's owner had not only signed her son but dubbed the young pitcher "Blue Moon" as well.

If Finley's cooking on the road was a deal maker, he really laid it on at home. Finley's farmhouse in LaPorte, Indiana, hosted many cookouts for his ballclub. It was a command performance for the players. If the team had time off after playing the White Sox or were on their way north to play Milwaukee, a party would invariably be staged with the A's as guests of honor. Finley showed off his prized possession to friends, business associates, or others he hoped to impress; the A's logo emblazoned on his barn now in the flesh in LaPorte. A charcoal barbecue pit more than 10 feet long served as the owner-chef's base of operations, and he supervised all preparations.

For the hard-charging owner, there was no time for rest, no chance of letting someone else handle the event. He made a rare exception for the farm itself, however, leaving its daily running mostly to caretaker John Mihelic, who had driven the owner daily from LaPorte to Chicago in the early 1960s until Finley tired of the 90-minute one-way commute and decided to stay in the city. It was in Chicago that Finley's larger-than-life personality, habits, and diet caught up with him.

On August 7, 1973, Finley had a heart attack and collapsed. He was rushed to the Passavant Pavilion of Chicago's Northwestern University Hospital. He was in intensive care for several days and in the hospital for nearly two weeks. When he was well enough to leave, the doctors sent him to the farm in LaPorte and prescribed a month-long recuperation: no entertaining, no traveling, no talking on the phone. Finley still sneaked away to make calls, but he couldn't meddle at his usual level with day-to-day operations of the club. The A's thrived on the field, winning nine in a row and 14 of 15 to go from two games out to five games up in the AL West. While it's tempting to draw correlations between Finley's relative silence and the A's finally firing on all cylinders, the more obvious reason was the return of Catfish Hunter.

Hunter's injury during the All-Star Game had resulted in short reliever Darold Knowles starting for just the third time in his career and for the first time since 1967. The durable left-hander had thrown 8⅔ cumulative innings over a three-day span when Dick Williams decided to have him start on three days' rest on August 1. He won, tossing five innings against Minnesota, and he pitched the first six innings of a 6–2 win in Anaheim four days later. Showing his versatility—and proving his manager's faith in him—Knowles was brought in to get out of a bases-loaded, ninth-inning jam in Detroit with dangerous left-handed pinch hitter Gates Brown coming up.

Knowles's presence made manager Billy Martin change to right-handed swinger Ike Brown, neither related to Gates nor the same kind of threat at the plate. Knowles fanned Ike Brown to end the game and earn the save before starting three days later at Yankee Stadium. Knowles was knocked out in the fifth inning as Oakland dropped its third straight and fell two games behind in the AL West, the farthest out the A's had been since June 17, when the White Sox led the division. Now the A's trailed the Royals, a club only in its fourth year of existence with no previous experience in first place outside of April. Now it was August—the dog days.

"Maybe there was a little rivalry because we had played there originally," A's outfielder Joe Rudi says of Kansas City. "They were an expansion team that had developed into a pretty good ballclub." But the Royals' August 1973 hold on first place wouldn't last the week.

⚾ ⚾ ⚾

On the afternoon of Saturday, August 11, 1973, the present gave way to the past at Yankee Stadium—for an hour or so. Old-Timers Day had been a Yankees tradition since 1947, but its genesis stretched back to Lou Gehrig's most poignant moment. Other teams had held special days to honor aging or unfortunate ballplayers (or their widows), but the 1939 ceremony for Gehrig, heart-rending for all who attended or heard it on the radio, became a touchstone of baseball tradition with its retelling in the 1941 film *The Pride of the Yankees*. Released a year after Gehrig's death from amyotrophic lateral sclerosis (ALS), a disease better known by the player's name, the last line of the film—moved from the beginning of Gehrig's actual speech for dramatic effect—was legendary: "Today I consider myself the luckiest man on the face of the earth."

Even Yankees haters couldn't help but feel a lump in the throat when Gary Cooper recreated Gehrig's farewell. In fact, Mickey Mantle was thinking about the Iron Horse the day that Mick's number 7 became the fourth retired by the team after Babe Ruth's 3, Gehrig's 4, and Joe DiMaggio's 5. The same day he and DiMaggio also received Yankee Stadium plaques. Mantle concluded his June 8, 1969, speech: "I've often wondered how a man who knew he was going to die could stand here and say that he was the luckiest man in the world, but now I think I know how Lou Gehrig felt."

Four years later, with Mantle's and DiMaggio's plaques in center field— in the field of play though beyond all reasonable range near the 463-foot mark in center field—Mantle was back in uniform for the last Old-Timers Day in the original stadium, the final time the old ball yard saw a crowd bigger than 40,000. The 1970s represented the heyday of Old-Timers Day, with still-in-shape players crisscrossing the country to help teams draw crowds with attractive guest lists. Some teams, including the Mets, invited other clubs to play against, but it was usually only Yankees playing in the Bronx for their Old-Timers Day. Theirs would also be the last such day to survive into the 2000s as an annual game for the stars of yesteryear.

The 1973 crowd roared as Mantle stepped up to the plate. Announcer Mel Allen, the Voice of the Yankees—fired by the team in 1964 but brought back for such festivities—called the game so that everyone in the park and at home could hear. Facing his old teammate, drinking buddy, and protector Whitey Ford, Mantle, batting right-handed against the old southpaw, lashed three straight fouls into the stands, each harder and farther than the one before. Moments after the third shot landed foul in the upper deck—with Allen encouraging him to "straighten it out, Mick"—Mantle did just that. "There's a long drive going deep to left field. It is going, going . . . it is gone!"

"It was fun," recalls Marty Appel, Yankees assistant PR man, on the field when Mick went deep one last time at the old stadium. "Whitey was laughing. Everybody wanted Mickey to hit one. He came through." Joe Rudi was watching from the visiting dugout. The A's outfielder had grown up on the other side of the country but idolized Mantle and the Yankees as a kid. "I always loved going into Yankee Stadium," he says. The Yankees were often the only team he saw on television as a child in the 1950s, before California had major league teams. "Every weekend CBS had the Yankees on. I became a huge fan of Mickey Mantle and that whole group. I followed them very closely, so the first time I went into Yankee Stadium it made the hair stand on the back of my neck. The stories . . . it was like going into a shrine. All those statues out in center field, an awesome place . . . a lot of history."

Reggie Jackson, who had a superb weekend in New York with three homers and seven runs knocked in, was prophetic in his praise: "There's something about playing in this city that means excitement. It brings out the best." When the generations of pinstriped heroes left and the gaudy-green A's took the field, Gene Tenace hit a ball into the seats that had the opposite effect on the crowd compared to Mantle's blast. The catcher's three-run drive against Mantle's and Ford's old teammate, Mel Stottlemyre, broke open a scoreless game on the way to a 7–3 Vida Blue win, snapping Oakland's three-game losing streak and New York's three-game winning streak. At that point in the season, the A's had 65 wins and the Yanks 64, though, at 1½ games behind Baltimore, New York was half a game closer to first than was Oakland in its division. The next day, everything would change.

Manager Dick Williams pulled Ken Holtzman, who entered the Sunday rubber-match with a 2.57 ERA and a 17-10 mark, after he allowed a leadoff single in the fourth inning with the Yankees up by a run. Left-hander Paul Lindblad gave up key hits to fellow lefties Bobby Murcer and Graig Nettles, the latter banging a two-run homer. Lindblad was in mop-up mode in a 9–4 game; by the time he was taken out in the sixth, the Yankees led, 11–5. Williams was ready to empty the Oakland bench and take out his regulars—after just one more at-bat.

"Sudden" Sam McDowell, purchased by the Yankees before the June 15 trade deadline from the cash-strapped Giants on the same day New York traded for Atlanta's Pat Dobson, seemed to be in command. The hard-throwing, hard-drinking McDowell allowed a two-out single to Reggie Jackson that made it 11–6. Houk decided not to push his luck and came out to remove McDowell. Though the Yankees still had a sizeable lead, the manager didn't fool around with anyone but his best, Sparky Lyle.

In 1972, the popular lefty had been the first reliever to enter to his own music—Elgar's "Pomp and Circumstance," PR man Marty Appel's touch—but Lyle thought it put more pressure on an already tough job, so they shelved the theme music. This time he entered with less fanfare, yet the same job awaited: Come in, get outs, and keep getting them until the game ends. That's how managers saw things in 1973 and for several years yet to come. If a manager was going to take out a starting pitcher late in a game that he felt his team could—or should—win, the first man in from the bullpen was likely to be the best candidate to finish the game, regardless of inning. The save rule had been adopted officially in 1969 to recognize the overlooked "fireman," but no manager of the day worried whether a reliever got credit for a save. Managing to the save rule—to avoid second guessing in the press and earn a Christmas card from relievers' agents—still lay a couple of decades away from universal adoption.

Lyle was in Sunday against the A's to get the last seven outs of the game. He didn't get any. A walk and three straight run-scoring hits sent him to the showers, the Yankees clinging to a now precarious 11–10 lead. Replacement Tom Buskey was greeted with back to back infield errors, and the game was tied. Another error, the Yankees' fifth of the game, gave Oakland the lead the following inning.

With the A's having pulled one out of the fire, Dick Williams not only kept in his starting lineup, he brought in a starting pitcher. Darold Knowles, who had started and lost on Friday night, pitched the eighth and ninth innings on Sunday. When the last out proved difficult, Rollie Fingers came in to retire Roy White to finish Oakland's unlikely 13–12 win. Sam McDowell, who had won five of his first six starts as a Yankee, didn't win any of his final 10 starts. The Yankees, 10 games over .500 heading into Old-Timers Day, had a dismal 16-28 finish. Oakland ended the season on a 30-17 run. The A's turned it on as needed.

"When you have that many guys living together for that amount of time, you're going to have disagreements," Fingers says of the somewhat fractious Oakland clubhouse. "But once we cross that white line, if you have a different uniform on, we're going to beat you. That's why we had so many fights on the field, too."

The A's fought the Royals for much of 1973, both on the field and off. The A's caught Kansas City in the standings in Boston, their next stop after New York. Odom, Knowles, and Blue allowed just four runs in a three-game sweep at Fenway Park that put the Royals and A's into a tie for first place in the AL West. Knowles was particularly masterful, going the distance to beat Bill Lee, 1–0, just two days after winning in relief in New York. The game's lone run scored on a squeeze bunt by Dick Green. The A's came home and swept Milwaukee to take over first place by themselves, then won two of three from Detroit, and stymied the Yankees again, allowing just one run in the three-game sweep. The series ended with a 1–0 shutout by Ken Holtzman, the lone run coming home in the eighth inning on a single by Vic Davalillo off poor luck loser Mel Stottlemyre. Two weeks after the teams had nearly identical win totals and positions in the standings in their relative divisions, the pendulum had swung completely to Oakland's side: The A's led the AL West by five games, while the Yankees, dropping like a stone, sank a full nine games out in the AL East.

Bill North's presence at the top of the lineup with Bert Campaneris redoubled Oakland efforts to disrupt the opposition. Nor was North afraid to settle scores right in the heat of a game. In May in Kansas City, North swung and missed a Doug Bird pitch and let go of the bat. He sauntered out to get the bat, which had flown beyond the pitcher's mound, but he suddenly stopped and said, "I remember." North decked the pitcher and landed several more blows as the benches emptied. What North remembered was a Class A game in Waterloo, Iowa, three years earlier, when two North home runs off Bird resulted in two balls thrown at North's head, the second cracking his skull and sending him to the hospital. In 1973, North was suspended for the rest of the May series in Kansas City, but the Royals and their fans remembered when the A's came to Kansas City on the last day of August holding a 4½-game lead.

The Royals had their first winning season in 1971, placing second to the A's, but that race was never close. Two years later, the teams were on more equal ground, the Bird attack creating an urgency and anger not previously there. The teams were close enough in the standings where a sweep by either could tighten the race or essentially end it. The Royals grabbed a 7–3 lead to chase Holtzman in the third inning, but the A's battled back to tie the game in the eighth. With Ray Fosse on first in the ninth, North singled him to third—against Bird, no less. The go-ahead run scored on a sacrifice fly, but North subsequently stole second and went to third on catcher Carl Taylor's errant throw. With North dancing off third base, Royals third baseman Kurt Bevacqua, perhaps still annoyed that he'd fanned with two runners on to end the previous inning, shoved North off the base before the next pitch. When Bevacqua did it again, North gave him a taste of what Bird had gotten in May.

Mike Epstein, the brawny former A's first baseman, was next on the North fight card when the A's stopped in Anaheim. After two successive bunts produced a run—including another squeeze bunt by Dick Green—Angels pitcher Dick Lange vented his frustration over Oakland's old-school run-scoring approach and new-school spanking of the lowly Angels. After a Lange fastball barely missed North's head, the A's center fielder chose a retaliatory tactic that harkened to the Dead Ball Era: a bunt along the first-base line that the pitcher fields, getting flattened by the runner. But Lange didn't take the bait, so Epstein intercepted the ball and North at the same time. Banished over the winter by Charlie Finley to last-place Texas, then shunted in the spring one rung up the ladder to the fifth-place Angels, Epstein exercised his frustration on the speedy North, tagging him so hard that the ball squirted out of his glove for an error. After Epstein and North traded insults, more hard tags from Epstein ensued as Lange repeatedly threw over to first base to try to contain the league's top base stealer. North got out of the firing line by stealing second and scoring an insurance run on a Bert Campaneris single. Victorious and defiant, North warned all comers after the game: "There's no one in this game who can intimidate me, including Mike Epstein. There will come a time for him."

The time proved short in coming for North. On September 20, he tore ligaments in his ankle crossing first base in a game against Texas. His season done, North wound up one shy of the league lead in runs (98) and steals (53), though his AL high with 20 times caught stealing held up. The big blow, though, was that the A's would be without his services for October, forcing the breakup of the best top of the order in the league with Billy and Campy. But Rudi, who missed 40 games in 1973 due to assorted injuries and ailments, finally returned to form, hitting .411 with 21 RBIs in his final 20 games of the season. Dick Williams moved up Rudi to anchor the second spot in the lineup, ahead of Sal Bando—who didn't miss a game and tied for the AL lead in doubles (32) and total bases (295). Hitting cleanup was Reggie Jackson, league leader in home runs (32), RBIs (117), runs (99), slugging (.531), and fewest at-bats between homers (16.8). Reggie was also a candidate to take over center field.

Though he had played just one game there during the '73 season—catching the two balls hit to him during a Catfish Hunter shutout in May—Jackson had played the middle pasture before. He was a standout center fielder at Arizona State, played 50 games in center for the A's in 1970, and started 92 games there for the 1972 A's. Bringing in the missing piece of the puzzle in Ken Holtzman after the 1971 season had cost them All-Star center fielder Rick Monday. North was a solid replacement, a switch hitter with great speed, glove, and grit. Plugging Jackson into that spot wasn't so easy.

Jackson pulled a hamstring, not only landing him on the bench for the second half of September but also starting a new round of Finley animosity. Not content simply to lead the American League in RBIs, Jackson wanted to lead the majors in that category, and Willie Stargell locked up the title in that category—as well as home runs—even as his Pirates tumbled in the National League East race. Dick Williams was inclined to let Jackson try DHing. After all, what was the designated hitter for but to let players hit when they were hurting a little or unable to go at full speed? Finley, still recuperating from his heart attack, denied Jackson. The Williams-Jackson relationship was complex. Williams, who with equal dexterity lambasted players in the press or to their faces, wasn't always easy to play for. When Reggie got defensive about a comment about his defense from coach Irv Noren, Williams backed his coach, much to the consternation of his star and the delight of his owner.

"Finley loved this," Williams wrote in *No More Mr. Nice Guy*. "He loved people to be uneasy, uncertain, worried enough about their jobs and their egos to play their butts off. I preferred to treat them like men and hope they'd play their butts off because they wanted to win. . . . Keep the players insecure and keep them hungry, that was Charlie's theme."

The day the A's clinched their third straight division title, Finley was in the house, so of course the game was played in Chicago. In the final road game on the schedule, September 18, Vida Blue picked up his 20th win of the year while handing knuckleballer Wilbur Wood his 20th defeat (against 24 wins). Blue joined Holtzman and Hunter (21 wins each) as a trio of 20-game winners. Though such a staff was exceptional, it wasn't exactly rare at the time. The Orioles had four 20-game winners in 1971, the year they swept the A's in the playoffs, and the O's had three 20-game winners in 1970. But the breed was dying. Never again would three teammates reach that milestone after 1973.

Four decades later, Holtzman was unaware of his part in this distinction—one that in the 21st century, where pitch counts rule and complete games are often as scarce as hen's teeth, has little chance of being duplicated. Holtzman didn't dwell on the achievement but on the teammates that made it happen: "Catfish and Vida were not only great pitchers but great guys as well," he says. "We helped and encouraged each other and felt that the success of the team was more important than any individual statistic. I never got a ring for winning 20 games or pitching a no-hitter, and that's what I think separates our staff from all others. Baltimore had four 20-game winners two years earlier but lost in the World Series. For me, the rings mean the pinnacle of achievement and the fact that I have a handful and never wear any of them is extremely self-satisfying."

But that self-satisfaction had to keep the A's going all through October, because some of them felt that the biggest obstacle they faced was the man who signed the checks.

Yankee Stadium, 1923–73 NATIONAL BASEBALL HALL OF FAME LIBRARY, COOPERSTOWN, NY

Nine

COMING DOWN

The Horace Clarke era was drawing to an end.

Clarke was a second baseman whose career as a Yankee from May 1965 to May 1974 cruelly coincided with the club's longest drought since the team called the Polo Grounds and Hilltop Park home in the 1910s. A contact hitter who rarely struck out or walked, Clarke annually ranked among the leaders in outs made in the field and, unfortunately, at the plate. (Teammate Roy White topped the majors in this latter category in 1973.) The Virgin Islands native lived within walking distance of the stadium in the Grand Concourse and loved being leadoff hitter for the Yankees. What still stings, though, is that for the team that has won more championships than any sports franchise his name became synonymous with losing.

"Horace Clarke was a very good second baseman—people don't remember that," says teammate Ron Blomberg. "I think they take it out on him because the name was Horace Clarke. It doesn't sound like a real big baseball name. But he was an excellent ballplayer and an excellent human being." Blomberg also notes ironically that if the Yankees hadn't been in such a tailspin during the CBS era, some other team would have had the number one pick in 1967. Or maybe he would have taken that scholarship and joined the John Wooden dynasty. "My story would be totally different. I was very, very lucky that the team was not a real good team, but it wasn't a bad team."

The 1973 team looked like it would turn the corner, that this might just be the beginning of another era of greatness in the Bronx. The Yankees swept a seven-game homestand in late June, taking two from the Orioles and then winning five straight from Detroit. The following weekend they won four straight from Cleveland, a series with its own set of drama. The Yankees had lost a game that week at Municipal Stadium amid a furor over Gaylord Perry's greaseball. After Bobby Murcer was fined for calling the commissioner "gutless," Howard Cosell and ABC's *Wide World of Sports* came to the stadium to see how Perry loaded up the ball—though, as everyone knows, a magician is very hard to catch in mid-trick. What the Yankees were doing wasn't magic, though Blomberg's .403 mark on June 28 might have quali-fied. The Yankees fashioned a 19-10 June and held first place for six weeks.

They opened August in Boston, leading the division by a game, eager for payback after losing four of five to the Red Sox a few weeks earlier in the Bronx. The teams split the first two games of their best-of-four series and tied 2–2 in the top of the ninth in the third game. Thurman Munson took a lead off third base with one out. Ninety feet away stood home plate—and Carlton Fisk. The two catchers in their early 20s had both been Rookies of the Year, Munson in 1970, Fisk in '72. Fisk was tall, strapping, and had a profile as rugged as the Old Man on the Mountain, the prominent cliff ledge in the White Mountains of his native New Hampshire. Munson, from a blue-collar upbringing in Canton, Ohio, was shorter and a little pudgy, even though Fisk had the nickname "Pudge." His Yankee teammates called Munson "Squatty Body" and "Tugboat," among other epithets.

Both were strong defensive catchers who could hit, a rare combination in baseball. Those qualities stood out in this era where the full offensive and defensive catching package coalesced in Johnny Bench, already a Rookie of the Year, two-time National League MVP, and five-time Gold Glove winner in his first five seasons in Cincinnati. Munson resented when praise went to other catchers—especially Fisk. Yankees pitcher Fritz Peterson recalls "the hatred each catcher had for the other—and the jealousy." "Munson genu-inely hated Fisk. And it was pretty much mutual," wrote Marty Appel in *Munson: The Life and Death of a Yankee Captain*. It also didn't help that the second-year Fisk beat Munson in the fan balloting to start the 1973 All-Star Game, played just a week earlier.

So with Munson on third base in the ninth inning of a tie game in Boston, Yankees manager Ralph Houk put on the sign for the suicide squeeze. Munson came charging homeward and never slowed, even as Gene Michael missed the pitch. Fisk shoved Michael out of the way, ball firmly in hand, to tag Munson. Munson flattened Fisk, who pushed the Yankee off him after recording the out. Then the punches started flying with Munson and Michael each hitting Fisk repeatedly as the two dugouts and bullpens emptied for a 15-minute Fenway Park donnybrook.

"You trace the rivalry of the teams to today, maybe it began with that fight," Appel says.

Dick Bresciani, working the same job as Appel that night at Fenway, only on the Red Sox side, saw it similarly: "In those days, a lot of the play-ers didn't like each other. From that aspect it was more intense. No matter where we were in the standings, there was no love lost between Yankees and Red Sox players. That was evident in some of the rough plays that happened during the games. It was a battle. They had some tough competitors that would battle—Thurman Munson, Nettles, Murcer, Roy White. They were good players, and they fought you to the end." Literally.

After the fight and the ejections of Fisk and Munson, Bob Montgomery, Boston's backup catcher replacing Fisk, scored the game-winning run in the bottom of the ninth. The tiebreaking single off Sparky Lyle—the second walk-off hit against Lyle at Fenway in 1973—came off the bat of Mario Guerrero, whom the Yankees had sent to Boston a year earlier in the otherwise one-sided Lyle-for-Danny Cater trade. With the loss, New York fell into a first-place tie with Baltimore—and the Yankees kept falling. They went 21-39 in the stretch run, as the promising season turned into a bizarre freefall that frayed nerves and tested character.

There was the wiener incident in Texas: a hot dog hidden in the fingers of Gene Michael's glove—a practical joke. The shortstop, who had a well-known fear of crawling things, flung the frank/cobra into the stands. Steinbrenner, on the road with the club, witnessed the episode from his seat next to the dugout at Arlington Stadium. He didn't laugh. Steinbrenner retrieved the wiener from the stands, demanding that Ralph Houk determine who was responsible. Evidence pointed to infielder Hal Lanier, who later won a division title managing Houston.

There was nothing funny about the callous Callison dismissal during the same visit to Texas. Johnny Callison, a former All-Star on his last legs at age 34, misplayed a flyball in his only inning in right field in an 8–1 loss to David Clyde, the 18-year-old wunderkind rushed to the majors to sell tickets in Texas after being chosen with the first overall pick out of his Houston high school. (Clyde blew out his arm at 20 and threw his last pitch in the majors four years later.)

When Callison's misplay turned a probable loss into a definite one, Steinbrenner required an instant sacrifice. "I will not have that man on my team," he fumed. Rosters expanded in September just two weeks later, which would have allowed Callison to ride out his final days in the majors anonymously on the bench. Instead, he was released on August 17, ending his career with 1,757 hits and 226 home runs, including a game-winning homer in the 1964 All-Star Game at Shea Stadium. Under Steinbrenner's wrath, the Yankees also sold two Alou brothers in one day in September: Matty to Montreal and Felipe to St. Louis for the NL East stretch run.

Neither Alou had much influence on the race, and both were done as players before the 1974 All-Star break. This flagrant disregard for veterans belied a later Steinbrenner obsession for such players that caused the Yankees to lose several future stars in the 1980s in pursuit of former name players with little left in the tank.

The bottom was coming into view in the closing days of wretched August 1973 as the deficit reached double figures. Starting with the June trade—that some might call a banishment—of Mike Kekich, the southpaw whose wife swap didn't take, the borderline personnel on the roster became increasingly worried that they were next to go. Mind you, many of these players *were* ideal candidates for shipping out, but the anxiety dragged overall morale lower and lower during the late-season swoon. The "absentee" owner generated much of the feeling. According to an anonymous quote in the *New York Times* that August, "Guys were thinking more of George Steinbrenner than what we should be doing on the field."

"We misread him," Phil Pepe, a Yankees beat writer for most of the 1960s and 1970s, says of Steinbrenner's debut season as an owner. "The reason we misread him was that when he came in he said he was going to be low-key and in the background. I don't know whether he meant it when he said that. Whether he did or he didn't, he didn't follow through with what he promised. We later found out that this was his personality. That was his nature, and to expect a person with that nature not to be hands-on would have been ridiculous. But we didn't know anything about him. Once we got to know about him, everything that he did was kind of understood and predictable."

Predictability may have been uncommon in the owner's box, but on the so-called idiot box it still reigned supreme. Family television in 1973 stretched credulity. *The Brady Bunch*, entering its fifth and final season on ABC in the fall of 1973, had New York Jets star quarterback Joe Namath visit the fictional family's youngest boy, Bobby, just as Dodgers star Don Drysdale had dropped by the same AstroTurf backyard to give the eldest Brady son, Greg, some pitching tips during the show's second season. The other top family shows of the time, including *The Partridge Family*, *Here's Lucy*, and *The Waltons*, used varying degrees of hipness and nostalgia to try to resonate with the viewing populace. But 1973 also proved that family in its pure form could be captivating and hazardous.

An American Family, the world's first "reality show," followed the Loud family of idyllic Santa Barbara, California, over a seven-month period—and watched them crumble. Contrasting with the contrived *Brady Bunch*, where each episode ended with the family of six stepchildren becoming an ever-closer unit cocooned in a world in which problems were small and fixable in a 22-minute arcing plot, *An American Family* worked the opposite side of the street. It began with a successful, stylish couple married for 21 years with five children and looking for all the world to be living the American Dream. But reality told a different tale.

The eldest son came out as openly gay—a first in American television history—and the 12-episode program ended with husband and wife splitting up. It's surprising now that this memorable dose of can't-turn-away reality that drew 10 million viewers to PBS didn't become a network TV staple until three decades later when ubiquitous cameras began capturing the semi-scripted lives of unknowns and called it drama on channels all over the dial. Other shows had been based on authentic human reactions, from *Candid Camera* in 1948 to any number of game shows where ordinary folks reacted to contrived situations. Yet network television held tight to its traditional model of scripted programming until cable TV, just starting to hit its stride in the early 1970s with the founding of Home Box Office, mounted enough of a challenge by segmenting the audience for networks to branch out into the genre of the "real." This made for engaging—and cheap—programming.

The state-of-the-art inconspicuous sound devices that picked up every word spoken in the Loud home disturbingly resembled the system installed in the White House during the same period. But whereas editors whittled 300 hours of footage captured in Santa Barbara in 1971 to 12 hours for TV broadcast in 1973, the voice-activated audiotapes in the Oval Office—and the unseemly truths they exposed—undid President Nixon.

The saga of the tapes, kicked off by the break-in at the Democratic National Committee headquarters at the Watergate office complex in June 1972, led to a round-the-clock crisis news cycle in the summer of 1973, when the Watergate hearings aired live during the day. Journalists examined them at night on the evening news and condensed them into print in the following morning's papers. The cycle proved so relentless that the networks agreed to broadcast the hearings on a rotating basis so that game shows, cartoons, reruns, and soap operas could continue to entertain and divert those who didn't like their drama quite so real or quite so close.

The scandal's events unfolded in such a way that the unthinkable just a few days earlier turned into fact upon entering the news cycle and then became another point on the Watergate timeline, which seemed as endless as it was incomprehensible. TV and the other media helped clarify it over the year and a half that the affair dragged on in public. During that time, the president transformed from a revered man in a position of power to one of derision, spat out in headlines and in the mouths of people who had voted for the man. Twice!

Even Archie Bunker had a harder and harder time defending the commander in chief on the top-rated show at the time, *All in the Family*. "Aww, geez . . . if Nixon keeps goin' on like that, he won't have Archie Bunker to kick around anymore."

George Steinbrenner had his own mire in which to wallow, but the reflection from the Watergate hearings threw more light on the American Shipbuilding president's problems. Steinbrenner did himself no favors in the way he handled the situation. He spent so much time at his Cleveland company's offices in 1973 not to honor his absentee ownership pledge made the day he took over the club; he was trying to get a handle on his own shady political dealings culminating into crisis.

Cargo ships trolling the Great Lakes were massive in size and cost to operate, so changes in legislation or to the party in control of said legislation could cost a ship-going concern a lot of money if the rules and contracts went against it. With Congress controlled by the Democrats and the White House in the hands of the Republicans, Steinbrenner needed to stay on friendly terms with both parties. Friendly in this case meant contributions—large ones—that turned out to be greater than the law allowed.

Steinbrenner already had a good rapport with Democrats, counting Senator Ted Kennedy among his close acquaintances. On the Republican side, Thomas Evans, a limited partner with the Yankees and AmShip's legal counsel, coached him. Evans put Steinbrenner in touch with Herb Kalmbach, president of the Committee to Reelect the President, the infamous CREEP. Because the law on the books at the time required that contributions larger than $3,000 disclose the donor's name, Kalmbach had Steinbrenner donate six checks in 1972 in the amount of $3,000 in the names of American Shipbuilding employees. Steinbrenner also made out two other checks for $3,500—against Kalmbach's instructions. These checks drew the attention of Watergate investigators. Steinbrenner also made out 25 checks for $3,000 each. Added together, the contributions totaled $100,000—and all they bought Steinbrenner was trouble.

Investigators subpoenaed eight American Shipbuilding employees to a grand jury in September 1973. Steinbrenner tried to get the employees, who had backed their boss during investigations by the FBI, to lie. They refused to perjure themselves. Still, Steinbrenner insisted on his innocence throughout the ordeal. Others caught in similar wrongdoings had come clean, including American Airlines, Goodyear Tire, 3M, Phillips Petroleum, and 10 other companies. In none of those cases was the chief executive indicted on felony charges. In the style that New Yorkers grew to love—and hate—Steinbrenner stuck to his story and hired one of the country's top defense attorneys, Edward Bennett Williams, himself a future owner of the Baltimore Orioles and Washington Redskins.

Indictment, suspension, and humiliation followed, and, through all this difficulty and stress in his shipping business, Steinbrenner still managed to create such an air of discomfort during his first year owning the team that longtime baseball men walked away from jobs they had long craved and once loved. Even Yankee Stadium called it a day.

On Bat Day two years earlier, the Yankees realized that their beloved stadium was falling apart.

Hillerich & Bradsby, makers of Louisville Sluggers since 1894, had started turning out their first aluminum bats in 1971, but on June 6 of that year, the Yankees of course handed out wooden youth-sized Sluggers. Kid after kid in the crowd of 59,348 who entered the stadium smiled as the wooden wands pressed into their hands. The name burned into every bat was Bobby Murcer, number 1, and in the late innings as the Yankees finished off Kansas City, 5–2, the fans all banged their bats in unison. That's when the people sitting beneath the overhang seats noticed chips of concrete falling down.

"We knew we had a problem," says Marty Appel. "Our security people walking the stadium would report that everybody was banging the bats last inning, and they would see chips of concrete fall from the second deck to the first deck and so forth. So it's not that I remember any incidents that spooked us into thinking that somebody was going to sue us, but more just the general security call-ins from the people around the ballpark."

Yankees president Michael Burke noticed, too. As a precaution during football Sundays security crews used long poles to poke "loose chunks of dank cement that needed little urging to fall," Burke wrote in *Outrageous Good Fortune.* "In football season, it was our urgent Sunday prayer that decay be spotted and knocked harmlessly onto the empty seats before it was jarred loose by the 62,000 Giants fans stomping for warmth or for a Fran Tarkenton touchdown." By the start of the 1973 football season, Burke was out as Yankees president and Tarkenton had gone back to the Minnesota Vikings, whom he led to a 12-2 season and a Super Bowl appearance against Miami. The stadium that both Burke and Tark had called home during their time in the Bronx was on its way out as well.

The National Football League was forged into the entity it has become at Yankee Stadium. Yet the NFL Giants had come into being at the Polo Grounds in 1925, proving that New York could be a player in the fledgling, fly-by-night league. The football Giants ranked among the most dominant teams in the up-and-coming NFL in 1956 as news started to circulate that the baseball Giants might ditch the Polo Grounds. The footballers beat the baseballers to the punch, lighting out a quarter of a mile down the road to Yankee Stadium. The 1958 NFL Championship Game in the Bronx between the Giants and Baltimore Colts was called—and is often still called—the greatest game ever played. The Colts tied the game in the closing seconds on a field goal and won it with a touchdown in the first sudden death in NFL history, the national audience rapt in the darkness of a late December night made bright by the aura of Johnny Unitas.

By 1973 Johnny U. was a San Diego Charger, wet-nursing a rookie quarterback named Dan Fouts, and playing a final year in the professional game that he and his crewcut helped build at Yankee Stadium in '58. The NFL had grown by leaps and bounds in the 15 years in which Unitas had gone from superstar to hanger-on. The pro game had grown up, absorbed a rival league, adopted the Super Bowl, annexed Sundays from September to January, and stolen the hearts and minds of casual and hardcore sports fans alike. Baseball—for decades the breadwinner in the sports family—had to wonder how its baby brother had grown so big so fast.

If America's youth was going to follow a sport in the early 1970s, it had to have action and appeal . . . in other words, football. The NFL had practically doubled in size with its merger with the American Football League in 1970. By January 1973, the NFL had reaped the rewards of seven Super Bowl Sundays to push past baseball in the national consciousness. Even college football was reaching newfound levels of popularity, especially in regions of the country with no professional sports franchises. College football's national appeal dated back more than half a century to an era when baseball reigned supreme and pro football stood about as stable as a Roaring '20s floating crap game. Even on campuses where protest had been a familiar form of expression since the late '60s, students could still spend a few hours worried about alma mater against State on a crisp Saturday afternoon.

Baseball in the early '70s was for many the establishment's game. Fathers and grandfathers took kids, but it had no real relevance to most people over 18. Kids grew out of baseball the way they grew out of playing with G.I. Joes.

By 1973, however, this perception had started to change. The DH made for a radical step compared to the game's normally glacial pace of change. Teams like the Oakland A's, with colorful uniforms and ballplayers alike, had shown that squares needn't dominate the game. Playing the All-Star Game at night—and experimenting with nocturnal World Series action as well—helped draw more eyes to TVs than the weekday mid-afternoon affairs that had played for decades while men and boys strayed from their age-appropriate desks to follow the action. The places where the games took place had changed as well.

Unlike the old stadiums, built for baseball and adapted to football, the new stadiums fit both sports by design, even if their homogenous environment, symmetrical dimensions, artificial surface, and overgenerous seating capacity screamed of a football-first pragmatism. The younger brother ill-content to share, the NFL was already engineering stadiums solely with football in mind. New artificial-surface, football-only stadiums—all financed through public coffers—had gone up in Foxboro, Massachusetts (1971), Irving, Texas (1971), Kansas City (1972), and Orchard Park, New York (1973). Detroit and New Orleans were planning new domed stadiums.

New Orleans offered a potential landing site for a major league ballclub. Speculation linked the Yankees to the Big Easy, but Michael Burke, according to his memoir, told New York Mayor John Lindsay point blank: "The New Orleans Yankees is beyond my ken." Seattle voters had approved a new domed stadium and started construction in 1972, even though they had neither a major league nor an NFL team. (The city soon got one of each, and both called the Kingdome home.) Looking around the country and seeing what was happening in these secondary markets—and what was happening to Yankee Stadium physically—it wasn't long before two linked New York sports teams seriously considered their alternatives.

Burke had architects make preliminary studies at Yankee Stadium to see how to renovate the place. He asked Lindsay for the same treatment for the venerable Yankees and the House That Ruth Built that the city had given an expansion team a decade earlier. "Simply put, we are asking the city to equate us with the Mets," Burke told the mayor. Lindsay authorized the expenditure, but his people didn't consider it a good investment—not at the $24 million price tag that Shea Stadium had cost. So even though he didn't want to move the Yankees to another city, it was in Burke's best interest at least to entertain the idea of moving them to another state.

East Rutherford, New Jersey, lies 14 miles west of Yankee Stadium and just 10 miles from the Lincoln Tunnel. Driving there in traffic might take as long as driving to Canada, but the New Jersey borough with a population of less than 9,000 stands close enough to think of New York as home, even if its address speaks differently. In the early 1970s, the Giants came to feel that New York City wouldn't make the needed renovations to Yankee Stadium, so they became the second Giants club in 15 years to leave the city, though their "New York" designation and their fan base remained.

Through the chairman of the New Jersey Sports Authority, Sonny Werblin, former owner of the New York Jets, the Garden State likewise offered the Yankees a new home. For the Giants, it meant considerably more seats to sell (76,000); the venue also provided a chance finally to shine as the main tenant in a stadium after nearly half a century of existence, though their initiation had them play in three states over four years: Connecticut, at the Yale Bowl for most of 1973 and all of 1974; New York, sharing Shea with the Jets, Mets, and Yankees in 1975; and New Jersey, finally, in 1976.

The Giants weren't the only ones leaving the city, though. New York's public services and infrastructure were cracking from age and neglect. During the 1970s, more than one million people left. But New York wasn't just some Rust Belt burg losing heads to other states; it was the Big Apple. The part of the apple most bruised was the South Bronx, home of the Yankees. The Polo Grounds in Harlem, like Ebbets Field in Brooklyn, had long since become a site for public housing, but the older buildings in the South Bronx, increasingly abandoned and more and more the target of arson, proved a major problem. Robert Moses, the city builder whose heavy-handed approach to neighborhood homogeny in the 1950s and 1960s caused the decay according to some, called the South Bronx "beyond tinkering, rebuilding, and restoring."

New York City was going broke. Asking for a handout from the hard-up metropolis for a stadium housing only one team was no easy matter, especially when the dollar amounts looked likely to grow as the project wore on. Michael Burke cited this as an underlying reason that CBS, the top network of the day and a cash cow, put the Yankees up for sale. The Tiffany Network preferred to sell rather than undertake the expense of building a new facility for a business that had proven unsuccessful, especially when every other city was footing the bill for new stadiums. CBS also didn't want to look as if it was getting the corporate equivalent of welfare. "It would be extremely embarrassing to have the city of New York renovate Yankee Stadium at great cost to the commercial advantage of the Columbia Broadcasting System," Burke wrote. He also noted that the chairman of CBS, the esteemed William S. Paley, "did not need the public outcry this would provide." Obviously Paley and Burke were working from the old ethics model.

Construction overruns upped the renovation cost to more than $100 million by the time Yankee Stadium reopened in 1976. Burke insisted that the new stadium eliminate the poles that had obstructed so many views through the years. He also wanted to retain the signature frieze that rimmed the top of the stadium. The 105 poles went, along with about 12,000 seats, but the new construction couldn't support the copper façade. A smaller imitation was erected above the scoreboards and billboards behind the bleachers at the new stadium. The original copper frieze was sold and melted down for scrap.

Renovated Yankee Stadium certainly saw its share of glory, and it worked well enough for those who didn't remember the way the old ball yard looked. For those who had fond memories of the old park, of the cavernous "Death Valley" in left-center that Joe DiMaggio defied to hit 148 of his 361 career home runs, of being allowed to walk on the field after games to exit the park, of the countless kids who looked at the monuments and thought Babe Ruth was buried in center field . . . well, that's progress. In the 1970s, new was better—at least on paper. But something got lost in the conjuring.

"That *was* the stadium," recalls Yankee Fritz Peterson. "I never felt like the revised stadium represented the real thing. I'm glad they have a new one altogether. That fake one didn't feel real. I got two seats from the stadium but later sold them. I took my dugout seat (stool) with me. I'll never part with that. Babe Ruth may have sat on it."

The Giants had the first round of goodbyes at the old place. When the Yankees headed out of town in mid-September after a brutal homestand that saw the club fall under .500 for the first time since May, goalposts went up— on the goal-line back then—and hash marks lined the field for the last time.

The Giants opened the season in the Bronx by pounding the Houston Oilers by 20 points. On September 23, the Giants faced the Philadelphia Eagles in the final football game at the old stadium, with New York pulling out a 23-all tie on the last play of the game on a Pete Gogolak field goal. NFL Films, which captured the game for posterity on its weekly *This Week in Pro Football* program, played "Auld Lang Syne" over footage of the flag coming down after the game, the sister kissed for the final time. (Regular-season overtime didn't commence until 1974.) The Giants, who had swept the preseason schedule and had high hopes for '73, moved to their new New Haven home at Yale Bowl . . . and won only once more all year. Only the 1-13 Oilers had it worse.

Matters had gone from bad to worse for the Yankees, returning to New York for the final weekend of the season from a four-city tour needing to sweep the Tigers just to finish the year at .500—the August 1 division leader having been eliminated from contention two weeks before season's end. The defending AL East champion Tigers had fallen on their own hard times after Billy Martin imploded against the Indians, ordering his pitchers to throw spitballs—and admitting as much—in order to show the umpires that they didn't know what they were doing in enforcing the rules when Cleveland's Gaylord Perry was standing on the mound. (It was a fit of pique with which the Yankees could sympathize.) Joe Schultz, blowhard manager in Jim Bouton's *Ball Four* with the expansion '69 Seattle Pilots, finished the '73 season as manager of the Tigers. It was the only managing job he ever had after *Ball Four*.

The last game at Yankee Stadium offered few televised or written retrospectives. United Press International didn't even bother sending a reporter to the game, asking Yankees PR man Marty Appel to file a story for them. The most lasting view of the old stadium hit movie theaters that September. Paramount released *Bang the Drum Slowly*, an adaptation of the 1956 Mark Harris novel of the same name, shortly before Labor Day, 1973. Feeding off interest in the baseball locker room stirred by Bouton's book, the story took place in the present and even had Major League Baseball approval to use uniforms, footage, and big league ballparks as locations. The film poster featured two players jogging in the outfield at the empty stadium, the low-slung box seats in the Bronx eyeing them as they ran past. The fictional team for which they played was the Yankees in everything but name; the Mammoths even wore old Yankees uniforms with a slightly altered logo.

Filmed in the spring of 1972 at Yankee and Shea Stadiums while the teams were out of town, *Bang the Drum Slowly* was the melancholy story of a backwoods backup catcher dying from Hodgkin's lymphoma. The actor playing the Georgia yokel with the tragic secret wasn't yet well known and not yet 30, but he went to see Bouton—the pitcher turned sportscaster—to ask for advice on how to act like a ballplayer. Bouton told him to ride the buses in the bushes for a few weeks and learn how to spit tobacco, which the character does in the majority of his scenes. "That young man grew up to be Robert De Niro," Bouton, ever the storyteller, told the *Wall Street Journal* years later.

De Niro made a bigger impact as a New York street tough in Martin Scorsese's breakout film, *Mean Streets*, released in November 1973, but it was *Bang the Drum Slowly* that offered the final cinematic glimpse of the original stadium. The Oscar-nominated portrayal of the Mammoths manager by Vincent Gardenia—also playing Archie Bunker's neighbor on *All in the Family*—read like a big-screen nod to actual Yankees manager Ralph Houk, all the way down to the number 35 on the back of the manager's uniform. That number also represented how many years Houk had been in the Yanks' employ, and that last day at the old stadium marked Houk's last day in pinstripes.

"The city was generally down on Ralph Houk, down on the Yankees," Marty Appel recalls. "The Bronx wasn't a very attractive place to go out of the way to go to a game. So all of these factors almost made it a non-moment. You had to be a pretty ardent fan and care about the history of the game to appreciate what was going on that day."

With both football teams playing on the road and the Mets playing for their postseason lives in Chicago, the game in the Bronx drew 32,238, far from a sellout but nearly twice as many as had come to the Bronx on Opening Day. The majority of the crowd didn't care so much about history or the giveaway, a Mel Allen–narrated LP called *Yankee Stadium: The Sounds of a Half Century.* No, they were there to see what they could steal.

Stealing is perhaps too harsh a word for what many considered mere souvenir hunting, as people in other cities had done as old stadiums had bid their adieus in recent years. The Yankees landed a win by forfeit, finishing above .500 in 1971 because Washington fans got an early start on trolling the field in the ninth inning of the last game in DC by the relocating Senators. After that embarrassing moment, teams didn't bother with fancy sendoffs for ballparks in the 1970s. No one wanted to see a 70-something Hall of Famer trampled by a mob more intent on stealing third base—literally—than on honoring a legend. That was what Old-Timers Day was for. Anyway, the Bronx address would host baseball again a couple of years later.

Construction at the new Yankee Stadium started the next day. Everything must go! Houk's exit, however, was a complete secret.

The Yankees had won the first two games of the series and held a 1–0 lead in the top of the seventh when September call-up Marvin Lane hit his first career homer with a man on for Detroit. Leading off the home seventh was Duke Sims, who had started the week as a Tiger. Many in the stands probably didn't realize that he had even become Yankees property in a waiver maneuver. A lefty-swinging catcher with power, Sims only played 10 games over parts of two seasons as a Yankee and hit just one home run—the final homer at the old stadium. Babe hit the first in 1923, and Duke hit the last 50 years later. Sims got the starting assignment by losing a coin flip.

"We didn't know that Thurman had gone home, so we came into the clubhouse, and it's the last day of the season," explains Sims. "I had just left the Tigers. I'm gearing myself up mentally to make the bus for the Tigers [after the game] because my car was sitting in Detroit. I was going to drive it home from Detroit, and I was going to fly back with them. When we got to the clubhouse, Ralph [Houk] came out. [Catcher Jerry] Moses and I had lockers next to each other. He said, 'Thurman has gone home. One of you guys is going to play today. Which one of you wants to play?' Neither one of us felt very good because we had been out the night before, figuring that Thurman was going to play. I didn't say anything. Jerry looks at me, and I looked at him, and Ralph said, 'That's what I thought. So I'm going to flip a coin. You call it.' I called it tails, it came up heads, and I lost the flip, so I was in the lineup."

Thus history was made.

After another immortal, Mexican League refugee Celerino Sanchez, singled in two runs in his last major league at-bat, the Yankees took the field in the eighth inning with a 4–2 lead and their top left-hander on the mound. It had been an interesting year for Fritz Peterson, to say the least. Being part of what some consider the most infamous "trade" in sports history—except of course for Peterson, who feels quite the opposite—had altered the Yankees locker room as well as the way the press handled off-field events in the lives of players.

But that wasn't all. Something else was going on with Peterson in 1973, a sore left shoulder. "Yes, my shoulder was starting to be the end of me," he says. "I got about 150 cortisone shots over those last two seasons I pitched." He managed to last long enough in the majors to pitch in the refurbished stadium—in another uniform—but among his proudest moments was getting the assignment to close the old place out. He would also have the distinction of owning the lowest earned run average (2.52) of any pitcher in pinstripes at Yankee Stadium, before or after renovation. Unfortunately for Peterson, that last starting assignment of 1973 ended soon after the eighth inning began.

The first two Tigers singled to open the inning, and Ralph Houk walked up the steps and out toward the mound as he had done countless times before. Removing a pitcher may often result in some displeasure from the crowd—often directed at the pitcher. This was different. Catcalls followed the manager every step of the way, a few hand-drawn signs demanding his ouster held up for emphasis. "It was the worst thing I ever saw," says Peterson. "If I didn't put a couple of guys on base that inning he would have never gotten booed, they wouldn't have a chance to get him. I've felt bad about it ever since."

It only got worse. Lindy McDaniel replaced Peterson and allowed three hits and three walks as six runs crossed home plate; two of the runs were charged to Peterson, but the loss fell to McDaniel. So Houk had to come out once more to the chorus of boos as he waited on the mound for the bullpen car to bring in Wayne Granger. It seemed to last so long that he might as well have driven the reliever down from Syracuse.

"It was very hurtful to everybody that liked Ralph a lot, which was all of us in the front office," says Appel.

News leaked out during the game that Houk was resigning. Appel called UPI back and told them they'd better send someone to the stadium to do a game story and probably a follow-up. Steinbrenner and general manager Lee MacPhail already knew and had tried to talk the manager out of leaving when he'd told them after Friday night's game. Steinbrenner had already assured the manager of his job for 1974 in the press—the press not yet knowing how tenuous the owner's assurances could be. Houk knew, as Michael Burke, Howard Berk, Lee MacPhail, and Bob Fishel all knew, that it was better to go out on your own terms than on the new owner's. Anyone who doubted it could ask Johnny Callison.

Tigers lefty John Hiller—ending a remarkable comeback season with a 1.44 ERA and a then-record 38 saves after missing a year and a half following a heart attack—got the final win and the final out at the old stadium on a flyball by Mike Hegan to center fielder Mickey Stanley. A few minutes later, their hard-nosed manager stood in front of the Yankees with red eyes and confronted them. This wasn't about the team missing the .500 mark by one game.

"We really thought we had a winner," Houk told the press shortly after addressing the players, his voice cracking with emotion. "A man has to go with his convictions. I blame no one but myself. It will be better for the Yankees to have a new manager." Asked four decades later about his feelings after Houk told the team that he was leaving, Fritz Peterson doesn't mince words: "I hated it! Not only were we losing our stadium to play in the next year, we lost Houk too. Horrible feeling, not to mention the humiliation of having to go to Shea Stadium the next season."

⚾ ⚾ ⚾

To Stanley Cohen, the boos for Ralph Houk didn't ring as loud as the sound of wood and metal pried from the past 50 years. Cohen, a Yankees fan since he attended his first game at the stadium as a child during World War II, brought his family with him to the final game of 1973. It was the culmination of a season in which he had toured many of the new stadiums throughout the major leagues for an extensive article in *Consulting Engineer*, the magazine he edited. Unlike many who considered the closing of the old stadium no big deal, Cohen knew the alternatives too well—the new circular two-sport stadiums with their "unrelieved monotony" that was "so insipid in conception and uninspiring in fact, that they might as soon have been stamped out on a mass production line."

Cohen had met with the head of the firm rebuilding the stadium, Praeger-Kavanaugh-Waterbury, which had overseen construction of Shea Stadium and Dodger Stadium in the 1960s. Cohen left the meeting with a copy of the plans and the hope that the new stadium might afford an experience akin to what he'd felt in the Bronx watching the Yankees in the spring and summer and the Giants in the fall and winter during years both lean and abundant. It was an unrealistic expectation.

"There are, in the end, only two guides to remembrance—time and place—and time has no memory," Cohen wrote in his 1981 book, *The Man in the Crowd: Confessions of a Sports Addict.*

It is place that endures and provides memory with its trigger to the past. I could not begin to recall just how many times I had been to Yankee Stadium, only that, since I was ten years old, I had been there in all the ages of my life, in all moods and all seasons, on the hand of my father and the hand of my son, and I knew that regardless of circumstances, I had always felt secure there, sheltered somehow from the thrusts of a harsher reality. Now I would be seeing it that way for the last time, and I knew that no matter how close a resemblance the new stadium might bear to the old, something I could not quite name would be lost to me forever with the first thud of the wrecker's ball.

As the title of the book suggests, Cohen was not the man above the crowd but the man *in* the crowd, and he joined the throng by grabbing his piece of history on the last day at the old park: a sign from section 5 and a block of three stadium seats. He insisted on going out as he always had, across the field and through the exit on the other side of the bleachers. His souvenirs didn't last long once he stepped on the grass. An usher calmly thanked him, took the seats and the sign, and tossed them into the first-base dugout, now devoid of Yankees but "already brimming with other lost mementos."

Many of those mementos ended up in the hands of Bert Sugar, a nonpracticing lawyer, practical entrepreneur, and prodigious writer. The 36-year-old Washingtonian turned New York raconteur negotiated with the club to "poke through all the storerooms under the stands." He carted away 17 truckloads of memorabilia at a time when many—including the Yankees brass—considered that kind of stuff to be junk, or at least not worth paying to store for two-plus years while the team operated out of temporary digs in Queens.

To fans not yet in the practice of draping themselves in team apparel—because there wasn't much available to the public beyond trinkets and nonadjustable hats—it was hard to put a price on what many deemed, wrongly, to be of little value on the open market. Future stadium closings became elaborate, sentimental affairs with most of the functional parts of the ballpark sold piecemeal by the team at an incredible profit. In the meantime, teams also figured out how to make merchandise readily available to the millions of people who walked through their gates or watched from the couch at home.

"Baseball hadn't yet embraced the whole marketing plan of selling licensed merchandise," Marty Appel says of the early 1970s major leagues. "That just opened up a tremendous new revenue stream for the game. People were happy to wear the brand and show their support. . . . Today you just ride the subway, and you're with your own people. Everybody's in their colors, their favorite player on the back of their T-shirt. It's a more joyous shared experience today that baseball was slow to recognize what it would be."

Bert Sugar ran ahead of the curve. Among the booty he hauled from the old stadium were the original Yankee Stadium cornerstone, Lou Gehrig's uniform, Babe Ruth's contracts, the papers of original owner Jacob Ruppert, a Miller Huggins statue, and lots and *lots* of seats. Sugar sold most of them to the chain discount store Korvettes, where the 40- and 45-pound seats went for $7.50 a pop, plus five empty Winston crush-proof cigarette boxes. Stanley Cohen even bought one.

Mayor John Lindsay got his own set of seats, which he donated to Gracie Mansion. Lindsay, who had given original approval for the stadium reconstruction and was long out of office by the time of its completion, got the project rolling by scooping the first hunk of formerly sacred ground from right field with a bulldozer the day after the final game. Also on-field for the ceremony at the empty stadium were a handful of construction workers, team employees, and dignitaries, including the widows of Babe Ruth and Lou Gehrig. Clare Ruth got home plate and Eleanor Gehrig first base. Bert Sugar got most everything else.

Ten

BELIEVE IT IF YOU NEED IT

*T*here was no shortage of major events during the first half of 1973: Watergate, Wounded Knee, *Roe v. Wade*, the end of Vietnam, inflation. New York seemed especially hard up for good news, but sports stories were putting much-needed smiles on people's faces.

"My teams were my teams—I lived and died with them," says Howie Rose, a future broadcaster for three New York teams but a Queens College sophomore in 1973. "The beauty of sports has always been to some extent that you could insulate yourself from the outside world. If you're not necessarily living vicariously through the teams, you're just immersed in what they're doing to the point where the heavy stuff can sit on the shelf until you get to it when the game is over. I was pretty aware of what was going on. I remember in '73 watching some of the early Watergate hearings, the Senate hearings. It was fascinating. It was a little scary because we'd never been through something like that."

"That year sports was on the front page," says Sal Marchiano, sportscaster for New York's ABC-TV in 1973. "Because of Namath, women started showing up at football games. . . . Then you had the Knicks winning with a team that was like a string quartet, with basketball being the city game. You had this incredible interest in sports, as a prelude setting up what happened later on."

The Knicks were the toast of New York, and plenty of teams were vying for that title. As of 1973, New York had two teams in every sport for the first time—including two tenants at the new Nassau Veterans Coliseum: the expansion Islanders, who won just 12 of 78 games (plus 6 ties) to earn *Sports Illustrated*'s designation as "one of the sorriest NHL teams ever," and the 30-54 New York Nets of the American Basketball Association, whose coach, Lou Carneseca, left the team in the summer of '73 to return to his alma mater, St. John's University in Queens.

Tug McGraw, left, and Jerry Koosman ham it up.

NATIONAL BASEBALL HALL OF FAME LIBRARY, COOPERSTOWN, NY

The Knickerbockers—a name that harkened back to the city's 17th-century Dutch roots—followed the world championship trail blazed by the Jets and Mets in 1969. The Knicks beat the Lakers for the NBA title in May 1970 with a limping Willis Reed providing the spark in the deciding seventh game. Reed was still at Madison Square Garden three Mays later, and all five Knicks starters in 1973 ended up in the Hall of Fame: '70 championship holdovers Bill Bradley, Dave DeBusschere, Walt "Clyde" Frazier, and Reed, plus superstar acquisition Earl "the Pearl" Monroe. The team also had Hall of Fame coach Red Holzman, team president Ned Irish, and sixth man Jerry Lucas, who became the first player in history to win a championship in high school, college, the pros, and the Olympics. The ninth Hall of Famer in the group was thinking man's forward Phil Jackson, who averaged 17 minutes per game for the 1973 Knicks after watching from the sidelines in 1970 due to back surgery; when his playing career ended, Jackson sharpened his focus to become a Zen master coach in Chicago and Los Angeles. At the LA Forum, New York claimed the '73 title by dispatching the Lakers in five games, with the Knicks flashing the "number one" sign in the visiting locker room and leaving no doubt as to the authenticity of their claim.

To get to the finals, the Knicks became the first team ever to beat the storied Celtics in a seventh game—and at Boston Garden. That came on the heels of the New York Rangers stunning the defending Stanley Cup champion Bruins in the quarterfinals, four games to one, winning all three games played in Boston. The previous spring, the Bruins had ended the Rangers' magical run in the Stanley Cup finals. Revenge was sweet, and Rangers fans were overjoyed.

"Yeah, that was an extraordinary year," recalls Marchiano, who called the series on TV. "The clincher was in Boston. . . . I was on the plane with the Rangers, and Bill Chadwick made the mistake of saying [on air] that we were coming into LaGuardia Airport. When we landed there were an estimated 10,000 people at LaGuardia Airport. They had broken down the fence. The plane had to taxi back out and the Rangers were put on a bus to be taken off the tarmac. The city was just full of exuberance over the Rangers."

Though the Rangers suffered a letdown against the Chicago Blackhawks in the semifinals, the bar rose high for other New York teams come summer. The Yankees took over first place and created excitement in the last year at the old stadium, but the Mets, still supposed to own New York since their Amazin'—with a capital "A"—1969 world championship, weren't making anyone forget the exploits at the Garden. In *Mets Fan*, his book about the psyche of rooting for the team, Hofstra English professor and baseball sage Dana Brand, a Columbia underclassman in 1973, paraphrased Mets manager and baseball sage Yogi Berra: "Nineteen seventy three was déjà vu all over again in spades. It was the pits."

⚾ ⚾ ⚾

After winning the 1969 World Series, the Mets had become a run-of-the-mill club. Pedestrian baseball was something new to Mets fans. Until the 1970s, it had been either top of the mountain or bottom of the pile. The team lost at least 100 games in five of their first six seasons, establishing the ceiling for losses for the 20th century—and beyond—with 120 in their maiden season of 1962. Seven seasons later, the team went the other way, winning 100 and continuing to stun the world in October, going 7-1 in the postseason, including a sweep of the first Championship Series in history. Since then, the team from Flushing had finished each year in third place with 83 wins. On July 9, 1973, the Mets sat at 12 games under .500 and 12½ games out of first place, but they were in the right division—and in the right clubhouse.

Ballplayers become used to non-uniformed personnel in their midst. To them, it's a hazard of the profession, and while it's understood that former ballplayers manage current ballplayers, often the person who signs the checks or negotiates their size is a man seemingly born in a suit. Mets chairman M. Donald Grant was such a man.

Yet Grant had an athlete's background. His first initial stood for Michael, after his father, a member of the Hockey Hall of Fame. At age 21, the revolutionary defenseman had become the youngest man to captain a team to the Stanley Cup, winning the first of five Cups for the Montreal Victorias in 1894. Don, as his son was known, was a good enough athlete that the Montreal Canadiens approached him, but his family knew too well the sporting life and the meager pay it provided at the time, so he gravitated toward business.

Grant moved to New York as a night hotel clerk, refereeing hockey games on the side. He married well and worked his way up in the investment business. He excelled at golf and squash, good enough to be invited to the most exclusive country clubs and the right parties. He was certainly at the right party when he met Joan Whitney Payson, heiress to the Whitney fortune. A parlor game asked each person to state his or her heart's desire. Grant confessed to wanting to purchase the New York Giants baseball team, of which he already owned a modest five shares. Payson, whose turn came next in the game, declared that she shared that desire. Grant became her friend, stockbroker, business advisor, and soon enough Payson's proxy for her newly purchased 10 percent of the Giants.

When the Giants moved—Grant-Payson providing the lone dissenting vote—it didn't take much for city leaders to form a group to try to bring a National League team back to New York. When the NL yawned at the suggestion, attorney William A. Shea formed a rival league: the Continental League. Shea gained everyone's attention when he announced Payson as one of the owners. Through bluster and bluff by Shea and Continental League president Branch Rickey—who had revolutionized the minor leagues in St.

Louis, integrated the game in Brooklyn, and helped rebuild the long-dead team in Pittsburgh—the National League eventually agreed to allow expansion for the first time since the 19th century. Though the Continental League existed only on paper, it set the standard taken up by very real rival leagues like the American Football League, American Basketball Association, and World Hockey Association, which all eventually merged with established leagues in the 1970s. The tireless Shea got the Mets and Astros into the National League in 1962 without having to produce so much as a catcher's mitt. That's how a lawyer gets a stadium named after him.

Payson and Grant finally had their own club. Though the press often pointed out Payson's wealth, Grant ensured that expenses stayed under control. Lou Niss, hired as the publicity director of the Continental League and who then served as traveling secretary of the Mets through 1979, knew all about the parsimonious ways of the organization. The old guard press corps—then known as the New Breed—all had heard the Niss joke about the title of his never-penned memoir: *The Club That Didn't Cost a Nickel and Never Spent a Dime*. The Mets only got into the special lottery for Tom Seaver in 1966—caused by the Braves signing him past the deadline—because general manager George Weiss assumed that many teams would be involved, thus making it unlikely that the Mets would have to fork over the $50,000 that the winning club had to pay for the contract. Only three teams took part in the lottery (Mets, Indians, Phillies), and New York had its first luck as a franchise with The Franchise.

But Grant was no Finley or Steinbrenner. They used their own money and earned the right to have their say, however much it grated on others. In the words of Steve Jacobson, who covered the Mets from the beginning for *Newsday* and had many dealings with Grant, "He was a big windbag in the first place, a stuffed shirt." Grant took a patronizing view of the players, bringing clients and stockholders into the clubhouse to introduce them to "the boys." Players didn't like being called that—especially the black men on the team—but everyone knew that standing up to management likely meant standing in another locker room in the near future—or winding up out of the majors entirely in the days before free agency.

Farm director Whitey Herzog never put up with Grant's foolishness, and it had cost him. "The guy who really should have managed the Mets in '72 was Whitey Herzog because he was there and had the résumé, but Grant hated Whitey," explains broadcaster Howie Rose, aficionado of all things Mets, about the possible line of succession as manager after the death of Hodges in April 1972. "Whitey, in so many words, told Grant that he didn't know shit about baseball. Grant, as stuffy as he was, didn't appreciate that. . . . The death of Gil and the failure of the front office to see what they had in Whitey Herzog combined to set them back almost a decade."

So when Grant came to the clubhouse to talk to "the boys," no one jumped for joy, but no one was going to say anything, either—except for Tug.

In 1973, Tug McGraw was the most combustible of ballplayers: a reliever who couldn't get anyone out. McGraw spent a lot of time talking with Joe Badamo, a Long Island insurance salesman and motivational speaker who had been good friends with Gil Hodges. After an especially insightful and enthusiastic talk with Badamo about believing in yourself, Grant, described by McGraw as "a martini guy," happened to be giving a clubhouse talk. "It was a good talk. The problem was it took twenty minutes for him to say what should have taken him five," McGraw recalled in his aptly named book, *Ya Gotta Believe!* When Grant said, "We believe in you guys, every single one of you," Tug could no longer contain himself.

"That's when I shouted out, 'Aaaaahhhh, ya gotta believe!' Real loud," McGraw wrote. "It stopped the speech in its tracks. I jumped up and ran around to a couple of lockers, grabbing guys and yelling, 'Do you believe? Ya gotta believe!'" M. Donald Grant didn't believe. He stormed out of the clubhouse while McGraw was still bouncing off the lockers. McGraw said both at the time and long after the fact that he wasn't trying to make fun of the boss, but just about everybody believed he was. Four decades later, memory of the actual locker room meeting has dimmed, but a few ya-gotta-believe teammates still believe that McGraw was mocking Grant.

"He was probably making fun of him," says shortstop Bud Harrelson, "but it became our war cry. It became Pittsburgh 'We Are Family'"—a reference to the Sister Sledge song adopted by the 1979 Pirates during their late-season run. "I think he mocked him a little bit," says third baseman Wayne Garrett. "You never know what was running through Tug's mind at any time. I thought it was bad timing to be doing that."

Teammates convinced McGraw to seek out Grant and apologize, which McGraw did. Grant said he was offended, telling the reliever, "The only thing that will keep you here is if we start winning some ballgames." The team still didn't take off, but McGraw's phrase certainly did.

Buzz Capra, an acolyte of McGraw in the bullpen, refers to how the players initially felt about McGraw's mantra as "that 'Gotta Believe' crap." The players were, however, far more receptive than the chairman of the board.

"Everybody kind of laughed at him at first—'Why don't you just shut up, Tug,'" Capra says of McGraw's overuse of the phrase as the team continued to struggle. "Then, all of a sudden, things started clicking, so it made that saying a little bit more . . . it started to catch on. But he was talking with this [motivational] guy, and he went off with that. Then, every day being in the outfield [during batting practice], things started to click, so we said, 'Let's believe.'" Pitcher Jon Matlack recalls how McGraw adamantly screamed out the saying "anytime that anything positive happened when he was on the field or in the dugout or in the bullpen. It sort of spread like wildfire."

Though the Mets beat the Astros in 12 innings on July 9, the night McGraw's message broke up Grant's talk, it proved only a momentary reprieve from an oppressive summer. The Mets put together just a 32-48 mark between the end of May and the middle of August, yet the division was so mediocre that the Mets lost a mere five games in the standings in that span. The last-place Mets stood 8½ games back in the NL East when they took the field in San Diego on August 15—four years to the day from when the second-place Mets began their climb from 10 games out to division champs in 1969. Just like '69, the surge started against the Padres. It began the way anything good often began for the Mets: with Tom Seaver on the mound. Trying not to get swept by the lowly Padres in the last game of a miserable 2-5 West Coast swing, Seaver tossed a two-hit shutout. His record stood at 15-6; his team was 53-65.

The Mets returned home from California to face the Reds, who were pursuing the first-place Dodgers. Despite what turned out to be the 660th and final career home run by Willie Mays, Cincinnati rallied to beat the Mets, 2–1, in 10 innings on August 17, dropping the Mets 13 games under .500—as many games south of mediocrity as they had been since 1968—but the 7½ games back in the standings made their perch in last place not seem as hopeless as it should have otherwise. Around this time *New York Times* writer Leonard Koppett, who had followed the Mets since their inception, opined, more prescient than optimistic: "The Mets remain on the fringes of what may yet turn out to be a memorable Eastern Division race." During that series with the Reds, the Mets, for the first time in three months, were whole again. Players had been coming and going from the disabled list all summer, but it was around this time that they began playing as a team—a healthy team.

"I had been hit in May by Ramon Hernandez [of Pittsburgh] in my fingers," explains Rusty Staub. "He hit [Jerry] Grote the same day. Here I thought Grote would be fine, and I would be done, but my fingers weren't broken, they were just beat to death, and Grote's arm was broken. Buddy [Harrelson] got hurt, this one got hurt, that one got hurt. In August, it all seemed to happen. I didn't play for three days [in the Reds series in August]. They injected my right hand four times and my left hand three times. When I played [on Monday], it was the first time I had pop all year. It was a very good job by the physicians, using cortisone as it should be used." Though the Mets lost the series finale to Cincinnati in 16 innings, Staub had four hits, the first time he'd had more than two hits in a game since June. From that point forward, *Le Grande Orange*—a name the red-haired slugger brought with him from Montreal—knocked in 21 runs, walked as many times, scored 24 runs, and batted .293 over his last 38 games.

When the first-place Dodgers followed the Reds into Flushing, the second game of the series looked for all the world like their 26th one-run loss in 47 tries. But with two outs in the bottom of the ninth and a man on second, Felix Millan, Staub, and John Milner all singled, and the Mets had a 3–2 victory—the first win of the year for McGraw, who had entered the game with an 0-6 mark and a 5.45 ERA. McGraw, the highest-paid reliever in the National League at $75,000, turned once more into the best reliever in the league, and cries of "Ya Gotta Believe" filtered from the clubhouse to the newspapers, from newsstands to every corner of the city. So went the humble beginnings of the signature phrase of a reliever and a franchise— which actually required an apology from the man who coined it.

⚾ ⚾ ⚾

The common perception is that the National League East was ridiculously mediocre for all of 1973, and the Pirates couldn't hold a lead they'd maintained for months. Not true. At the end of June, the Cubs had the second best record in the game at 47-31 and had the largest lead of any team in baseball's four divisions: 8½ games ahead of the Cardinals. (The 31-39 Mets were last, 12½ games back, though their .443 winning percentage was almost 80 percentage points higher than any other cellar dweller in any other division.)

St. Louis had its own remarkable comeback in '73. By the All-Star break on July 22, the Cardinals, who lost 12 of 13 to start the year and reached a nadir of 15 games below .500, had already caught the Cubs. The Cards went 26 games over .500 between May 14 and August 5. On the latter date, the standings looked like this:

	Won	Lost	Percent	Games Back
St. Louis	61	50	.550	--
Chicago	56	55	.505	5
Pittsburgh	54	55	.495	6
Montreal	53	56	.486	7
Philadelphia	52	60	.464	9½
New York	48	60	.444	11½

Over the final 50-plus games of the season, the division turned almost upside down. Baseball-Reference affords a look at who did what in that final third of the season:

	Won	Lost	Percent	Games Back
New York	34	19	.642	--
Montreal	26	27	.491	8
Pittsburgh	26	27	.491	8
Chicago	21	29	.420	11½
St. Louis	20	31	.392	13
Philadelphia	19	31	.380	13½

So what happened? How did the race turn around so quickly, and so completely? All the theories and bits of conjecture are inconclusive. It may be more insightful simply to go with the explanation of the day: God took an apartment in Flushing.

⚾ ⚾ ⚾

After winning the series against the Dodgers at Shea, the Mets lost two of three to the Giants but didn't lose another series for the rest of the season. The Mets finished an 8-5 homestand with a sweep of San Diego—their first sweep since the Padres last had come to New York in mid-June. The Mets split a four-game series in St. Louis, but took three of four at Jarry Park in Montreal sandwiched between series wins over the Phillies both at Shea and the Vet. When the Mets won the series against the Cubs on a Jerry Grote squeeze bunt, the army of believers in New York was growing. Their faith would be tested, though, with five games in five days in a home-and-home series with the first-place Pirates.

Pittsburgh had its own mission of belief. They still had the best hitting in the division, but the team's heart had been torn out. Roberto Clemente died when his plane went down on a humanitarian mission to earthquake-ravaged Nicaragua on New Year's Eve, 1972. Fans in America and especially in his native Puerto Rico were devastated. The Hall of Fame waived its five-year wait for induction, and Cooperstown honored him in the summer of '73 along with contemporaries Warren Spahn and Monte Irvin.

In Pittsburgh, though, going on without the "Great One" had left a giant hole not only in the outfield but in the clubhouse and the greater community. Manny Sanguillen, an All-Star catcher, was chosen to replace his close friend in right field. Manager Bill Virdon didn't admit to the mistake until June and didn't play hard-hitting rookie Richie Zisk in right field every day until late July. (Another rookie with a deadly stroke, Dave Parker, also spent an inordinate amount of time on the bench.) The Pirates gained a first-place tie with St. Louis at the end of August after three straight wins against the Cubs at Three Rivers Stadium. The Bucs lost to the Cubs the next day to fall back to second and then dropped three of four to the Cardinals to sit three games back in the standings. The Pirates, winners of the last three division titles, made the radical decision to replace Virdon with the man whom Virdon had replaced: Danny Murtaugh.

Under Murtaugh, Pittsburgh surged . . . or rather, as the NL East was going in September, lurched forward. Murtaugh epitomized blue-collar baseball in Steel City. The Pirates had employed the Pennsylvania native and former paratrooper since the late 1940s, and he spent the last four years of his up-and-down playing career as the club's second baseman before calling it quits and asking general manager Branch Rickey about a managing assignment in the minor leagues. Rickey's replacement, Joe E. Brown, chose Murtaugh to take over for Bobby Bragan at the helm of the big, bad Bucs in 1957—and "bad" is an accurate description of the team. Three years later the Pirates shocked the Yankees in the World Series. Despite twice retiring due to heart problems, Murtaugh guided the Pirates to another seven-game series triumph in 1971 against the Orioles in Clemente's signature baseball moment. Then he retired again, seemingly for good and on top. Now 55, gruff, grizzled, and on his fourth go of managing the Pirates, his craggy face stared out from the shadow of his gold Pirates hat on the cover of *Sports Illustrated*.

The Cardinals, who had so quickly and efficiently dispatched the Cubs from first place in July, were rudely bounced from the penthouse in

September during a seven-game losing streak that started when they were swept—where else?—in Chicago. The Pirates, who had been 10½ games out in July when St. Louis was making its run to take over the division, now owned first place. Pittsburgh missed its chance for the sweep on the second Sunday of September against the Cardinals, but the Pirates at least picked a day when the locals were less inclined to notice. Sunday, September 16, opened the NFL season, and all eyes in Pittsburgh trained on a Steelers team coming off the first playoff win in its 40-year history, the Immaculate Reception game of December 23, 1972 against the hated Oakland Raiders.

So on Monday, September 17, 1973, many in Pittsburgh were still relishing the Steelers' 24–10 demolition of the Detroit Lions the previous day even as the Pirates took the field against the Mets on the same Three Rivers AstroTurf that Bradshaw and Co. had so recently consecrated. Not all eyes in New York were on baseball, either. Joe Namath and the Jets were facing Green Bay in the *Monday Night Football* season opener. ABC's psychedelic Scanimate intro fed into the voice of Howard Cosell—a man with whom more Americans disagreed than Archie Bunker—yet people were more inclined to turn him up than turn him off. Cosell and Namath? Jets iconoclast John Riggins with a Mohawk haircut? The first Monday nighter of the year? The nation watched for the next 13 Monday nights.

Three years of beaming one game per week into every living room, basement, and bar in America had proved a winning gamble for ABC. The other networks had passed when Pete Rozelle ran Roone Arledge's idea by them. *Monday Night Football*, along with new blackout policies that finally allowed sold-out games to be shown locally, not only didn't hurt attendance, but the NFL actually set a record in 1973. All other interests went out the window on Monday nights, whether bowling leagues were folding, restaurants were closing, or kids were hurrying through homework. The 1973 *Monday Night* opener took no prisoners on other channels, be they Lucille Ball's or Dick Van Dyke's latest shows on CBS, Clint Eastwood's *Play Misty for Me* on NBC's *Monday Night at the Movies*, or the Mets on WOR-TV in New York—except a local station wouldn't put a baseball game on television opposite Cosell, Frank Gifford, and Don Meredith, especially with the Jets playing.

So while New Yorkers watched the Pack pound Namath and Co., 23–7, in muddy Milwaukee County Stadium, a segment of the audience listened— for a while, at least—on WHN and the Mets Radio Network's 21 affiliates in five states as Pittsburgh peppered Tom Seaver in the rain, 10–3. The fourth-place Mets were now four games under .500 and 3½ games back with just

12 games to play. A loss the next night against the first-place Pirates, and you might hear *MNF* QB, announcer, and crooner Dandy Don Meredith warming up the pipes: "Turn out the lights, the party's over."

The party seemed just about over. For the second straight night, the Pirates knocked out a Mets starter after three innings, and Pittsburgh took its 4–1 lead into the ninth inning. Lefty reliever Ramon Hernandez, in his third inning of relief, got the first out, but Jim Beauchamp singled, Wayne Garrett doubled, and Felix Millan tripled, suddenly making it a one-run game. Hernandez walked Rusty Staub, setting up a potential game-ending double play with pitcher Tug McGraw's spot due up. Duffy Dyer was announced to pinch-hit, but when Murtaugh summoned fireman Dave Giusti, Yogi Berra countered with Ron Hodges to face the right-hander. Hodges, a lefty-swinging rookie catcher drafted from Appalachian State just a year earlier, stepped out of the on-deck circle and into the week of his life.

Hodges, a lowball hitter, turned out to be ideal to bat against Giusti's palmball, which sank heavily. Hodges singled to right field to bring in Millan and tie the game. After a walk to Cleon Jones, Don Hahn, who, like Hodges, had been in the minors until June, singled to center to score two more and cap a five-run ninth. Ron and Don were sudden heroes, and Yogi Berra intended to forge even more before the ninth inning ended.

Early in the season, Met-turned-Yankee Ron Swoboda had taken a swipe at his old team: "I think there are a lot of people who put their uniforms on over there who aren't sure Yogi can manage in the big leagues." Now in the visitor's dugout in Pittsburgh, a few Mets—"prima donnas" Swoboda had called them—might have been inclined to agree with their former teammate. Not to mention plenty of people watching the Tuesday night broadcast in New York on WOR-TV. As inspired as the decision to have Hodges bat with the season on the line had been—he could have tried an ailing Willie Mays—Berra summoned another unknown in a 6–4 game against the Pittsburgh Lumber Company.

Coming back from commercial, fans saw Bob Apodaca making his major league debut. Even frantically reaching into their Mets library—a collection that announcer Bob Murphy always suggested the discerning fan should have—and flipping to the pages of obscure Mets in the back of the yearbook couldn't conjure up the name or face. Nothing. Apa-*who*? When he walked the two batters he faced, Apodaca was banished to the future, where he became a trusted Mets reliever and later an esteemed pitching coach. For now, though, the season rested on the right arm of Buzz Capra.

"I don't know how much faith Yogi had in me, actually," says Capra. "He brings in Bob Apodaca, which of course is a tough situation for a guy from Triple-A. His blood isn't even cold yet. He just got up there, and he [Berra] puts him in the game. I was kind of perturbed about that."

Capra had pitched twice in the past week in mop-up outings, but he hadn't appeared in a close game since blowing a save in a loss to St. Louis on September 2. With Ray Sadecki and Tug McGraw already used in the game and Harry Parker ailing, Capra came in to save the season. "That's the Lumber Company," Capra says. "Those guys are mashers."

Dave Cash sacrificed the tying runs into scoring position, which gave Capra an out but put him in the unenviable position of navigating the toughest lineup in the division with little margin for error. "So I go out there, start cranking up, and I got to face Al Oliver, Willie Stargell, Richie Zisk, and Manny Sanguillen—in that order," he says, getting more animated in the re-telling. Oliver grounded to first base, resulting in the second out but allowing a run to score to make it a 6–5 game and move the tying run to third.

"Yogi comes out to the mound asking what I want to do. I said, 'For crying out loud, you're the manager. If you're going to walk him, you already got the [tying] runs on base. . . . I can get Richie Zisk because I face Richie Zisk in Triple-A a lot.' I got a right-hand hitter coming up. I'm not going to face Stargell. Lefty-righty, who cares? We have a force play anywhere." Capra walked Stargell and, it turned out, Zisk. So the bases were loaded, the tying run at third, the winning run at second, and Sanguillen up. Capra fell behind 3-and-1. Another ball and the game would be tied.

"He's one of the best bad ball hitters," recalls Capra. "He could hit balls off the shoetops, swinging that 30-ounce bat that he used to swing around like it was a toothpick. He would hit balls a foot over his head, literally. The guy was a Yogi Berra–type hitter, bad ball hitter. I'm just cranking it—here we go. I said, 'I'm throwing this next pitch as hard as I can. It's going to be a fastball. I'm not going to throw a curve.' I threw him a fastball right down 'powder river.' I'll never forget it. *Boom!* He hits a little dinky shallow flyball to Cleon, game over. I go on *Kiner's Korner.* I get my 50 dollars, and I never got in a game after that."

As Capra smiled in the postgame interview with announcer Ralph Kiner, appearance fee in hand, the Mets and their fans could breathe again. It was a two-game swing in the standings, from the oblivion of 4½ back to a doable 2½ back, and the showdown still had three games to go—in New York.

Thursday, September 20, began in New York with Willie Mays on NBC's *Today Show* announcing his retirement from the game. The day closed in jubilation at Shea Stadium, the biggest day for the club since 1969. It proved a significant day in the women's movement as well.

As the Mets and Pirates clashed at Shea, the Battle of the Sexes raged at the Houston Astrodome. This exhibition tennis match had a bit more hype than your average ballgame. Promoted like a boxing match on ABC, the biggest voice in the country, Howard Cosell, called it. In this corner was Bobby Riggs, 55, former men's amateur and pro tennis champion, well-known hustler, and male chauvinist, who relished his straight-set beating of the top-ranked women's player in the world, Margaret Court, in a challenge match on Mother's Day. And in this corner: Billie Jean King, 29, Wimbledon champion, at the top of her game, and tired of listening to Riggs rant. She had turned Riggs down when he wanted to play her instead of Court. Now the ball was in her court to defend not only the women's game but her gender as well.

King, already in Houston playing the Virginia Slims tournament, rode into the Astrodome like a queen, astride a chair carried by four bare-chested men. Riggs arrived in a rickshaw drawn by bikini-clad models. The *New York Times* declared: "This was an event more like a Super Bowl game than a lawn tennis match." The $100,000 winner-take-all match went to King, 6–4, 6–3, 6–3. Her husband, Larry, helped her, teary-eyed, off the court. Her father, Billy Moffitt, a former college basketball player, fireman, and current scout for the Milwaukee Brewers, erupted in shouts of "Go, baby, go!" joined by heavyweight champion George Foreman. King's brother, Randy Moffitt, wasn't at the Astrodome, but he was also a winner that evening, getting a key out in relief as the Giants beat the first-place Reds at Candlestick Park.

A year earlier, Congress approved the Equal Rights Amendment— which would have guaranteed that the rights affirmed in the Constitution applied equally to all, regardless of sex; clarified legal status of sex discrimination in courts; and deterred those who might try to enforce laws inequitably. In 1973, the ERA was in the process of gaining approval by the states. It eventually fell three states short of ratification, but Title IX—forbidding discrimination by gender in any educational program or activity with federal funding—had recently become a law. As such, the Battle of the Sexes made for a huge prime time spectacle and a stereotype-bending occasion all at once. A crowd of 30,492—the largest in history to see a tennis match—witnessed the two-hour event, while an estimated 50 million people tuned in around the world. The duel even had an encore during the sweeps period that November when Riggs and King appeared side by side on an episode of *The Odd Couple*. The title of the episode, in which Riggs hustles sportswriter Oscar Madison, played by Jack Klugman, until King comes to the rescue on the Ping-Pong table, was called "The Pig Who Came to Dinner."

The game at Shea Stadium didn't have a worldwide audience or gender-wide implications, and the crowd of 24,855 was closer to the number of copies sold by New Jersey native Bruce Springsteen's just-released second album of 1973, *The Wild, the Innocent & the E Street Shuffle*—a follow-up to his debut earlier that year, *Greetings from Asbury Park*—than it was to a sellout. But like Springsteen, the critics fell in love with the effort and the energy generated by a tight ensemble, and the crowds followed.

George Stone and Tug McGraw had combined the previous night to beat the Pirates at Shea, 7–3, bringing New York's deficit to 1½. The last time the Mets had been that close to first place had been May, which was also when the Mets had last seen .500. Now they were two games under .500 and tied for third with the Cardinals. Gene Mauch's fourth-year Expos, bolstered by ex-Met Ken Singleton in the outfield, Twins castoff Mike Marshall in the bullpen, and rookie Steve Rogers atop the rotation, giddily stood in second place just one game out. Pittsburgh was the only NL East team with a winning record—and they had dropped three of four.

The Mets, using a four-man rotation down the stretch, started Jerry Koosman against the Pirates on Thursday night. He had played as big a part in the team's resurgence as anyone. On August 19, saddled with an 8-14 record and a 3.47 ERA, Koosman allowed an unearned run in the fifth inning against Cincinnati. Koosman didn't allow another run until September 7. His 31⅔ consecutive scoreless innings remained a Mets record for 39 years until surpassed in 2012 by R. A. Dickey. (In 1985, Dwight Gooden passed Koosman's '73 effort with 36⅔ consecutive innings without an earned run.) More importantly, the Mets won all five of Kooz's starts during his streak. He had been hit pretty hard in his two starts since then, but on September 20 he matched pitch for pitch with another 30-year-old crafty lefty named Jim Rooker.

Pittsburgh nicked Koosman for an unearned run in the fourth inning, but he began the game-tying rally by drawing a leadoff walk in the sixth. After Richie Hebner tagged Koosman for a home run in the seventh, it was Rooker's turn to be victimized by an error, this one by center fielder Al Oliver to tie the game. After the Pirates took the lead in the ninth against Harry Parker, the Mets once again stood one pitch away from a stinging defeat at a crucial time. With Dave Giusti roughed up the past two nights, Murtaugh brought in southpaw Ramon Hernandez to face left-handed pinch hitter Ed Kranepool with a runner on second and one out. Berra countered with righty George Theodore, his first at-bat since breaking his hip in July. The Stork struck out, and Duffy Dyer came out as a pinch hitter as he'd done two nights earlier in Pittsburgh. That time, Murtaugh had yanked Hernandez for Giusti, and Berra countered with Hodges, who delivered the game-tying hit. This time, the Pirates stayed with Hernandez . . . and Dyer got the game-tying hit.

Four tense innings later, with two outs in the top of the 13th and Richie Zisk on first, Dave Augustine, a September call-up who had entered the game as a pinch runner and remained in center field, blasted a Ray Sadecki offering well over the head of Cleon Jones in left. The ball struck the very top of the wall, and . . . well, let the witnesses call it.

"I grew up in a garden apartment development, so we all had stoops or steps. We used to play stoopball with a rubber ball," explains Howie Rose, Bayside native, Queens College student, future Mets broadcaster, and among those at Shea that night. "Sometimes you'd hit one right off the edge of the step; it was called a 'pointer.' The ball would hit the edge of that step and pop straight up. Sometimes it would go way out, and sometimes it would go straight up but that's exactly what Augustine's ball looked like. It hit the top of the fence. It was a pointer. It came right to Cleon. Everything happened as if it were in slow motion to my memory. I could feel it like it was yesterday."

"Cleon got it and threw it to me," says Wayne Garrett, who'd moved to shortstop in extra innings. "I just relayed it home."

"He made a perfect throw to me," says catcher Ron Hodges, who entered the game in the 10th inning. "We got Richie Zisk sliding in at the plate. I felt that collision, and I remember the umpire at the time, John McSherry, yelling, 'Show me the ball, show me the ball!' I'm on one knee, and I pulled the ball out of my glove and hold it up. He said, 'Yeah, you're out.' The crowd just went nuts."

"Once he was tagged out," recalls Rose, "I looked at my cousin and said, 'That's it, man. We're winning this whole thing.' Not just the game. At that point I knew they were winning the game. I said, 'We're winning this whole thing.' Plays like this aren't wasted on also-rans." Even Cleon Jones, who manned left field at Shea Stadium for eight years and saw plenty of odd doings in that little corner of Queens, admitted in '73 that he was stunned that the ball didn't bounce into the bullpen for a home run: "When it hit the top of the fence, I said, 'Hey, what's going on?'"

What's going on was that Shea Stadium had been visited by another miracle, plain and simple, one as unlikely as the events visited upon the club four years earlier. Yet those unexplained moments of baseball magic in September and October of 1969—the black cat suddenly appearing to jinx the first-place Cubs, two pitchers driving in the only runs in a doubleheader sweep of powerful Pittsburgh, Steve Carlton fanning 19 Mets in St. Louis only to lose on two Ron Swoboda home runs, a throw glancing off the runner's wrist and bringing in the winning run in Game Four of the World Series, or, the next day, a bit of shoe polish on a baseball starting the rally that led the Mets to a world championship—had been bestowed to a talented young team coming together, growing up as one. Those Mets deserved the breaks and made the most of them. The 1973 team had done little to deserve anything over the first five months. Perseverance and memory—the events of '69 were still fresh enough for ballplayers and ballfans to hold out hope. Maybe there really was something to "Ya Gotta Believe."

With two men on in the bottom of the inning and Giusti pitching once again, Hodges victimized the Pirates reliever's palmball for the second time in three nights. His hit scored John Milner to end what became in Mets lore the Ball on the Wall Game. Mets fans never forgot it, nor would Hodges. "That play there and the game-winning hit, that was almost unbelievable," says Ron, no relation to Gil—though the catcher came through off the bench as if he'd been beamed down from Gil's '69 club. "We come running off the field—a walk-off game-winning RBI—Yogi and everybody else beating me on the back, saying, 'Nice job, nice job.'"

"The wisecrack around the league," says Steve Jacobson, watching from the press box, "was that God had taken an apartment in Flushing. Only God could have created a play like that."

Only through divine intervention, as Ron Hodges called it, still chuckling four decades later at the unlikelihood of it all, could a team in last place on August 30 rise to first place on September 21. But that's exactly what happened the next night when the Mets won for the fourth straight night against the Pirates, giving New York the season series by a commanding 13–5 margin. Steve Blass, a 1971 World Series hero, who had won a career-best 19 games as the Cy Young runner-up in 1972, simply couldn't throw strikes in 1973. He walked 84 in 88 innings and led the majors with 12 hit batsmen. His malady of shattered control with no known origin or cure became known as Steve Blass Disease.

In the series finale Blass walked only one Met—intentionally—but two-run doubles by Cleon Jones and Jerry Grote ended the pitcher's night and his season in the first inning. His season ERA of 9.85 was three runs higher than any pitcher with at least 80 innings pitched in 1973—even in the "DH league." Tom Seaver, knocked around for five runs in three innings by the Pirates earlier in the week to raise his ERA all the way to 1.88, dominated Pittsburgh in a 10–2 win. The Mets, on the verge of oblivion in the ninth inning on Tuesday, were in first place on Friday. Shea was packed with its first 50,000-plus crowd since before Memorial Day. Belief is in the eye of the beholder.

⚾ ⚾ ⚾

When Willie Mays told the press that he was retiring on September 20, he had been surprisingly unemotional for a man who had given everything to the game over 22 years in the majors, and before that as a teenager in the Negro Leagues.

Mays had seen plenty, done even more, and spent the majority of his time considered by most observers to be the best player in his league. The Mets wore a public smile for Willie, the Say Hey Kid, whom the owner so desperately wanted to bring back to New York. Yet beyond Joan Payson, the front office generally was unmoved about honoring the baseball legend. The Mets promoted Willie Mays Night—the penultimate game on the regular-season home schedule—and the turnout of 43,805, plus almost 10,000 more nonpaid visitors to the house on a Tuesday night in late September, pleased them. It was by far the biggest weeknight crowd of the year. Most of the planning of the event, however, fell to Mays himself.

Mays wasn't playing. His last regular-season game had been as a first baseman on September 9 in Montreal, where he had slammed into a chest-high dugout railing chasing a foul pop. He finished the game, striking out in his final regular-season at-bat. Because of soreness in his chest, he asked to return to New York on the off-day. Berra approved, telling him to meet the team in Philadelphia on September 11. At game time at the Vet, unbeknownst to his manager, Mays was still in his Riverdale apartment awaiting a return call from the doctor. Even at age 42, batting .211, and contributing little, reporters quickly noticed when Mays didn't show. For the second time in 1973, Berra had to deal with a legend gone AWOL.

When his phone kept ringing and he heard the press and the front office on the other end of the line rather than his doctor, Mays got the hint and drove to Philadelphia, arriving not long before the September 12 game began. But Berra didn't fine Mays, even putting his name on the lineup card the next day. When Mays tried some swings and told his manager he was too sore, 23-year-old John Milner took his place as the Mets won in 12 innings. Maybe it was this that Mays was talking about when he spoke to the crowd at Shea on his night on September 25.

Dabbing his eyes and speaking without notes, he told the adoring crowd: "I look at the kids over here, the way they're playing, the way they're fighting for themselves, and it tells me one thing: 'Willie, say goodbye to America.'" It was a long goodbye, as companies lavished Mays and his family with gifts for an hour.

"They gave Willie all sorts of trinkets, automobiles and things," recalls Steve Jacobson of *Newsday*. "Willie wanted more. He says, 'What's there for my son?'" Jack Lang of the *Long Island Press* later noted that as a result of this comment, "Before the night was over, a Honda motorbike was delivered to Shea for his adopted son, Michael."

"I find Willie always a far cry from the jolly, cheerful player that his reputation was," says Jacobson, a sentiment echoed by many in the press who covered his final years as a Met. "He was always cranky and suspicious when I was around." Anonymous quotes from Mets veterans at various times hinted at resentment about there being one set of rules for him and one for everyone else. Yet to the young ballplayers on the team, he was, well, Willie Mays.

"Absolutely, it was special. I mean, how could it not be special?" says Jon Matlack now, 23 at the time. "The guy was and is a phenomenon in the game and still at his age brought such instinct and life to playing the game. He was great to be around. He was a phenomenal influence."

Though the ceremony was long and the Mets had an important game to play, watching Mays's tearful goodbye wasn't easy for a ballplayer who understood that the glory years for even the greatest of players had their limit, the accolades fleeting. Explains Matlack, "It was something that I watched some of . . . I don't think I watched it all because it was something you don't want to end. You don't want to see the end for somebody else, and you certainly don't want to think about that it could end for you. It was a wonderful tribute and all that kind of stuff, but it was like looking at what's coming for me at some point. I don't know there's ever going to be a day for me. But it meant the end for his existence and for baseball, and I didn't want to look at that."

The fans couldn't get enough of the ceremony or of Mays. Karl Ehrhardt, Shea Stadium's "sign man," a fan who carried dozens of signs suitable for numerous points in a ballgame, summed up the feelings of the crowd: WE WHO ARE ABOUT TO CRY SALUTE YOU. Joan Payson joined the throng in crying as Willie came over to her seat near the Mets dugout. Mays, who a week earlier had told the press during his retirement announcement, "Maybe I'll cry tomorrow," was crying today.

⚾ ⚾ ⚾

The Mets, who had swept two from St. Louis after the Pittsburgh conquest, beat Montreal on Willie Mays Night to make it seven straight wins. The Mets were three games over .500 and had a 1½-game lead with five games left on the schedule. But in this insane NL East race, the lead ship generally started taking on water the moment that sailing looked smooth—as had happened to the Cubs, Cardinals, and Pirates before them. Quoth Shakespeare: "Uneasy lies the head that wears a crown," but quoth Yogi, during what seemed to everyone else like a lost summer: "It ain't over 'til it's over."

The Mets lost their final home game to the Expos, 8–5, ending their winning streak at seven and leaving them just a half-game ahead of the Pirates heading into the last weekend of the season. Five teams in the National League East still had a mathematical shot going into the final four games on the schedule, with the National League office racking its brain for how to settle the issue in the case of a five-way tie. While every other division in the major leagues was settled, with the winner of each guaranteed at least 92 wins, the only sure thing in the NL East—or "NL Least" as it was being called—was that every second-place team in every other division, not to mention a couple of third-place teams, would end up with a better record than a champion of the NL East.

Despite what seemed like a laughable farce, the pressure was intense for the five clubs involved, and, if the mediocrity of the division hadn't been enough of a godsend to the Mets, yet more divine intervention came in the form of rain. While the Pirates lost an excruciating 13-inning game at home to Philadelphia, the only team in the division not involved in the race, the Mets were idling damp in the Windy City.

"The Mets were in a strangely relaxed mood," *New York Times* beat reporter Leonard Koppett later wrote. "In a sense, the act of reaching the top, from where they had been in August, had already established their self respect. They wanted to win a pennant as much as anyone, but there was something less than desperation in their feeling. Perhaps the main motivation was to avoid the nagging regrets that would follow them all winter if they didn't make it now. But there was neither the unreal exhaustion that marked 1969, nor the painful tension that marked the late stages of 1970."

So the Pirates lost to the Expos on Friday and again on Saturday, increasing the Mets' lead by two full games without New York doing a thing, and assuring the Mets of the title if they won three times—if the Pirates won their final two games. Despite doing the Mets' dirty work, the valiant Expos were eliminated from contention. The Cardinals stayed in the race by beating the Phillies twice. The Cubs were done, but they might still perhaps exact some revenge for 1969 by bedeviling the Mets during four games in two days. Chicago had a 9-5 season record against the Mets heading into the final weekend.

NFL or no NFL, 33,000 Pirates fans turned out for the Sunday game against Montreal at Three Rivers Stadium while the 2-0 Steelers traveled to play hapless Houston. Both Pittsburgh teams won. So did the Cubs. Chicago knocked off Jon Matlack in the opener of the doubleheader, 1–0. The Mets poured it on at Wrigley in the second game, 9–2, with Cleon Jones opening up a close contest with a two-run homer off Fergie Jenkins in the sixth; Rusty Staub sent Fergie to the showers an inning later. Jerry Koosman went the distance to assure the Mets of at least a tie for the top spot in the bottom feeder division. The Cards completed their sweep of the Phillies that Sunday to finish at 81-81 and could only wait and hope for the others to screw up.

The Pirates had a makeup game Monday against San Diego. The Bucs had to win and hope the Cubs swept the Mets in another makeup doubleheader in Chicago. It was still overcast, sodden, and murky at Wrigley, so just 1,913 fans—the smallest Cubs crowd of the season—came out on the day that once and for all decided who wanted to win this damned division.

Burt Hooton, who had thrown a no-hitter at Wrigley as a rookie in his first start of 1972, needed to be near perfect against a team that had played near flawless baseball in September in a very flawed race. Hooton didn't have his no-hit stuff against the Mets. He retired the first four batters, but Cleon Jones clubbed his sixth home run in his last 10 games in the second inning. Hooton allowed just 12 homers in 239⅔ innings in 1973, but at this point in the year Cleon could hit the ball out of any ballpark at any time. September was actually Cleon's worst month of the season in terms of batting average (.224), but Jones, finally healthy for the home stretch, knocked in 17 runs in his last 13 games. For a team with the lowest slugging percentage in baseball (.338), a burst of power at the right time could perform miracles.

Hooton filled the bases with nobody out in the fourth, and Jerry Grote singled home two runs. The Mets chased Hooton with two more runs in the fifth. With the best pitcher in the National League on the mound and a 5–0 lead, it looked like the forecast called for champagne, but the four-man rotation during the stretch run had taken a toll on Tom Seaver. Yogi Berra could have gone with George Stone in the first game of the twinbill and saved Seaver and his sore right shoulder for a must-win second game if needed. Yogi went with Seaver in the first game in the hopes of making the second game a moot point. It's not the last time this argument would come up.

Seaver had thrown 284 innings already in 35 starts coming into the season finale. Based on some methods of analysis that came along much later, such as Wins Above Replacement (WAR), 1973 was considered Seaver's finest year—though he missed the most important mark of the day, 20 wins, after averaging 21 over the previous four years. He led the league in strikeouts (251), ERA (2.08), complete games (18), strikeouts per walk (3.922), fewest hits per game (6.797) and baserunners per inning (0.976). Nailing down the clincher might also clinch his second Cy Young Award, but the game wasn't yet nailed down.

Cubs Don Kessinger and Billy Williams, who had watched sizeable early division leads dissipate both in 1969 and 1973, singled runs home in the fifth. Seaver got through the sixth unscathed, and a two-out error by Ron Santo, in his last game as a Cub, plated a run that looked even bigger a few minutes later when Rick Monday launched a home run with Dave Rosello aboard in the seventh to make it a 6–4 game. Berra had gone with his best to start the game, and now he went with his best to finish it.

Tug McGraw had been flawless since August 27, winning four, saving 12, and putting together an ERA of 0.88 over his final 41 innings. Along the way he also became the face of the club's unlikely 24-9 finish. Besides barking "Ya Gotta Believe" at every available opportunity, he'd incorporated a thigh-slapping routine that became his signature move. It had a purpose. McGraw's wife, Phyllis, had given birth that month to their second child and his third (considering a tryst in the minors in Jacksonville that produced a son he didn't acknowledge for many years, a boy named Tim who became a pretty fair musician). Tug admitted to his serial philandering, but his signature on-field antics were for his first wife, Phyllis.

"The batting of glove on the leg that went along with the 'Gotta Believe' thing was a message to his wife," says Matlack.

"I just remember him having told Ralph Kiner on *Kiner's Korner*," says Howie Rose. "It was kind of a shout-out to his wife. I don't know if was 'Hi, honey,' or 'We got them, honey,' or whatever it was, but I remember him specifically mentioning that it was designed as a message. It was the same thing as . . . I don't know if you remember Carol Burnett tugging on her ear . . . but it was the same thing. It was neat, but he probably would have done it whether he was saying anything to his wife or not because it was Tug's nervous energy, which was infectious."

The Mets needed all his energy and skill to secure one more victory. McGraw retired his first six batters in Chicago before Ken Rudolph led off the bottom of the ninth with a single. He notched his third strikeout for the first out. Then—just as the season had begun—an opposing manager went by the book and sent up a right-handed batter to face McGraw when a lefty might actually have had a better chance against the southpaw's pile-driving screwball.

Like Phillies manager Danny Ozark replacing young lefty slugger Willie Montanez with righty veteran Deron Johnson on Opening Day, the last day of the season saw Rick Monday, having a breakthrough year with 26 home runs—not to mention having hit one out against the best pitcher in the league his last time up—called back to the bench for a right-handed bat. Manager Whitey Lockman sent Wrigley favorite Glenn Beckert to the plate in a spot where a home run was needed, even though he hadn't hit one in 1973 and had just 22 career homers while playing in a hitter's park. Beckert hit a soft liner that first baseman John Milner caught, took a step forward, and doubled off Rudolph to end the game and the most convoluted chase for postseason glory that the game had yet seen. The day after the season was supposed to have ended, the NL East was finally decided. Believe it or not.

The Mets had earned the right to celebrate. Yet interfering in the clubhouse once again came the chairman of the board—not Frank Sinatra, in the midst of a comeback of his own in '73. M. Donald Grant was in the clubhouse.

"That was my eleventh year, and it was the first time I was going to get into postseason play," recalls Rusty Staub. "I remember Mr. Grant said, 'Don't open the champagne, we have another game to play,' and I said, 'Mr. Grant, I'll play that game drunk. Don't worry, we're opening that champagne.' So we all opened the champagne." Staub stopped for a second at the memory and shook his head. "My God, how can you say, 'Don't open the champagne'?"

Especially with God watching from his Flushing apartment.

Then, as if sent by angels, the umpires quickly sent word to the locker room that the second game at Wrigley, now meaningless, wouldn't be played due to wet grounds. As the celebration began in earnest, the cramped visitor's clubhouse at Wrigley became pretty wet, too.

"That six-week stretch was the most enjoyable, exciting thing that I participated in in my career," says Staub. When asked how the champagne was, he smiles. "It was good."

Eleven

"And a Fight Breaks Out!"

While the Pirates were winning the National League East in 1970, 1971, and 1972, the Mets were finishing third with exactly 83 wins each year. In 1973, the Mets won 82 games and claimed the division title. Their unfathomable comeback and incredible good fortune made them the toast of New York, but with the lowest winning percentage of the 20th century for a playoff team (.509), these Mets looked like a guy with long hair and torn jeans who crashed a black tie event and asked for a can of Rheingold.

Cincinnati won more games than any team in the 1970s, an impressive feat given that the A's, Yankees, and Pirates also won multiple World Series during the decade, while the Orioles captured five division titles, three pennants, and one world championship. The Reds won six division titles, four pennants, and two World Series while averaging 95 wins per year for a decade. The Reds had a manager, Sparky Anderson; first baseman, Tony Perez; second baseman, Joe Morgan; and catcher, Johnny Bench, all bound for the Hall of Fame. Left fielder Pete Rose, declared ineligible for the Hall of Fame for gambling while managing in the 1980s, beat out a strong field to be named National League MVP in 1973. He led the league in plate appearances and times on base, and produced more hits in a season (230) than any switch-hitter in history. Cincinnati's rotation couldn't match its offense, but it was solid, finishing fourth in ERA (3.80), third in saves (43), and having more shutouts (17) than any team while completing 39 games under a manager known as Captain Hook for yanking pitchers off the mound. The Reds were also one of just two teams—the Dodgers being the other—to draw two million fans in 1973. The Mets were third with 1.9 million attendance.

Like the Mets, the Reds had gone into September trailing the division leader, but Cincinnati had already reached the final Mets win total for '73 before Labor Day, powering past the Dodgers with a late 31-6 run to go from four games behind to six games ahead. The Reds won more games than

Tom Seaver, 1973 Cy Young Award winner NATIONAL BASEBALL HALL OF FAME LIBRARY, COOPERSTOWN, NY

any club in baseball in 1973, even if they lost three of their last four to fall one win shy of 100.

But the Reds were also taking heat. Having won the pennant in 1970 and '72, losing both times in the World Series, it was starting to be said—as it's always said when a team gets to the pinnacle of its sport only to fall short of a title—that they couldn't win the big one. Las Vegas is known for looking right through "good stories" for the bottom line, and odds maker Jimmy "the Greek" Snyder installed Cincinnati as 3-2 favorites over the Mets. The Reds, who'd gone 8-4 against the Mets during the season, weren't taking Yogi Berra's team lightly, but it was hard to get caught up in the New York hype when the Mets would have finished a distant fourth if they'd been in the NL West—just a half-game ahead of Houston. "For some reason," said Reds second baseman Joe Morgan, "people seem to think we're afraid of the Mets. I don't understand it. We've faced good pitching all year." True, but the Reds hadn't faced Tom Seaver in the glare of late afternoon.

The four-day layoff between the regular season and postseason provided the Mets yet another break. It allowed the maxed out pitching staff a much-needed rest, especially Seaver and his ailing right shoulder. Three days before the playoff opener he said, "If my shoulder is tender, I wouldn't mind if Yogi decided to open with Matlack." A couple of days later, team doctor Peter LaMotte gave Seaver a shot of the nonsteroidal anti-inflammatory drug Butazoldin, and the pitcher declared himself ready to start the opener.

The game was a four o'clock start, with glare and shadows that made it harder for hitters to see the ball. NBC decided to run the Orioles-A's ALCS game first, followed by the Mets-Reds—a night playoff game not entering into their thinking. Of course both the Mets and Reds played in the same tough twilight conditions, but even Jack Billingham, the NL leader in starts (40), innings (293⅓), and shutouts (7), conceded, "Once we get in the shadows, Tom has the advantage. He starts throwing smaller baseballs."

Seaver fanned 13 Reds to set a new Championship Series record, but, too often the case for Mets pitchers, the offense afforded precious little support—so Seaver provided his own. His two-out double off Billingham made it 1–0 in the second inning. The Mets didn't get another hit the rest of the day.

He held the Reds scoreless until the eighth inning, when cloud cover gave Cincinnati a reprieve. Pete Rose lined a home run to right to tie the game. Johnny Bench homered in the bottom of the ninth, and the Reds, who had clinched the pennant the previous year in walk-off fashion against the Pirates at Riverfront, looked like they'd gone a long way toward claiming the 1973 flag. As the next day's starter, Jon Matlack, charted Seaver, marking down each pitch and result, the second-year southpaw wasn't exactly feeling overconfident.

"It was a masterful job of pitching," Matlack says of Seaver's hard-luck loss. "He really made two bad pitches. Each one was hit for a home run . . . and we lose, 2–1. I'm looking at this chart after the game, thinking, 'How in the world do you do better than this?' You can't give them anything, or they are liable to beat you. It was that sort of a mindset that went into the next day."

Game Two matched the hardest-throwing young lefties in the league: Matlack and Don Gullett. At that point, no team had ever come back from two games to none since the best-of-five Championship Series format had begun in 1969. Of the eight Championship Series in both leagues through 1972, five had seen one team take a two-games-to-none lead, and only the '72 A's had not picked up a three-game sweep. In the '69 World Series, after Seaver lost the opener to Baltimore, Jerry Koosman went out and took a no-hitter into the seventh inning and allowed just two hits as the Mets evened the Series. They never looked back.

"It wasn't like you're trying to pitch a shutout," Matlack says of his mind-set going into his Game Two start in the '73 NLCS, "but you pitched the pitch, batter to batter, out to out, staying in the moment, trying to win that moment." Again, a Mets pitcher had little offensive support for most of the game, but Matlack had received some promising intel from one of his top hitters. Rusty Staub saw something in Gullett's delivery and told his pitcher between innings, "Don't worry, before the day is over I'm going to get you some runs. You keep them close." Staub homered off the Cincinnati lefty his second time up, and Matlack, like Seaver, had that tenuous one-run lead. But everything was clicking, his fastball and curve baffling the Big Red Machine. Andy Kosco, starting in right field over rookie Ken Griffey, had the only two hits of the game against Matlack. The only time the Reds got two runners on base in the same inning actually benefited the Mets as it forced Sparky Anderson to bat for Gullett in the bottom of the fifth—something that wouldn't even have been a consideration in the same situation in the ALCS. Phil Gagliano whiffed as a pinch hitter, one of nine strikeouts by Matlack.

The Mets eventually wore down the Reds bullpen in the top of the ninth. Cleon Jones singled in a run against lefty Tom Hall. After Pedro Borbon came in for Cincinnati, Jerry Grote knocked home two, and Bud Harrelson finished off the scoring with an RBI single. The notoriously light-hitting

Mets shortstop observed to the press afterward that the Reds hitters looked like himself at the plate. It was self-deprecating humor, but, to a Reds team that now had to win two of three on the road to claim the pennant that seemed theirs for the taking, it didn't sit well. With the playoffs still a year away from including an off day—and with home field advantage alternating annually rather than being determined by best home record (a change not instituted until 1998)—the team with the most wins in the league was at a sudden disadvantage.

The next day in New York, Cincinnati second baseman Joe Morgan found Harrelson before Game Three. Morgan and Harrelson, who both grew up near Oakland, had formed the National League's late-inning double-play combo in the 1970 All-Star Game, a game that ended famously in extra innings with Pete Rose crashing into catcher Ray Fosse to score the winning run. That was Rose's most notorious altercation—until the '73 NLCS.

Harrelson recalls a less-than-neighborly meeting with the Reds second baseman during batting practice at Shea Stadium: "Morgan came out and said, 'You ever say that about me again, and I'll punch you.' And I said, 'What?' I knew Joe, we grew up in the same area. I knew it was only a joke. . . . He said, 'Pete's going to use it to fire up the team. He's going to come get you.'"

Harrelson knew Rose, too. It was a small league, especially among its elite players. A solidarity held among National Leaguers, an unwritten understanding that they would pull for each other in the World Series and fight tooth and nail to win the All-Star Game for the sake of league pride; the National League won all but one All-Star Game between 1963 and 1982. Though fraternization between players on different teams was frowned upon, an encouraging word to a younger player from a competitor could go a long way. Harrelson recalls his first encounter as a rookie with Rose. "He and Tommy Helms [1966 Rookie of the Year] said, 'Can we talk to you?' They talked to me about relaxing. 'You're going to be a good player, just relax.' Stuff like that. . . . I said, 'Wow, Pete Rose and Tommy Helms. They didn't need to do that.'"

It also wasn't necessary to knock Harrelson into left field in Game Three of the 1973 NLCS, which Rose admitted to trying to do. With the Mets leading 9–2 on a pair of Rusty Staub home runs and some shoddy Reds pitching, Rose singled with one out in the fifth inning, and Joe Morgan—well, he started the whole thing.

Morgan hit a sharp grounder to first baseman John Milner, who threw to Harrelson to start a 3-6-3 double play that ended the inning. "I got the ball and threw it and was watching it go to first," Harrelson says. "He slid, and when he got up he hit me in the side of my head with his elbow. I said it was not nice of him. I was mad. I called [it] a cheap shot."

After that, words on the field became rather unintelligible. Ringside announcer Bob Murphy called Flushing's "Fight of the Century" on WHN:

And a fight breaks out! A fight breaks out! Pete Rose and Buddy Harrelson. Both clubs spill out of the dugouts, and a wild fight is going on! Jerry Koosman's in the middle of the fight. Everybody is out there. Buddy Harrelson and Pete Rose got into it. Rose apparently thought that Harrelson had done something in making the double play. Rose outweighs Harrelson about 35 pounds. And now Buzzy Capra is in a fight! Capra is in a fight out in center field. Another fight breaks out!

Some of the Mets involved in the play were the last to know what was going on. Milner, the ball in his glove, was running off the field, along with right fielder Rusty Staub, who was hustling in to back up the double play. "The crowd screamed, obviously," explains Staub. "I put my head down, and I was very close to the fans because I wasn't on the grass. I was on the track coming in [toward the dugout]. All of a sudden, there was a lot of noise. I looked up, and everybody was running out of the dugout. . . . Then I looked where everybody was running, and there was dust in the air, and people were swirling around. I didn't know what was going on. I just ran to the group, like everybody else, and it got pretty frisky."

"I don't think I had seen it start instantly," says Jerry Koosman, who, many people forget amid the day's hoopla, tossed a complete game. "I know I had thrown four pitches at Rose because he had screamed at me from the dugout after his first at bat where I popped him up. . . . He took it out on Buddy Harrelson."

And there was the third baseman, the third man in.

"I saw Pete hit him [Harrelson] pretty good—he knocked him on his back," says Wayne Garrett. "I was going to see if he was going to get up. I wasn't running . . . I was trotting that way, and I saw Buddy get up and run right at Rose. Rose grabbed him and threw him on the ground and was sitting on top of him. That's when I took off and dove into Rose. I tackled him. He let go of Harrelson . . . he lost his momentum and went on me. I had my arms around Rose, then I became the bottom of the pile. Rose was on top of me, looking up at the sky, then everybody started jumping on. I was there to break it up. I knew it was a mismatch there, in size. Rose is a lot bigger. He's bigger than I was, too. Whatever happened above the pile, I had no idea . . . I was on the bottom of it. Everybody was on top of me."

Above the pile, Reds catcher Johnny Bench, in his shin guards, pulled Rose away and held him. For a moment, it seemed like order might return. Then came round two: Lee William "Buzz" Capra vs. Pedro "Dracula" Borbon.

"Yeah, I like seeing replays of that [fight], and there I am. I'm in my Met coat coming in right from the dugout, and I held somebody," says George Theodore, who'd broken his hip two months earlier and had batted only once since. "I can't remember who I grabbed, but I grabbed somebody from behind, and like the rest of us we were all pretending, until Pedro Borbon came in from left field and hit Buzz Capra in the back of the head. That started it again."

"We opened the gates there at Shea and took off to the infield," says bullpen catcher Ron Hodges, part of the blue-coated cavalry charging in from the right field bullpen. "About the time that we got there, the fight was almost over already. People started backing up and yelling at each other. . . . As soon as we got there Pedro Borbon came out of nowhere and whacked Buzz Capra on the back of the head. When he did that, Capra went crazy and went after Borbon. When that incident happened, we were out there pushing and shoving and in each other's face after that."

"Buddy and I are probably the two smallest guys," says Capra, who, like Harrelson, stood a shade under six feet and weighed around 160. "Here we go—they're coming from the left field bullpen, and we're coming from the right field bullpen. I'm milling around. All of a sudden I get popped in the ear by Pedro Borbon, who was like a stark raving maniac. . . . I saw it at the last second. *Bang!* He hit me, and my hat went flying off. I came back, and Duffy Dyer was there. He had him around the neck. In the '73 highlights, you can see I'm getting some pretty good punches in. Then we start wrestling to the ground. Willie Mays came over there and starts peeling guys off. They weren't going to mess with Willie. He had that respect where no one's going to screw around. He peeled me off the ground. I got my shirt pulled out. My hat is gone. People are going crazy."

Then came the donning of the mistaken Mets hat, which became Dracula's dessert.

"Borbon [was] coming off the field with my hat on his head," Capra says. "When he saw it was a Mets hat, he starts eating it. He rips it in about three pieces. . . . It was on the ground and still held together by the front part, the other two sections—a baseball hat has four sections sewn together. He ripped apart two of them with his mouth and threw it down. So I still have that hat."

Then there was the guy who missed everything, though Pete Rose later claimed the Met had been in the middle of the donnybrook.

"Truth be known, I wasn't even there until the thing broke up," says Jon Matlack. "I was inside using the restroom. I hear on the radio what was going on. I come out from the clubhouse as things were breaking up. I saw the trading of the hat with Pedro Borbon and having Capra's hat. I had nothing to do with the actual incident, except what I saw in replays on TV."

But he did get to see everything that happened in left field the next inning.

⚾ ⚾ ⚾

Tug McGraw didn't have to say "Ya gotta believe!" to Bob Heussler—the man was born believing. Graduating from Essex Catholic High School in Newark in the spring of 1973, Heussler started at the University of Bridgeport in Connecticut that fall. When the Ball on the Wall play occurred a couple of weeks into freshman year, Heussler jumped so high that the blanket hanging over the fluorescent light in his North Hall dorm room came down with him. "It was like a parachute coming down on the three of us," Heussler recalls. "My college roommate was from Long Island, was a Mets fan, but he thought we were taking it to ridiculous levels because when I moved into the room, I had this habit of taping *Daily News* back pages on my wall of the latest win or latest achievement of that month of September."

Luckily, his high school friend Tom Hassan was just as rabid a Mets fan. He waited all night in line along with 15,000 others outside Shea and scored tickets to every postseason game in New York that fall. The seats for Game Three and for the whole postseason run were ideal: in the loge section right above the auxiliary scoreboard in left field. It was a front-row seat for mayhem.

After the fight, the umpires didn't eject Rose, Harrelson, or any of the other four dozen on-field combatants. When Rose went out to his position in left field after the brawl subsided, he soon found out that 53,967 people didn't think the fight had ended.

"One of my earlier courses was sociology, and I clearly got a lesson in mob psychology that day," Heussler says. "It was unbelievably powerful how incensed you were by the whole situation. Not wanting to inflict harm, but hurl whatever you could, literally and figuratively—verbally or heaving whatever garbage you could get your hands on—at Pete Rose. It was really powerful, and in retrospect it was really scary. It was . . . wow! Overwhelming. And I was part of it."

Heussler mostly tossed balled-up pages from the *New York Post* and *Daily News*, but others heaved more solid objects: cups, cans, coins, batteries, and anything else on hand. If Felix Millan had been retired a little more quickly, the bottom of the fifth would have ended, and the fans might have calmed down by the bottom of the sixth. But as the home fifth continued, debris kept flying and growing larger, like a hailstorm. Then came the last straw.

"I didn't see exactly where that whiskey bottle came from, but I saw it whiz by onto the field," recalls Heussler, a future New York radio voice at WFAN. "I always thought it was from the lower field boxes, but I've read that it came from the mezzanine or the upper deck. . . .When you saw the whiskey bottle come flying out on the field, you knew this was pretty much out of control."

Rose had been hurling some of the debris out of his path, but when the bottle came down, he jogged off the field. Sparky Anderson said he wasn't going to let his team back on the field until the rain of abuse stopped. Anderson related after the game, "An umpire said, 'We better get this straightened out.' And I replied, 'Let me know when you do.'"

"I didn't pick it up, but there was a Jack Daniels bottle out there," says Pete Flynn, who worked on the Mets grounds crew for the club's first 50 seasons. "A lot of beer cans. Shortly after that, I think they put a stop to it [selling cans to fans]. That way they couldn't throw them out [on the field]. If you throw a full beer and hit somebody with it, you could kill him."

A beer can, its contents partially consumed, hit Reds pitcher Gary Nolan in the head. The Reds relievers huddled for cover on their sheltered island in the left field bullpen. But the Mets were just as concerned as the Reds. There had never been a forfeit in postseason play. In Game Seven of the 1934 World Series in Detroit, the pelting of Cardinals left fielder Joe Medwick with debris following an altercation at third base resulted in Commissioner Kenesaw Mountain Landis ordering Medwick off the field with his team winning, 11–0. Now National League president Chub Feeney came knocking on the Mets dugout looking for a solution. He suggested sending an emissary out to mob nation in left field. The Mets were already discussing the same move among themselves.

"We'd been talking about Willie and Yogi going out there," said Cleon Jones, who joined the ensemble, along with Rusty Staub and Tom Seaver. They were well received. "They hadn't seen Willie in a while and they were glad to see him."

"The players went out there and talked to them so they [the fans] behaved themselves," says groundskeeper Pete Flynn in his Irish brogue. Imagine if the fans hadn't calmed down? What level riot would a forfeit have created? Perhaps it would have resembled an urban combat version of the '73 summer movie *Battle for the Planet of the Apes*, the fifth installment of the franchise about a future in which apes ruled the world. Rose did call Shea Stadium "a zoo" after all.

Order was restored—for the time being. "I can remember holding up the peace sign," says Heussler. "I don't know if Willie or one of them was giving it back or initiated it, but holding up the two fingers—'Yeah, peace, we're cool, we got it. We're going to calm down. Everything's going to be all right.' And luckily, it was."

For anyone who didn't already have a severe case of Met Fever in Met City, as the *New York Times* was calling the five boroughs, the fight and its aftermath gained the interest of the previously uninterested and uninitiated. Like the previous year's ALCS in Detroit—when Oakland's Bert Campaneris's bat heave lit a fire under the Tigers—the defending NL champion Reds, the odds-on favorites to win the 1973 NLCS, wouldn't go quietly. The zoo had rattled their cage.

⚾ ⚾ ⚾

The next day, scrawled bed sheet sentiments like ROSE IS A WEED and THIS ROSE SMELLS proliferated in the stands at Shea—along with boos that followed Rose in New York for the rest of his long career as a player. But a day after instigating the most memorable fight in Shea's history, the left fielder played the role of zookeeper.

"Rose is doing long toss in the bullpen, warming up, hanging out in left field," says Heussler, who got to his seat above the auxiliary scoreboard in the left field loge section in time to see the Reds practicing before Game Four. "What impressed me about Rose is that he almost relished this. Maybe he did relish it. He fed off this stuff. The stuff that was being said to him was vicious, still emotional from the previous day, and he's going with the flow. And people are yelling, 'Rose, you suck!' and Rose this and Rose that. And he's basically having fun with it. He's like, 'C'mon, bring it on.' Some people start yelling out to him, 'Throw us a ball! Throw us a ball!' Sure enough, Rose turns and throws a ball, lobs it, into the stands, into the loge. As God is my witness, the ball smacks into a guy who had no idea it was coming, and it knocks him to the ground. It was softly thrown, but it hit him hard, *thwack*, right in the temple. And the chant began, 'Sue Pete Rose! Sue Pete Rose!'"

Left-hander George Stone, acquired from Atlanta with Felix Millan the previous winter, hadn't lost since before the All-Star break and finished the year with a career-best 12-3 mark and 2.80 ERA. With the teams playing for the fourth time in four days and Tom Seaver's shoulder not 100 percent, Stone was the only choice. Like Seaver in his start, Stone got just one run to work with.

The Mets got that run in the third inning on a run-scoring single by Felix Millan, New York's only hit off Cincinnati starter Fred Norman. Stone, with the help of some brilliant defense, kept the Reds off the scoreboard until Tony Perez homered in the seventh. Tug McGraw kept the game tied at 1–1 when Rusty Staub slammed into the wall next to the "371" mark in right field to haul in Dan Driessen's drive with two on and two out in the 11th. Staub, who'd made an over-the-shoulder catch earlier, went shoulder first into the wall this time and ricocheted onto his back. He finished the game but was finished for the series.

Batting left for the first time since his Game One homer off Seaver, Rose drove a Harry Parker fastball well over the wall in right-center in the 12th inning. Rose circled the bases with his fist raised. Pedro Borbon chewed through the heart of the Mets order for the save as the Mets mustered just three hits against four Reds pitchers.

"We couldn't believe it," Heussler says of the tiebreaking blast from Rose, who hit all of five homers during the season. "Then Borbon closes it out. That was funny having these two freakin' guys, Rose and Borbon, stick it up our freakin' you-know-what the next day. Then we had the final word."

Tom Seaver was the period after the final word. The Reds had him on the ropes in the first inning of Game Five, however. After retiring Rose to start the game, he walked Morgan and allowed a single to Driessen. With Tony Perez at the plate, Seaver wild-pitched the runners to second and third. He got two strikes on Perez, and the slugger got a piece of a fastball, but it landed in the glove of catcher Jerry Grote for the second out.

After the game, Seaver effusively praised his catcher; that moment might well have changed the game and the series. Perez, who in 1973 had produced his seventh straight season of 90-plus RBIs (racking up 11 such seasons in a row), was a tough out, but right after him in the lineup came two-time MVP Johnny Bench.

"It's a tough pitch, he fouled it, and he caught it in the web," Seaver said of Grote in the locker room after the game. "That's a big pitch for me. It gives me two outs, gives me an open base to put Bench on. I can't walk the guy [Perez] in that situation is the thing. You can't pitch to Bench there. You've got to strike Perez out and get Bench to first base. . . . Your thought in the first inning is you want to go to the dugout, give your hitters a chance to go, like in a horse race, to go from the start even. We've been fighting uphill all year long, and you don't want our players to have to fight uphill again on the last day. That was my thought, and I had to strike him out. God bless Jerry Grote, he made a great play."

God bless Ed Kranepool, for that matter. After having not batted at all during the series, the last original Met started in the outfield in place of the injured Staub. Kranepool's two-out, two-run single off Jack Billingham in the bottom of the first changed the momentum of the game and the—

⚾ ⚾ ⚾

We interrupt this game with breaking news from Washington.

"Vice President Spiro Agnew resigned today, the first man holding his high office to do so under fire," reported Harry Reasoner on ABC. "Agnew then pleaded no contest, in effect, guilty, to income tax evasion. The court placed him on probation for three years and imposed a maximum fine of $10,000."

Reporters outside the Federal Courthouse in Baltimore didn't know of the breaking news until US Attorney General Elliot Richardson appeared shortly after 1:30 p.m. Agnew arrived at 2:00 p.m. In court, it quickly became obvious that an arrangement had been worked out between the VP and AG, with Agnew's resignation accepted by Richardson at 2:05 p.m.

Agnew's meteoric rise had begun a decade earlier as a Baltimore County executive, running unopposed, before becoming governor of Maryland four years later and winning the vice presidential nomination in a landslide over George Romney (Mitt's father) in 1968. It was one of the fastest political ascents in history, but Agnew's fall came just as swift. Investigators accused him of taking more than $100,000 in bribes during his two years as governor before leaving for Washington. Nixon had chosen Agnew as veep to gain southern votes, but he had little use for Agnew in the White House with the ever-running audiotapes even catching Nixon considering a replacement for him on the 1972 ticket. Nixon reluctantly renewed Agnew, but the second in command became the first VP to resign. With Watergate at full throttle, many believed that Agnew's resignation formed yet another White House plot to take the glare off Nixon, but the president's continuing abuses of power soon turned Agnew into old news and small potatoes.

Known for turns of phrase from White House speechwriters—like wordsmith William Safire's precious "nattering nabobs of negativism"—Agnew didn't sound very elegant on the afternoon of October 10 in Baltimore, agreeing to income tax evasion for the year 1967. The justice department didn't pursue the case further. He received a $10,000 fine and three years probation but no jail sentence. Agnew, amid the whirl of cameras and scrambling newsmen, stated outside the courthouse that a drawn-out case didn't serve the national interest and would have a "brutalizing effect" on his family. He also "categorically and flatly" denied the assertions of bribery and extortion. Not everyone bought his act or, frankly, cared.

In the midst of hearing oral arguments in the Supreme Court that afternoon, a note was handed to Justice Potter Stewart: "V.P. Agnew just resigned!! Mets 2, Reds 0." Potter, a devoted Reds fan and Republican, glumly passed the note on to Harry Blackmun, another dedicated baseball fan on the bench.

Many miles from the Beltway and just a few miles from Shea, updates did not come so readily. Ten-year-old Greg Prince was at McDonald's in Oceanside, the closest golden arches to his Long Beach home. He was there only in body. Prince, who three decades later cofounded the website *Faith and Fear in Flushing* with Jason Fry, wrote a well-regarded book of the same title, and penned articles for numerous outlets, obsessed over his team at age 10 just as he did at 50. He was off from school as part of the Jewish festival of the fall harvest, Sukkoth, described by Prince as "the Harry Parker of Jewish holidays when compared to the High Holy Days one-two punch of Rosh Hashanah and Yom Kippur." Half of his mind focused on Bob Murphy's voice on WHN in his ear, and the other half relayed Murph's descriptions and accounts from Shea to the girl behind the McDonald's counter. Ball one, now ball two! It was a day he would remember forever, his first win-or-go-home postseason game. Now the real world intruded, creating another level of memory and meaning as the news bulletin interrupted the action.

"Agnew just resigned," he announced in the fast food joint.

"Who cares?" the girl replied. "What's the score?"

"The Mets were still winning, 2–0," Prince later said, "and we let Spiro be."

Back in Manhattan, the throng on Fifth Avenue and 56th Street watching through the window at the Sony showroom booed Agnew's visage across 18 television screens, not so much for disgracing the office of vice president as for interrupting a rally in the crucial game. For those with the sound up, NBC's two-minute report ended with an almost cheery, "And now back to the ballgame."

It all took place in "God's own sunshine"—a phrase curmudgeons used as a lament in the coming years as postseason games invariably switched from day to night and future 10-year-old Greg Princes had to break curfew to follow the postseason. On the afternoon of October 10, 1973, baseball took precedence over all else in New York City. The vice president, or ex-VP, and even the president could wait. Willie Mays was coming up.

Lefty Don Gullett, who'd pitched four innings in relief the previous day, walked John Milner. With the bases loaded in the deciding game of the playoffs, with the Mets holding a 3–2 lead thanks to a Cleon Jones RBI-double, and with a chance to bust the game open, Berra called back Ed Kranepool for a man whose major league career began the same year Gullett was born. Sparky "Captain Hook" Anderson countered by summoning Clay Carroll, his most trusted reliever, in the bottom of the fifth. The pitching change allowed fans to get a longer look at Willie and love him a little more.

No longer a mere ornament telling them to cry as sponsors showered him with gifts or a peacemaker telling them to stop showering Pete Rose with different types of gifts, Mays was again a bona fide ballplayer—his first at-bat in more than a month. Mays had thought about leaving the team before the season ended, but Berra, who'd twice been shown up by Mays during the year, and Payson, who'd brought him back to New York for an encore, asked the star to stick around for an occasion such as this. "Spiro Agnew resigns as Vice President" crawled silently on the bottom of the screen as the crowd roared at Shea. Unlike the disgraced ex-veep, Mays intended to give the home crowd one last thrill.

"I'm very emotional about a lot of things, Lindsey, but that time I blocked everything out," he told Mets announcer Lindsey Nelson in an interview a few days later. "When I play ball, I play ball like there's nothing there in my way. When I walked to the plate I didn't hear anything. I understand that the people love me around New York, but my main thought there is, 'Hey, you've got to get this run in.' . . . I was trying to concentrate on just hitting the ball rather than going up there saying, 'Hey, they like me, I don't have to do anything.' I wasn't concentrating on that. I was worried more about the run than I guess the people at that particular time."

Spoken like the Say Hey Kid—with 3,283 hits, 660 home runs, 338 steals, 1,903 RBIs, and New York in his back pocket.

Mays hit a Baltimore chop high off home plate, and Felix Millan raced home. Don Hahn and Bud Harrelson also knocked in runs, and the Mets rose to a 6–2 lead—the same lead the Mets handed Seaver nine days earlier that soon became precarious at Wrigley Field. Today, though, Seaver would have none of it. He not only shut down the Big Red Machine, but he created another insurance run in the sixth with his second double of the NLCS and then clapped his way home on a single by Cleon Jones. Only the fans could hold Seaver back.

With too big a lead to worry and too much time before the pennant officially wrapped up, the minds of many drifted toward obliteration—not of the Reds or even of Rose, but of their own ballpark. Fans crowded the aisles with riot on their minds. They harassed and jostled the Reds wives to the point that the game was stopped, and the Cincinnati delegation was led out of the stands and into the visiting dugout on the third-base side to wait under the stadium, some of them and their children crying from the fans' abusive treatment. Reds reserve Phil Gagliano punched one fan near the visiting dugout who pulled the hair of a woman. With Rose batting, the fence on the first-base side collapsed from the weight of the impatient mob. Even Seaver yelled at the crowd to stay off the field. He said afterward, "At that point, they couldn't have cared less who won the game."

His concentration gone, Seaver walked Rose to load the bases. Berra signaled to the bullpen for Tug McGraw, who had pitched 4⅓ innings the previous day and hadn't expected the call. His mind wasn't on the bases-loaded, one-out jam with the heart of the Big Red Machine coming up; he was thinking of how the players were going to get off the field alive.

"When I came in from the bullpen, I had been watching what was happening in the stands," McGraw explained to Lindsey Nelson a few days after Game Five. "It was like they were filling the place up, and it was just about to overflow. And the people were just getting to the point where they were not going to be able to hold them back much longer and you could see this happening from the bullpen. We had our cart that we usually ride in on, we had it down the tunnel, out of the way so that wouldn't get damaged. I got finished [warming up], and they said, 'McGraw, you're the pitcher,' and I said, 'Where's the cart?' They said, 'You've got to walk in'. . . .

"While I was walking, I was thinking that yesterday, the game before that, the game before the final game, I came in, I didn't feel good . . . Well today, not today, but the final game, I felt great, but I wasn't really worried about getting out of the bases-loaded situation. I felt like I could do that. But my main concern was: How in the heck am I going to get off the field when this game is over? I'm just glad the game ended in a way where you could run to first base. You had your momentum going and just make the turn and head for the dugout."

After getting Joe Morgan to pop up, Dan Driessen's grounder to John Milner allowed McGraw to receive the throw on the run, but by the time he touched first base people had already flooded the field. Thousands of them. Running, pushing, shoving. The dust they kicked up made it look like a stampede—which it was—and, like stampeding cattle, they had little regard for what they trampled.

The helmeted Pete Rose ran off the field dodging would-be tacklers like Buffalo's O. J. Simpson did when he surpassed the 2,000-yard rushing barrier in December against the Jets on the same Shea turf—actually the turf laid *after* the playoff riot. Rose understood the animosity of those around him, but Mays, who figured he'd be retired by now, played the last four innings in his old familiar spot in center field. He found himself stranded in no man's land as the game ended. A fan tried to steal his cap, but Mays fought his way to where the bullpen car was stashed.

"It's the only cap I have right now, and it's sort of good luck to me," said Mays, more relieved than elated to be in the locker room as the champagne corks popped and Mayor John Lindsay, along with several other Mets veterans of 1969, got another October shower. "I realized he just wanted a souvenir," Mays said of the overaggressive fan, "but if he asked me I woulda given him my shirt." The team had already given the shirts off their backs to win this unlikely pennant.

Sirens sounded on Fifth Avenue, people willingly joined the Hare Krishnas dancing on 46th Street singing Mets chants, and reporters out to get man-on-the-street reactions about Agnew's resignation got plenty of "Ya Gotta Believes" instead. In the Bronx, the *New York Times* dutifully reported, "The demolition of Yankee Stadium went on apace."

Back in Flushing, the 340 policemen and private officers on duty could do little more than watch the destruction of the field and help collect the wounded. The stadium's first aid room treated some 30 people. Destruction took place inside the stadium as well: The Reds tore apart the visiting club-house, smashing chairs and pounding bats against lockers. Above them, on the field, the rampage continued, the fourth such desecration in the stadium's history. The first three had taken place in less than a month during the fall of 1969.

"It was unsettling, it was disturbing," says Bob Heussler, who easily hopped onto the field between the field-level seats and the left field wall. He stepped into the middle of a full-fledged riot. "My frame of reference was 1969. People enjoyed themselves on the field then. Even though the field was being torn up and people were taking their souvenirs, it was a happy kind of mob scene.

"Winning the division was great, and upsetting the Big Red Machine was phenomenal. That final moment with the swarms of people. . . . Mostly young, mostly male—so I fit the profile that day—not good. Really not good. I took a piece of turf, but I felt guilty later for doing it. They were worried about having the place ready for the World Series. It was the equivalent of strafing the field. It was like carpet-bombing except it was done by the fans. I apologize to Pete Flynn or anybody else that had to clean that up. I didn't go down there in malice. I went down there thinking it would be a good time. It was not. . . . This was really ugly. It was an unfortunate P.S. to the pivotal moment of 1973."

Lost in the din was the sound of God shutting off the TV set in his Flushing apartment.

Reggie Jackson, Swingin' A RON RIESTERER

Twelve

THE PLAYOFF VAULT

At 4:00 a.m., the alarm clock sounded.

Fifteen-year-old Nancy Finley pried herself out of bed in her family's Oakland apartment. She heard her father, Carl Finley, already on the phone down the hall with his cousin, Charlie. An early riser with a two-hour head start in the Central Time Zone, Charlie Finley operated on Finley Daylight Time and expected the world to follow suit. Carl had agreed to set his watch to that time zone when he consented to operate the baseball portion of the Finley empire in Oakland. It took a lot of convincing from Carl's very persuasive cousin.

Charlie's calls had begun a decade earlier, back when Carl was still in the Central Time Zone in his native Dallas. Carl, who had studied law at Southern Methodist University, went instead into education. He was content with his job as a vice principal in the Dallas school system, but Charlie, as always, pushed. Saying "no" to Charlie Finley was often a beginning point; the born salesman worked his array of angles from there, and it took an iron will or a seething hatred of the man not to come around either to what he wanted or at least to his line of argument. When Charlie Finley wanted something, it took nothing short of a court order to stop him. It had required several years and much maneuvering for Charlie to realize his dream of purchasing a major league franchise. But even after purchasing the Kansas City A's in 1960, the Chicago-based Charlie, who had his farm in Indiana as well, had no plans to relocate full-time to Missouri. Many business moguls before and since have owned sports teams outside their home states; most have hired people with industry experience to run them. Charlie tried that—hiring and firing the volatile "Trader" Jack Lane, replacing him with Pat Friday, an employee from his insurance firm. Charlie wanted to do everything himself and often did, but he needed someone whom he could trust absolutely to run his team, even if that person knew relatively little about the baseball business. He knew who he wanted, and, well, Charlie Finley could be pretty stubborn. Stubborn as a mule—and not just the mule that shared the owner's name.

Carl and Charlie Finley were close, despite not having lived near each other for most of their lives. They shared the same grandfather, but their families went in different directions. Carl's family moved from Alabama to Dallas—where Carl was born in 1924—while Charlie, six years older, had stayed in Birmingham with his family until the steel mill jobs started disappearing in the 1930s. When Charlie's family relocated to work in the mills in Gary, Indiana, Charlie lived with Carl's family in Dallas while he wrapped his mind around becoming a Hoosier. Charlie joined his family in Indiana and worked to make a name for himself in his adopted Midwestern home. But he always maintained the bond with his cousin Carl.

For his part, Carl became intrigued with the concept of a life change during his cousin's relentless pitching of his new baseball team. Not surprisingly, Charlie won. At age 37, Carl Finley changed careers. After two years of going back and forth from Kansas City to Dallas, Carl's family came with him to Missouri in 1964, just in time to witness the Beatles perform their first concert in a baseball stadium.

Charlie had talked—that is, bribed—the Fab Four into squeezing in a last-minute show at Kansas City's Municipal Stadium. The notorious penny-pincher paid the Beatles $150,000—about six times the going rate for their other gigs on their first US tour—to give up a day off to play in Kansas City. Beatles manager Brian Epstein turned Finley down several times until he hit the magic number and agreed to pay the group almost $5,000 per minute for a half-hour gig for the appreciative, if half-full, house. The tickets, which ranged from $2 to $8.50 per head, featured on the back a picture of Charlie Finley in a Beatles moptop wig.

Carl learned quickly and could multitask—a must given the skeleton staffs his cousin employed. Carl's greatest skill, however, was his ability to patch over problems caused by his boisterous relative. Though some have characterized Carl as simply a messenger for Charlie, those pre-dawn conversations didn't only contain one-way orders. When Charlie decided to create a sporting empire by purchasing the California Golden Seals of the National Hockey League and the Memphis Pros of the American Basketball Association (renamed Tams by Finley for Tennessee, Arkansas, and Mississippi), Carl told Charlie no.

With the pipeline of quality ballplayers finally showing results in Oakland, Carl didn't want to dilute his energies or Charlie's resources on other enterprises even if the Golden Seals played in the adjoining arena in Oakland. "No one liked it," Nancy Finley said of the bogus brand of hockey played by the Seals—and she still has numerous sheets of unsold Seals tickets to prove it. "Dad was actually the most frustrated about it because he did not want to participate in any other team. He wanted to focus on the A's. It seemed that Charlie thought if he could do it for the A's, he could do it for another sport. Charlie wanted him to do the same thing with the other teams that he was doing with the A's, and Dad refused. Dad said, 'We got into this to build a team, and that's what I'm going to do—concentrate 100 percent on the A's.' Charlie could buy a team, but he couldn't follow through with it. He didn't have the time, he didn't have the knowledge to put in."

He didn't have Carl Finley. Carl concentrated his energies on the A's and ran the day-to-day operations of a championship major league team with fewer front office employees than man a baseball diamond at any given time. "Carl was wonderful," says longtime Bay Area writer Art Spander, who wrote for the *San Francisco Chronicle* in the 1970s. "He was P.R., he was tickets, but he could only do so much. I remember going in there once saying, 'Is anybody here?' There was nobody in the entire A's office."

Others recall walking into the vacant office and seeing a sign that said: "Dial this number," in order to roust somebody. Phones formed the lifeblood of the A's. While working the night desk at the *Chronicle*, Spander was the point man for locating Charlie Finley. "Find out about this trade," an editor ordered. So Spander went through the many phone numbers in various states to locate the owner-GM. "You'd get him on the phone, and you couldn't get him off. He talked and talked and talked. His favorite phrase was 'Money talks, and bullshit walks.' I must have heard that 100 times from him."

Steve Somers, on the other hand, managed the feat of getting Finley to hang up on air by insulting him as an absentee owner. Instead of Finley's boisterous voice there was silence during a live TV interview with KOVR in Sacramento.

The tortoise to his cousin's hare, steady Carl was right about the other clubs Finley owned. These other teams had little in common with the A's, other than their uniforms of Kelly green and Fort Knox gold—a color scheme that even the Beatles joked about at their Kansas City press conference in 1964. Both the Seals and Tams were abysmal. Neither garnered even minute interest, and both lost money. The Golden Seals never won more than 21 games or came close to the playoffs under Finley rule, and the Tams had even fewer wins and fewer fans. Beyond a few Finley gimmicks, all the Tams managed to prove was that it took more than a $300 mustache bonus to make a cohesive team.

In 1972 Finley had taken a negative—Reggie Jackson growing a mustache, not done since the 1930s—and turned it into a gimmick, paying any A's player who grew one $300 as part of "Mustache Day" at the Oakland Coliseum. "The Mustache Gang" even held sway on future hirsute ballplayers. San Francisco native and future MVP Keith Hernandez, a 20-year-old first baseman in the Cardinals minor league system in 1973, acknowledged that the Swingin' A's influenced his decision to grow a mustache—and not just any mustache but the Greatest Sports Mustache of All Time as recognized by the American Mustache Institute. (Hernandez shaved his trademark stache in 2012 for charity, a move that positions runner-up Rollie Fingers to one day wear the coveted crown.)

The facial hair on Charlie Finley's hockey and basketball players, however, was like a silk purse on a sow's ear—or lip. Losing money even faster than they lost games, Finley returned the teams to their respective leagues in 1974. The Tams folded, but three relocations and a merger later the spawn of the Golden Seals, the Dallas Stars, finally won the 1999 Stanley Cup.

Finley's A's, meanwhile, kept on winning. One of the byproducts of this success was Nancy Finley's 4:00 a.m. wakeup. Nancy and her father had breakfast, made a special trip to the post office, and arrived at a secret location around 6:00 a.m. There, in the vault of a relocated bank, resided the team's allotment of postseason tickets. A few words on the broadcast by Monte Moore, who directed fans to mail their money to an Oakland post office box, generated thousands of orders. No credit card paperwork or computers tracked any of it—it was all done by hand. Inside the envelopes lay cash, checks, money orders, and loose change. Sometimes there was a little something extra in the envelope.

"Oh, my gosh, they sent a lot more," Nancy Finley recalled. "Gift certificates would fall out, cash would fall out, jewelry would fall out. We had a bin to put that stuff in." The extra largesse went for naught, though. Season ticket holders and baseball dignitaries still wound up with the best seats. What Charlie Finley did with the excess isn't known, but the A's owner had a reputation for bestowing jewels on dazzling, young acquaintances. With all the cash on hand and more than $1 million in tickets in the vault, security was a priority on the long days of envelope stuffing. What A's employees could be spared were brought to the vault, along with Nancy's friends from Oakland High School. Nancy missed school to help get the tickets organized, but the daughter of a former principal got her homework done, often finishing it in the team offices at the Oakland Coliseum during games.

While the arrangement sounds bizarre and perhaps even inefficient, it was the way the Finleys liked to do business. The family preferred to have inexperienced but trustworthy people handling the tickets and the money, which might otherwise prove too tempting to temporary employees. This practice of hiring worked for ballgirls, too. Local girl Debra Jane Sivyer was the younger sister of one of the team's switchboard operators, and she brought her friend, Mary Barry, to guard the other foul line. The teenaged Sivyer delivered refreshments to umpires between innings, including her homemade cookies. The cameras always found her pretty face, especially during the World Series. She later became famous as a baking entrepreneur by the married name she took after leaving the A's: Mrs. Fields.

Despite all the care and the hush-hush nature of the task, however, breaches of security still happened. One day an elderly gentleman found his way inside the former Oakland bank and became incensed that he hadn't been informed about the institution's relocation. He demanded the money from his account from Carl Finley, who was using the former bank president's desk. Carl—perhaps fighting the urge to put the gentleman on the phone with his cousin Charlie—sent the old man on his way.

Those who successfully completed the transaction for American League Championship Series tickets arrived at Oakland Coliseum on Columbus Day to find the series between the A's and Orioles tied and the field swamped by a torrential downpour. Charlie Finley cursed both the weather and the American League president.

Joe Cronin's watch as AL president coincided with Finley's arrival in the league in late 1960, and Cronin endured Finley's constant threats of relocating and incessant calls for votes on the topic. By October 1973, Cronin, long ago elected into the Hall of Fame, had decided to leave the game after almost five decades. But Cronin wasn't going to glide out of office without a Finley challenge—or two. With the Coliseum field flooded and rain pounding the area, Cronin postponed Game Three of the 1973 ALCS on Monday afternoon. He got a faceful of Finley for his trouble, a shouting match in front of reporters with no game stories to file who were hungry for good copy.

Though after his heart attack Finley was supposed to avoid getting excited, the team with the smallest front office staff in the majors got even smaller come playoff time. Seven people listed in the team's Championship Series program were no longer with the club, nor was their announcer. TV and radio color man Bill Rigney had been taken off the air in September for the important assignment of scouting the Orioles in preparation for the playoffs, but he left to come home to his ill wife after Baltimore clinched the AL East and began playing its backups. The resulting stir left Rigney no longer in the booth, so White Sox announcer Bob Waller filled in for the postseason on radio.

The rain wasn't doing anything good for Charlie's health, either. The A's owner fumed at losing the large gate for the one game that week held while many people had the day off. With the A's hosting three afternoon games during the week—as were the Mets in the National League—Finley knew that Columbus Day was the one day that he had a shot at a decent crowd. Cronin was right about the weather: It poured well into the night. Finley was right about the crowd: Fewer and fewer people showed as the series grew more tense. But there was plenty of tension to go round on the other side of the world.

Saturday, October 6, was Yom Kippur, the most solemn day on the Jewish calendar, a day of fasting and prayer. Egyptian and Syrian forces—aided by other Arab countries and supplied by the Soviet Union—launched an attack on Israel, shattering the day's solemnity. The Arab coalition pushed beyond the Suez Canal, the Israelis both caught by surprise and outnumbered. Aided by US supplies and intelligence, however, Israel soon pushed back, moving into Syria through a gap left by the two forces. More than 2,500 Israelis were killed, but there were five times as many Arab casualties during the 18-day struggle known as the Yom Kippur War. It was the region's fourth war since the UN had carved out a homeland in the desert for the Israelis in 1948 from the British Mandate of Palestine, a holdover from the ruins of the Ottoman Empire. Never had Israel come so close to losing everything. It was a tremendous victory, the costs of which reverberated far from the Golan Heights.

Eleven Arab countries cut off oil shipments to the United States in retaliation for their aid of Israel. As if President Nixon hadn't delivered enough bad news in the past year, he addressed the nation with winter coming: "We are heading toward the most acute shortages of energy since World War II." It was no exaggeration. Fuel shortages of every kind changed the way people looked at how they heated their homes and what they drove. Consumers paying 38 cents per gallon for gasoline (leaded gasoline, which was just starting to be phased out) were soon forking over twice as much—if they were lucky enough to get through the long lines before gas stations ran out. Cars soon got smaller, imports with better mileage suddenly became popular, and the environmental, financial, and legal battles that had halted an Alaskan pipeline to that point gave way to America increasing its domestic oil production. Skyrocketing energy prices caused by the embargo—and worsened by Nixon price controls—resulted in improvements in energy efficiency of nearly every household product, reducing the amount of US energy generated by petroleum, and sweaters long stored in the backs of closets helped pass those cold nights with thermostats set at record lows.

⚾ ⚾ ⚾

On a sun-splashed Tuesday in California, Finley sent the A's out onto the field at Oakland Coliseum in the "wedding gown whites," a resplendent ensemble normally reserved for Sundays. The A's bats responded like they were sleeping in. Oakland had seen tremendous success in the past year, but there was something about Baltimore. A little sting still remained from when the Orioles had knocked the high-flying A's to earth in 1971, sweeping that Championship Series in three games.

"In '71 we blew everybody away during the season," recalls Rollie Fingers. "That was the year Vida had an incredible year. He was a day off for me. . . . I would just walk down and plop down in the dugout and say, 'Game's over.'" Out of the blue, Vida, who had started just 10 games in his career before that, won 24 times at age 21, completing 24 games, tossing 312 innings, and fashioning a 1.82 ERA. The way things rolled for the A's that season, winning 101 times to take the division by 16 games, who was going to say the A's couldn't just keep on rolling?

Baltimore, that's who.

"We got into the playoffs against Baltimore, and everything just went wrong," Fingers says of the 1971 ALCS. "Everyone went cold. We couldn't score any runs, too many runs [allowed]. That's why we lost. We learned how to lose. Now we had to learn how to win." The three-game sweep in '71 had made Dick Williams and Charlie Finley see the need for another top-notch starter. The A's acquired Holtzman from the Cubs for center fielder Rick Monday that November. Holtzman could match Baltimore's third-best pitcher: 1969 Cy Young co-winner Mike Cuellar, who won 18 or more games for six straight years.

The Baltimore lefty held the A's to only one hit and had a 1–0 lead entering the bottom of the eighth in Game Three of the 1973 ALCS. After keeping the lineup card clean for seven and a half innings, tactician Dick

Williams went to work. He sent Jesus Alou to bat for Ray Fosse, and the pinch hitter lifted a single to left to start the wheels moving in earnest. In came pinch runner extraordinaire Allan Lewis—a Finley favorite but loathed by the other players for being one-dimensional, as evidenced by the big fat zero under the column for at-bats by the Panamanian Express in 1973. Mike Andrews batted for Dick Green and laid down a bunt. Though Cuellar had a chance to get Lewis at second, he opted for the sure out. The lefty retired Bert Campaneris for the fourth time, but Joe Rudi produced a game-tying single.

"Mike Cuellar seemed to have their number," says Steve Jacobson, assigned to cover the 1973 ALCS for *Newsday*. "The Orioles had the really good pitching staff at that time. This was a breakthrough for the A's."

A subtle yet ironic decision, given the way October went, was the new defensive alignment in the ninth. With the A's needing to insert a new catcher, first baseman, and second baseman, Gene Tenace was the only choice to take over at catcher, Vic Davalillo assumed Tenace's previous spot at first base, and Ted Kubiak manned second. Though Andrews, the manager's old Boston ally, had been the man he trusted most to get down a bunt at a key moment in a tied playoff series, Williams chose the superior defender, Kubiak, to play second base.

A throwing error by Davalillo put an Oriole on third with two outs in the ninth, bringing up the powerfully built Don Baylor, a future All-Star and league MVP. It was the most tenuous situation Ken Holtzman had faced in the game. Baltimore's only run, and last hit before the ninth, had come on a third-inning home run by Earl Williams.

Holtzman had been one of the National League's top lefties and had twice thrown no-hitters as a Cub, but he had never gained the confidence of his manager, fiery Leo Durocher. In big spots, the legendary manager never fully trusted the left-hander, both college educated and Jewish. After being traded to Oakland in 1972—a move both Holtzman and Durocher wanted—the lefty found Dick Williams to be a manager who backed him up both on and off the field. After the tragic killing of 11 Israeli athletes during the Munich Olympics in September 1972, Holtzman and A's first baseman Mike Epstein, a slugger whose nickname was, yes, "Super Jew," had black armbands sewn on the sleeves of their uniforms out of respect. Holtzman recalls that his manager was "very respectful" of the decision, as were his teammates, with Reggie Jackson even wearing the armband in solidarity.

Now, in the ninth inning of Game Three of the '73 ALCS, with the league's top bullpen at his disposal, Williams left in his starter to face a right-handed batter whom he'd retired three times already. Leo Durocher this was not. "Dick Williams had complete trust and faith in his starting pitchers and let them pitch out of trouble on occasions where Leo might have pulled them from the game," Holtzman says. "Both were good tacticians, but I appreciated the confidence that Dick showed to Vida, Catfish, and I." Holtzman fanned Baylor to end the threat and retired the side in order in the 10th and 11th innings. Cuellar matched his opposing southpaw, each hurler allowing just a run and three hits until Bert Campaneris led off the 11th inning.

Retired all four times up against Cuellar, a fellow Cuban, Campaneris dug in, his mind set on starting the decisive rally in this taut pitcher's duel. As the team catalyst at the top of the order, Campy just had to get on first base, steal or claw his way to second, and try to cross home plate any way possible. Yet October 1973 saw Campy Campaneris transform into the unlikeliest of sluggers. He lifted a high drive off Cuellar that sailed just over Baylor's glove and into the seats in left field. Dick Williams hugged Holtzman in the dugout while Campy was rounding the bases. In the locker room, Campaneris was short on pithy quotes for the media, but not shy on emotion: "I be happy . . . I be lucky." The A's were neither the next afternoon.

It seemed like Oakland had everything going its way in Game Four. Back to back doubles by the two players pinch-hit for in the previous game, Fosse and Green, built a 3–0 lead that knocked out Jim Palmer, who barely got through the order once after fanning the A's 12 times in his Game One shutout. The lead became 4–0 when Fosse drove in his third run of the game with a sacrifice fly in the home sixth. The champagne was already in the Oakland clubhouse as Vida Blue took the mound in the seventh, working on a two-hitter. Blue retired good friend and former teammate Tommy Davis to start the inning but then walked Earl Williams. Don Baylor's single prompted a visit from Dick Williams, and no sooner had the manager returned to the dugout than Brooks Robinson's single to center broke up the shutout.

Veteran catcher Andy Etchebarren, the right-handed portion of Baltimore's perennial platoon behind the plate, stepped to the plate a prime candidate for hitting the double-play grounder to get Blue and the A's out of this jam. In seven previous postseason series, Etchebarren had never hit higher than .143 or even driven in a run. Yet he jumped on Blue's first pitch and crushed it deep into the seats in left to tie the game. Everything had fallen apart in just two pitches.

"That got our attention when Andy hit that home run, the last guy on that team that you'd expect to do that," recalls A's captain Sal Bando.

The still stunned A's and the Coliseum crowd watched in disbelief an inning later as Bobby Grich launched a homer off Rollie Fingers. Dick Williams made so many moves trying to tie the game that he became the first manager to lose the designated hitter in a postseason game. Mike Andrews (the third player used in the DH spot in the game) was forced onto the field at first base in the top of the ninth to replace Gene Tenace, who moved to catcher after Ray Fosse was pinch-run for. All the maneuvering came to nothing.

Though very much down, the A's had experience in this situation. A year earlier, Oakland had a two-games-to-none lead against Detroit, but the bench-clearing melee that occurred after the enraged Campaneris hurled his bat at Lerrin LaGrow lit a fire under Billy Martin's Tigers. The A's seemingly had the 1972 pennant won in the 10th inning of Game Four, but Detroit scored twice in the bottom of the inning to force a deciding fifth game at growling Tiger Stadium. The A's regrouped and held on to win the pennant in 1972. They needed a repeat performance after another heartbreaking Game Four loss in '73.

Luckily for the A's, they had Catfish Hunter on the mound. A clubhouse clown when he wasn't the best big game pitcher in the league, he faced a power-packed Orioles club that had played in three straight World Series from 1969 to 1971. Hunter calmly held the O's without a hit until a fifth-inning double by Etchebarren—starting against the A's righty after his stunning homer the previous day; platoon be damned. By then, Catfish already had all the runs he needed. Again the A's cracked the ice with two unheralded hitters in Vic Davalillo and Jesus Alou, both in-season Finley acquisitions. With the A's up, 1–0, two outs, and nobody on base in the fourth, Gene Tenace singled. Davalillo's triple to right plated a run while Alou's single brought home Davalillo and sent Doyle Alexander to the showers. Jim Palmer pitched for the third time in the series, but it proved too late to catch Catfish.

Hunter toyed with the O's all afternoon, striking out only one and letting the Orioles have one baserunner—but never more than one baserunner—in eight of the nine innings. At his best, Hunter let his opponents get themselves out, just as he'd done in a 6–3 win in Baltimore in Game Two to even the series. The A's had clubbed four home runs off Dave McNally, the same pitcher who two years earlier had won the opener of the 1971 ALCS over wunderkind Vida Blue. Hunter had then been lit up the following day for four home runs as the O's swept an AL West club in the playoffs for the third straight year.

Since that time, the A's had not only worked on their rotation but on their swagger as well. In '72 they rolled to the AL West title, beat the Tigers for the pennant, and knocked off the Reds in the World Series even as Reggie Jackson watched from the dugout on crutches. The O's didn't intimidate the A's any more, and they weren't letting Baltimore stand in the way of reaching the World Series for the second straight year. The fans weren't standing for it, either.

Much to Finley's consternation, the crowds at the Coliseum were disappointing. It followed a trend from the season, when Finley fudged the crowd total on the final regular-season game to eke over one million fans. The 1973 Championship Series crowds at Oakland Coliseum had grown progressively smaller with each game: 34,367 in Game Three; 27,947 in Game Four; down to a scant 24,265 in Game Five. The attendance for the deciding game remains the lowest figure by any club in Championship Series history—but that didn't stop the riot.

In the ninth inning, just like at Shea Stadium a day earlier, a retaining wall collapsed with fans pushing forward in anticipation of flooding the field. Hunter calmly stood on the mound like he was waiting in the woods with his shotgun for a buck—or a Boog or a Blair or a Brooks—to come into his sights. *Blam!* When Bobby Grich grounded out to Campaneris, the walls came down again, and the modest gathering became an urgent mob. The A's had been on the road when they clinched the 1972 pennant and World Series as well as the '73 division title, so the fans, denied their hunt for souvenirs and other on-field booty, were hungry.

Fans storming the field after clinching a championship—or even after an old ballpark witnessed its final pitch—was rather common in the 1970s, before security beefed up to include mounted police, dogs, and riot gear. No one ever condoned fans taking the field by force, but in Oakland, where owner and players alike frequently questioned fan loyalty, management didn't seem to mind seeing the patrons follow their heroes onto the field after winning the big game. "We saw it as a compliment," said Nancy Finley, who had helped fill many of the playoff orders for those who looted the field. "Our fans felt the same way we did."

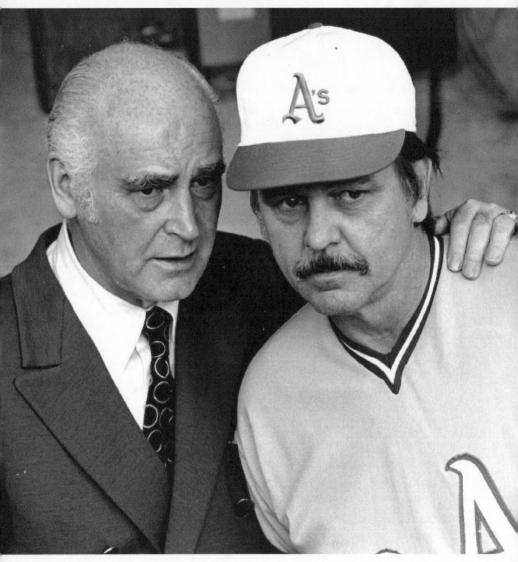

Charlie Finley talks into Dick Williams's ear. RON RIESTERER

Thirteen

SCAPEGOAT BY THE THROAT

On paper it looked like a mismatch.

The Mets had crept into the playoffs against the mighty A's, but a year earlier Oakland seemingly had no chance against Cincinnati. Great pitching always seemed to make up for most other deficiencies come World Series time, especially in an era when starters pitched on short rest and relievers threw as many innings as needed to get the job done.

"Will the real New York Mets stand up for the 1973 World Series?" asked Curt Gowdy at the top of the opening broadcast. When he asked his partner for the series, A's broadcaster Monte Moore—the home team's broadcaster working the booth in the World Series then—if the A's were better than they'd been in 1972, the answer came out, "Yes, we're better." As Spanky McFarland said in Depression-era *Little Rascals* shorts syndicated coast to coast in the 1970s: "What do ya mean 'we'?"

"Anybody who says they worked in the big leagues and traveled with the team all year and don't pull for them, there's something wrong with them," says Moore today. Hired by Charlie Finley while riding with the owner in an elevator when the team was still in Kansas City, Finley didn't even ask the voice of Kansas Jayhawks basketball if he could call baseball. "They've always said that Finley would make you be a 'homer.' That's not the case at all," Moore says. "I always felt that the local broadcasters of baseball—if your home fans were satisfied with your local broadcasts, that's all that counted."

Because the A's said the marauding fans stole it after the playoffs, no customary red-white-and-blue bunting hung from the facing of the Coliseum decks. In Oakland, there was just the red of the American League umpires' jackets, the blue of the National League arbiters' coats, and the white shoes of the home team. The biggest hand in the pregame introductions went to Willie Mays, the San Francisco treat doing an encore and surprising fans by starting in center field in a World Series game for the first time in a dozen seasons. Rusty Staub's separated shoulder left him in extreme pain, so Mays took over for him, getting a 40-second ovation that rivaled the reception a few days earlier when he stunned the New York crowd by pinch-hitting. On the A's side, an almost unnoticed man among the players introduced was Manny Trillo. A September call-up, the 22-year-old second baseman had been on the roster for the ALCS, though he didn't play. He was one of the 25 players introduced by the A's for the World Series, but he wasn't eligible to play.

When Finley sold third-string catcher Jose Morales to Montreal in September, it left the roster one player short of the 25-man limit. Players who landed on a team after the rosters expanded on September 1 weren't eligible for the postseason. The Orioles had allowed Trillo a place on Oakland's roster. The Mets, however, didn't. Finley had an announcement read before the game telling the crowd that Trillo was ineligible—the first of three Oakland offenses for which Bowie Kuhn levied fines.

With that bit of angst, the World Series began.

$$\oslash \ \oslash \ \oslash$$

In Game One left-hander Ken Holtzman faced lefty-swinging leadoff hitter Wayne Garrett, who in his last 23 games of the season had batted .345 with 6 homers, 17 RBIs, 20 runs, 11 walks, and a .655 slugging percentage as the Mets finished 17-6 to claim the NL East title. He singled in the NLCS opener in Cincinnati but was kept off base 20 straight times until his double started the decisive rally in Game Five. Second on the team during the year in home runs and first in steals—16 and 6 respectively for the offensively challenged Mets—Garrett started the series by popping up to the infield. After Felix Millan grounded out, another rousing ovation greeted Mays. He singled for the first hit of the 1973 World Series. The Mets stranded him in the first and Bud Harrelson in the third while Jon Matlack retired the first seven A's. He walked Dick Green, then up stepped pitcher Ken Holtzman, who was batting because the leagues had agreed the previous winter to keep the DH out of the World Series—for the time being.

This being the first year of the designated hitter, you would think that hitting was a complete afterthought for American League pitchers, but Dick Williams had the pitchers take batting practice late in the year. The day after the A's clinched the AL West title, Williams sent Catfish Hunter and Holtzman up as pinch hitters. Hunter singled, and Holtzman walked in either pitcher's only plate appearance of the season. A left-handed thrower but righty batter, Holtzman had a .158 career batting average in 606 career plate appearances to that point, with 18 extra-base hits, the kind of batting record that raised many a cheer at the elimination of hurlers hitting in the AL. His inability to get down a bunt in the World Series cut down a base-runner. After fouling off one bunt, a pitch in the dirt got far enough away that Green thought he could take second, but catcher Jerry Grote threw him out. So there were two strikes, two outs, no one on, and a pitcher without an official at-bat all year at the plate. The turning point of the game lay one pitch away.

Holtzman drilled a ball down the line, left fielder Cleon Jones got to it and made a strong throw to second, and Holtzman slid in late, banging up his knee. Bert Campaneris followed with a grounder to second that went right through the legs of second baseman Millan, a two-time Gold Glove winner who had made just nine errors in 153 games during the year. Holtzman scored the first run of the series. Matlack, with a high leg kick and superb move to first that Campy had never seen before, caught him leading too far.

"He fooled me," Campaneris says. "He made kind of a different move. I say . . . God, he got me." But the Mets didn't get him. Campy took off for second, beating first baseman John Milner's throw. Joe Rudi, considered in the Mets scouting reports to be the toughest right-handed hitter in an A's lineup stacked with seven such swingers, punched a single to right to give the A's a 2–0 lead. Sal Bando, another pretty dangerous righty, followed with another single—bobbled by Willie Mays in center—and the A's had men on the corners, only to have Reggie Jackson strand both. The A's didn't have another hit until the eighth inning.

The Mets hit the ball hard, but the only run they could muster was Milner singling Cleon Jones home in the fourth. They might have gotten more, but Jackson, playing center for Oakland, got a good jump on a hard liner by Grote and tracked it down in the gap. Holtzman lasted just five innings. After the game, Williams said he removed his starter early because of how hard he'd run the bases, banging his knee in the process. Fireman Rollie Fingers proved worthy of the designation by *Oakland Tribune* beat writer Ron Bergman as a "bullpen in himself." In 21st-century baseball parlance, Fingers served as middle reliever, set-up man, *and* closer.

"You don't see guys going out there, today . . . relief pitching three, four, five innings—it doesn't happen," says Fingers, the second relief pitcher elected to the Hall of Fame. "Everybody is a one-inning pitcher. There are so many pitchers in the bullpen now." The A's had eight pitchers on their

World Series roster, the fewest by a team since, well, the 1972 A's. But before that you had to go back to the 1944 St. Louis Cardinals—during the World War II manpower shortage—to find a team that brought that few pitchers to a World Series.

Fingers entered Game One to begin the sixth inning and navigated trouble for the next 3⅓ innings. A one-out walk in the ninth brought Rusty Staub into the on-deck circle as a pinch hitter and Williams out of the dugout to summon lefty Darold Knowles. Yogi Berra, using the injured Staub as a decoy, sent up right-handed Jim Beauchamp instead. Dick Green snagged his soft liner, and Garrett popped up to end the game.

Game One marked the sixth straight postseason game in which Mets pitching had allowed two runs or fewer, and New York had won only three of those games. That streak quickly came to a halt the next afternoon.

⚾ ⚾ ⚾

After getting bounced from the 1971 playoffs, A's owner Charlie Finley had changed from sleeveless uniforms with Kelly green and somewhat muted gold to an almost fluorescent version of those colors with pullover tops in yellow, green, and wedding gown white. The hats for the players went two-tone, though the heads of the coaching staff remained covered in white and green. Captain Sal Bando said the uniform greeted the players upon arrival in the clubhouse, the color of the day by whim of ownership. "They would always put the uniform in your locker," he says. "Every Sunday, our best uniform, the white one."

For Game Two the A's were resplendent in their Sunday whites. The A's started out playing their Sunday best, too, collecting three extra-base hits against Jerry Koosman in the first inning. The A's were up 3–2 in the third inning and stood a hit away from blowing the game—and the World Series—open. An error by Koosman loaded the bases with one out when Yogi Berra replaced Koosman with Ray Sadecki. The batter was Dick Green, who had four career grand slams, including one in Anaheim that August, but he squared around for a suicide squeeze—and missed. Gene Tenace was caught in a rundown, which the Mets nearly botched, but they got the out and got out of a big inning for the second time by fanning Green with multiple runners on base. In just three innings, fans already had seen one error, two misjudged flyballs by the Mets, two A's thrown out on the bases, and runners repeatedly taking liberties on Rusty Staub's arm.

Vida Blue staggered through five innings holding the one-run lead, but three Oakland pitchers allowed six straight Mets to reach base—with only one hitting the ball out of the infield. Staub, playing despite his separated shoulder and looking pained both at the plate and in the field, made the first and last outs in the four-run sixth. The Mets bullpen held the line, though a two-out hit by Reggie Jackson plated a run in the seventh.

For the Mets, the sky was quite literally the limit. The haze—the Northern Californian term for what Southern Californians called smog, broadcaster Monte Moore pointed out—and the high sun created a bedeviling combination for Mets outfielders. Cleon Jones lost a ball completely in the first inning, and in the ninth Willie Mays had his own problems. Mays, who had gone in to run for Staub but had tripped over the bag rounding second, now stumbled in center field, letting Deron Johnson's liner fall in for a leadoff double. Mays ironically had gone out to play right field for Staub, but once out there he switched positions with Don Hahn for old familiar center field, where he'd won 12 Gold Gloves but had also committed an error in Game One. Moore winced at the mic as he watched the legend stagger on the big stage.

"Boy, Curt, this is the thing I think all sports fans in all areas hate to see," Moore said, "a great one playing in his last years having this kind of trouble standing up and falling down."

"Ten years ago he would have put that ball in his back pocket," partner Curt Gowdy lamented.

McGraw almost survived the gaffe, getting the next two outs and going to a 2-and-2 count on Sal Bando. The next two borderline pitches were called balls, putting the tying run on first. Jackson collected his third straight hit to make it a one-run game. On the next pitch, Tenace laced a single to tie the game and delight the raucous Coliseum crowd.

The Mets got a rally going in the 10th inning, but Augie Donatelli, umpiring his last game behind the plate before retirement, wasn't moving away from the spotlight so soon. The former minor league infielder had started umpiring softball games at a prisoner of war camp in Germany during World War II, not able to play after breaking his ankle jumping out of his burning B-17—though the injury didn't stop him from twice trying to escape. After the Soviets liberated Stalag Luft IV in May 1945, instead of returning to the Pennsylvania coal mines, Donatelli attended umpire school. After 23 years in the National League, having helped start an umpire's union, working 10 no-hitters, and now his fifth World Series, Donatelli watched Bud Harrelson tag up from third on Felix Millan's short flyball.

Joe Rudi's one-hop throw veered to the left, allowing Harrelson to slip past the tag of catcher Ray Fosse and score standing up. Or not. "Out!" called Donatelli, who had dropped on his belly behind the plate as the ball arrived, obscuring his view of the tag. The Mets dugout exploded, with Yogi Berra leading the contingent onto the field to crowd around the 59-year-old umpire. Willie Mays, the on-deck hitter, with the best view in the house, fell to his knees to beg his team's case as Fosse casually rolled the ball back toward the mound and walked off. Side retired.

Donatelli—a man used to having his judgment questioned by large numbers of people—withstood the wrath of Hahn . . . and Jones . . . and Milner . . . and Mays. He didn't eject anyone, though he had to be tempted. Harrelson got in the best insult: "You can't kick me out for your inadequacies!" When Berra repeatedly asked Donatelli where Fosse tagged Harrelson, the ump patted Berra's rear and told him: "On the ass!" The animated dispute, caught by field microphones, served as the lead-in to the 1973 World Series Highlight Film, though it proved far from the most memorable confrontation of the series—or the day.

After the Mets wasted another chance the next inning, Harrelson led off the 12th with a double. Reliever Tug McGraw, batting for the third time in the game, bunted over the head of hard-charging Sal Bando, and now the Mets had runners on the corners. But Garrett and Millan were both retired, and the game was still tied with two outs and the Say Hey Kid at the plate. Now past five o'clock, the shadows, sun, and more of that haze made his task even tougher against the top reliever in the American League, Rollie Fingers. After taking a slider, Mays commented to Fosse, "I can't see, man." Figuring he couldn't catch up to the fastball in the fading light of a fading career, Fosse signaled for a fastball. Mays hit a dribbler up the middle, past the pitcher, past the infielders trying to knock it down, and into center field. Experience had pulled one over on youth.

Back in Queens, Howie Rose was jumping for joy. "When Willie hits a little 38-hopper through the middle, when it gets past the mound, into center field, Rollie Fingers throws his mitt in the air. It's great."

It was the last hit for Willie Mays.

Cleon Jones followed with a single hit too hard to score McGraw from second. That was all for Fingers, as southpaw Paul Lindblad entered to face Milner. Now the unwanted spotlight found Mike Andrews. Subbed in when the A's were still trailing, Andrews had recorded one putout in four innings, but now it all fell apart. Like Felix Millan the day before for the Mets, the ball went right through the legs of the second baseman. The only difference was that Millan was a superb infielder; Andrews embodied the old baseball axiom: "The ball will always find your worst fielder at the worst moment." Gene Tenace's misplay at second base in extra innings had cost the A's a game in the 1972 playoffs—and now Dick Williams was burned again. The manager later claimed "the ball hit something" just before it reached Andrews. However it occurred, two runs crossed the plate, Milner reached second base, and it was 9–6, Mets. Nor was the ordeal over yet.

Jerry Grote hit a ball close to the same spot. Andrews fielded this one, but his throw to first sailed, and Tenace—not the most graceful of first basemen—stretched awkwardly, pulling his foot off the bag. Williams later said, "It was clearly Tenace's fault, but I didn't call up the press box and didn't yell at the scorer because I didn't give a damn. We'd given up four runs, and that was all that mattered. Or so I thought."

The Mets still had to get three outs. Minutes after being the hero, Mays misplayed another ball in center field, giving Jackson his fourth hit of the game and putting him at third with no one out. Oakland may have committed five errors in the game—one shy of the series record—but Mets outfielders botched three flyballs, two by "the greatest center fielder who ever played this game," according to Jackson after the game. "That's not Willie Mays out there. That's Willie Mays in nomenclature."

If Mays had caught the ball hit to him in the ninth, the teams would have already been at the Oakland Airport, not still on the field at the Oakland Coliseum. Instead manager Yogi Berra went to the mound after McGraw issued a walk to the 27th batter he faced.

"Are you tired?" Berra asked.

Reliving the moment that winter in his book, *Screwball*, McGraw reflected that he had pitched eight innings of relief over the past two days. "I guess I am," he told his manager.

George Stone entered and surrendered a hit to his first batter and later issued a walk—to Andrews, of all people—to put the tying run on base, but the Mets got through it. Stone retired Vic Davalillo and Bert Campaneris with the bases full to notch the save and finally end the longest (4 hours, 13 minutes) and most inclusive (38 players used) World Series game played to that date. For the A's, though, the aggravation was just beginning.

In Oakland's locker room, Charlie Finley hurried into the manager's office and slammed the door: "Dick, we're putting Andrews on the disabled list and activating Manny Trillo." Six weeks earlier, this would have been fine. Andrews, picked up on waivers in July, was slightly damaged goods and had throwing problems that made him a liability in a critical game. Trillo had a great future—though not with the A's—and later won three Gold Gloves as a second baseman. But once the rosters were frozen on September 1, he couldn't put Trillo on the team. The commissioner and the Mets had made the fact clear the previous day that neither Trillo nor anyone else could be added to the team—unless a player on the existing roster was hurt. Team orthopedic surgeon Dr. Harry Walker, at Finley's request, examined Andrews in the training room. The infielder said his shoulder, which had bothered him with the White Sox in 1972, was fine.

John Claiborne, then A's farm director, recounted to the authors of the book *Charlie Finley* that he told the owner that Bowie Kuhn would shoot down the idea of disabling Andrews, and "the only way you're gonna get him on there is if Andrews will sign a letter saying his arm is no good." So the next step was to convince Andrews to sign the letter. Less than an hour later, the deed was done. "I should have walked out on the doctor and Finley in the first place," Andrews admitted at a press conference three days later. "But I was tired and ashamed, and I just hung my head." His attorney, Harold Meizler, said his client "had not been in complete control of his emotions" and "had reached the lowest level of humiliation."

When Williams next saw Andrews after Game Two, the infielder was taking his luggage off the bus to the airport: "He had been torn from the inside out, and was crying." Williams was in tears as well.

During Boston's "Impossible Dream" pennant season in 1967—a combination of Rodgers and Hammerstein's *Cinderella* and the New York Mets in the final months of 1969 and 1973—the rookie Andrews had been a revelation for the Red Sox. He started 135 games at second base. Batting near the top of the lineup, he tied for the league lead in sacrifices and was second on the team in runs. Of course, he'd also committed 16 errors, but a rookie manager doesn't forget a rookie infielder who helps him win a pennant and then hits .308 in the World Series. Williams wasn't forgetting Andrews now.

"At the moment I grabbed Mike's limp hand and wished him good luck," Williams later wrote, defying the title of the book, *No More Mr. Nice Guy*. "I decided that I'd need good luck, too. Because I was getting the hell away from Charlie Finley."

The film scheduled for the A's flight, *1776*, a musical on the signing of the Declaration of Independence, was cancelled by Finley. Revolution was in the air regardless.

Forty years can make players, managers, announcers, fans, and writers a little iffy on details, but everyone even remotely involved in the 1973 World Series remembers the Andrews incident. Even if they don't exactly recall the name of the person involved, there's no forgetting that betrayal of a ballplayer on baseball's biggest stage. There are so many methods to get rid of a player that the word "fired" is seldom used, but that was exactly the language used, starting with the lead sports story in the *Oakland Tribune* the next day: "Was Andrews Fired?" Even some members of the opposing team still get annoyed thinking about it after all these years.

"He's a professional player, and he made an error, and the ownership is going to get rid of him? C'mon, that's not very professional," says '73 Met Ed Kranepool. "How many base hits did Charlie Finley get in his career? Or how many groundballs did he catch? There are people that make decisions and dictate what's going on in the game, not knowing what's really happening. Not knowing how to run a ballclub."

"To embarrass a guy like that for making an error, that's ridiculous. That's something the Japanese do," says Mets third baseman Wayne Garrett, who spent his last years as a player with the Chunichi Dragons. "They don't even go to that extent. They may take him out of the game, but they don't take him off the roster."

To the A's, it still resonates as something personal, an event that nearly cost them their dynasty. And the scapegoat might have been any one of them if the circumstances were different.

"One of our own was getting shafted," says team captain Sal Bando. "We felt like we had to rally around him in [that] there was an injustice."

"We were going to strike unless he put him back on the team," says Oakland left fielder Joe Rudi.

Before the A's even got on the plane to New York, Reggie Jackson said the attitude of the team was "near mutiny." By the time they took the field for their Monday workout in New York, they were all the way there. The players wore Andrews's number 17 crudely taped to their sleeves—even Trillo wore the number in tribute. The team's sporadic feuding fostered the idea that they didn't like one another, but their actions regarding a teammate who had only been with Oakland for a couple of months told a different story.

Commissioner Kuhn had the last word, and, as predicted, he disallowed the move, admonishing Finley for "unfairly embarrassing a player who has given many years of able service to professional baseball." Esteemed *New York Times* columnist Red Smith referred to Finley as "Charlie I" and said that the A's owner suffered from a "Napoleonic complex."

Before Game Three, Dick Williams held a closed-door meeting with the team. The manager told them, "This is the hardest thing I've ever done, but somebody has to stand up to this man, and it's going to be me." Williams planned to resign at the end of the World Series, regardless of its outcome, and he would deny it if anyone leaked it to the media.

"We were a little shocked because nobody expected it," says reliever Darold Knowles. "Everyone knew that through the years he had his differences with Finley. Then after the Mike Andrews incident, that was the real big thing. He said that was going to be it, and, yeah, we were shocked."

Even the unflappable Catfish was rattled. Hunter spoke with Andrews on the phone shortly before Game Three, the team welcoming him back from his home in Peabody, Massachusetts, confident in knowing that he would return in time for the next night's game. Hunter's mind was on many things, not the least of which was hosting 30-plus people who had come to New York from his little hometown of Hereford, North Carolina. On the field, he ran into a promoter he knew who said he had bet $50,000 on him. Hunter quickly moved away from the man, retreating to the bullpen to warm up. Warm was a relative term because the weather was like they were playing on Pluto.

The first postseason night game in New York baseball history blew windy and cold. In truth, the weather wasn't so different than a night game in the Bay Area with the wind howling, but with Hunter's supporters on hand, not to mention meeting the gambler on the field, and everything going on in the clubhouse, it took longer than usual for him to implement his game plan. "Maybe I tried to smoke the ball by people," Hunter later pondered in his book, *Catfish*, "instead of pitching smart. Whatever." Whatever he threw that inning, the Mets hit hard. Wayne Garrett crushed Hunter's second pitch for his second home run of the World Series. Felix Millan and Rusty Staub singled to put runners on the corners, and a slider went to the screen, making it 2–0. Then Hunter committed an error. The Mets were verging on blowing things open, on taking the A's out of the game after they'd gone through so much the past two days. That's when cool Catfish took control. The Mets didn't score again.

Tom Seaver was sharp, his fastball ripping through the chill. He already owned the major league record with 10 straight strikeouts in a game in

1970, and then he came within one strikeout of the World Series consecutive mark by fanning five A's in a row. He fanned 10 batters through the first five innings and finished with a still-standing club World Series mark of 12. Meanwhile, the Mets stranded runners in all but one inning—the big cold crowd into every pitch, oohs and ahhs on each remotely close play, and cheering when "Sign Man" Karl Ehrhardt flashed a beaut after a grounder bounced off Bando's chest. YOU'RE FIRED, it read.

The A's finally got on the board in the sixth, with an inadvertent assist from Mets fans. Because of field repairs in the wake of the sacking of Shea six days earlier, the grounds crew had to fill in some of the bald spots on the infield with grass from the outfield, extending the warning track. Mets center fielder Don Hahn hesitated just enough for Bando's drive to hit the wall for a double, later coming around to score.

No one had told Hahn that the warning track had become two feet wider since he was last at Shea. A's left fielder Joe Rudi sympathizes with Hahn, conceding that "the footing was bad." Rudi turned in a couple of stellar plays and set a World Series mark for a left fielder with seven putouts in Game Three, despite never having played at the stadium before. Shea's toughest feature for him was the "large area right behind me that was all clear Plexiglas. You couldn't tell where you were."

The A's were still in the game, but time was running short. Seaver retired a trio of pinch hitters in the seventh, but in the eighth the A's used the same formula that had foiled Jon Matlack's brilliant Game One effort. Campaneris reached first, stole second, and came around on a hit by Rudi. The Mets also had some tough luck. John Milner crushed a ball early in the game that hit the brick wall in right field and went for a single. (At the end of the decade, the Shea ground rules changed so that a ball hit to that area was a homer.) Milner scalded another ball with two on and two out in the ninth that looked like it might end the game, but Reggie Jackson tracked it down on the run.

With extra innings required for the second successive game, Tug McGraw threw two more frames to push his innings total to 10 so far in the World Series. "McGraw might not be able to shave when this Series is over," NBC announcer Curt Gowdy said of Tug's overburdened left arm. The Mets might have squeezed yet another inning out of the arm they'd ridden into mid-October, but a two-out single by Harrelson brought up McGraw's spot in the 10th. Willie Mays grounded to short in his last career at bat.

Just as had happened in Game Four of the NLCS, McGraw left, and trouble entered. The 11th inning began innocuously enough when A's pitcher Paul Lindblad was retired to open the inning; playing with just 23 players on the roster this night left the A's with little alternative but to have the pitcher bat. Mets reliever Harry Parker walked Ted Kubiak—the only time he reached base in the 1973 postseason. A passed ball by the normally sure-handed Jerry Grote put Kubiak on second base. Then once again Campaneris came through for Oakland. His two-out single gave the A's the lead, and Rollie Fingers finished the job.

⚾ ⚾ ⚾

Game Four belonged to the "Little Guy." Mike Andrews was back in town, and the A's and every other person, save for a small contingent above the visiting dugout, seemed to be pulling for him. After Tuesday night's win, Bando had told reporters, "The Mike Andrews stuff was actually good for us in the end. For two whole days, it made us completely forget we were facing Tom Seaver." But lest anyone forgot how tough Jon Matlack could be, he reminded them in short order on Wednesday night.

Matlack allowed just three hits and one unearned run in eight innings, and this time the Mets didn't let Oakland off the ropes after the opening inning. After the first two batters singled off Ken Holtzman, Rusty Staub took the tall lefty deep, somehow clearing the wall in left-center despite his painful shoulder.

"Never in my wildest dreams did I think I could hit a home run, much less go four for four with five RBIs," says Staub. "By the grace of God I found a way to play, or I never would have played in a World Series. . . . I just felt that if I didn't play we weren't going to win. Maybe that's being a little bodacious about yourself, but I just seemed to be the guy to drive in the runs at the right time."

The Mets were up by enough runs that Staub played the whole game despite having to throw the ball underhand. It afforded the Mets the chance to give the ill Cleon Jones, caught getting sick in the outfield by NBC cameras, a couple of innings off. It also supplied George Theodore with his World Series moment.

"I haven't played in two, three months," says Theodore, whose last inning in the outfield had ended with the horrific collision with Don Hahn on July 7. "I'm out in left field, and my knees are shaking. I don't know if it's from the cold or just being there. Wouldn't you know, the first player, Sal Bando, hits a line drive into left-center field. I, reacting on instinct, ran over, got the ball over my head, throw it in like I've done it forever. The next ball was hit to me as well—a ground ball single. I go down to get it, it hit the dirt clump and jumps up. It was going over my head. I catch it with my bare hand, throw it in, and I thought it was one of the great plays of the Series, but nobody else remembers it."

What everyone remembers is Mike Andrews pinch-hitting in the eighth inning. The capacity crowd of 54,817 gave him a standing ovation on the way to the plate. He meekly grounded out to third in his final career turn at bat as the fans stood again. That he got the chance to get that at-bat was the victory. So what if it was a lopsided game?

"The most amazing thing wasn't that these tough New Yorkers were cheering for the enemy—it was that Charlie Finley was in the club box near the dugout cheering with them," Dick Williams wrote of the satisfying moment. "People wondered if I had used Andrews just to spite Finley. If they could have heard me say, looking into the stands, 'Take this, you son of a bitch,' while Andrews walked to the plate, they'd have had their answer."

⚾ ⚾ ⚾

With the series even, Jerry Koosman faced Vida Blue in Game Five in a rematch of wild Game Two. But this game lacked the off-field drama, errors, timely hitting, and, most notably, the sun. "It was the coldest I had ever been at a ballpark," says Howie Rose, the Queens College student in 1973, who later as a Mets broadcaster logged many frigid nights at stadiums. "It was a challenge to take my hand out of my coat pocket to keep score. It was brutal; '73 was like Antarctica."

It was also beautiful to look at that box score as a Mets fan. New York never lost any of Koosman's six career postseason starts as a Met, and he got an early lead on a second-inning RBI by John Milner. Kooz allowed just two hits through the first six innings and erased that pair with a pickoff and a double-play ball. After Don Hahn's triple in the home sixth made it 2–0, a one-out double by Gene Tenace in the seventh put the tying runs on base for Oakland. After a night off, Tug McGraw was ready to resume his duties. He walked pinch hitter Deron Johnson but got Angel Mangual to pop up and then caught Campaneris looking, bouncing off the mound with glove slapping thigh, sending a message to his wife and everyone else that "Ya Gotta Believe!" was working in October, too. Just a few nights earlier, when McGraw and his family had arrived back in Long Island from Oakland in the wee hours, their Manhasset neighbors, whom they didn't know all that well, emerged from their homes to welcome them back. A bed sheet slung across the house simply said: WE BELIEVE.

McGraw pitched out of trouble in the eighth and caught the last two batters looking in the ninth, and the Mets miraculously stood a game away from a world championship. Ron Bergman, the *Oakland Tribune* beat writer, noted, "About the only thing the A's averted in losing two out of three in slummy Shea was the obligatory victory riot of the fans."

Howie Rose and 54,816 others spilled down the ramp from Shea's glacial upper deck for the last time in 1973. Already the question was forming that still hangs in the air 40 years later and will remain without a definitive answer 40 years after you read this.

"So what do you do now? Who pitches Game Six?" Rose asked his friend, somewhat rhetorically, as they descended. The stranger in front of him emphatically interjected, "Stone!"

"The more I thought about it, the more it made sense to me," Rose recalls. "To try to piece it together in Game Six and still have the best pitcher in the world, on full rest, to drop the hammer in Game Seven. I didn't know it then, but I've learned over the years that there's no such thing as house money. You don't play a game with house money. I understand the concept of trying to get the choke hold when you have the chance. But in retrospect, I do remember the thought of having Seaver on full rest in Game Seven. That's pretty good because if Seaver gets in trouble, you can go to Matlack as early as you want."

The George Stone/George Thomas Seaver Game Six conundrum has become one of the great what ifs in Mets history. Every team has its own what ifs: What if Vernon Stouffer had accepted George Steinbrenner's bid for the Cleveland Indians in 1971 instead of changing his mind at the last minute? What if Charlie Finley paid an insurance premium to Catfish Hunter and kept him from going to the Yankees as the first free agent? What if Nolan Ryan was still in the Mets rotation and able to pitch Game Six of the '73 World Series? It can keep a person up nights.

But at the time, the hypothetical repercussions of the pitching matchup for Game Six didn't get much ink. Pitchers starting on short rest, sore shoulder or no, were no big deal at the time. Dodger Sandy Koufax in 1965 and Tiger Mickey Lolich in 1968 had pitched on two days' rest to win those World Series. Wasn't Catfish Hunter, whose hand had been in a cast in August, pitching on the same amount of rest as Seaver? Hadn't Seaver pitched Game Five of the NLCS on three days' rest? While the sun was just rising on the West Coast, anxious New Yorkers were already reading the *New York Daily News*. The headline screamed: "For the A's There's No Tomorrow—Seaver Figures to Wrap It Up Today."

In Oakland, page one of the *Tribune* featured stories about President Nixon agreeing to provide a summary of the White House tapes, the headline about the court battle with Special Prosecutor Archibald Cox culminating with an ominous, "Cox Must Stop." Meanwhile, Secretary of State Henry Kissinger had gone to Moscow for talks on the Middle East War threatening to involve the Cold War superpowers as Israeli soldiers continued to push into Egypt. No baseball story ran above or even below the fold on page one of the 15-cent Oakland paper, but stenciled across the front page were four huge letters and one necessary apostrophe: "Go A's."

Asked about the Game Six pitching assignment four decades later, several Mets say that talking about anything besides what actually happened is hindsight—there's nothing to do about it now.

"That's what second guessing is all about," says right fielder Rusty Staub. "However Seaver got to be the pitcher, he did pitch and pitched a pretty good game . . . and we didn't score enough. That's just the way it is." "Stone was funky, but he wasn't our best pitcher," says shortstop Bud Harrelson, who never asked Seaver—few ever getting an answer on the subject—but Harrelson always thought his roommate lobbied for the Game Six start. "The way it works out, Seaver went on short-days' rest rather than having Stone pitch."

"I think Yogi made the right decision at the time," says third baseman Wayne Garrett. "I would have pitched Seaver on three days' rest. Why do you want to save him until the last if you can win it before? Why do you want to give them a game? If George Stone had pitched, maybe he would have beaten them. Who knows?"

"That question has been debated for 40 years, I suppose; all the armchair quarterbacks say whatever they say, and the pundits have all the reasons for this, that, and the other," says pitcher Jon Matlack, to whom the burden for Berra's decision ultimately fell. He looks at it now not just as a ballplayer but as someone who has spent a quarter century as a pitching coach in the majors and minors. "To me, it comes down to the guy making the decision. Yogi went with his gut, with all the statistics, he went with what he felt based on what was going on with the team at the time. To me, that's making the right decision. I would rather see more managers in today's game manage along those lines than what appears to be managing, sometimes, to avoid criticism and follow the statistics where the news media is less apt to find out where they made a mistake and more apt to say the odds were in my favor, but the players didn't get the job done."

Mets teammate Ed Kranepool, on the club before any other '73 Met and who stayed with the team after all had left except for Ron Hodges, offers a dissenting opinion. "We didn't have to win the sixth game; Oakland did. We had to win the seventh game, if I do my math, you have to win four out of seven. The sixth game . . . we don't have to win, we have to show up, we have to play. We might win, we might lose. But that's [not] the end of the World Series, correct? The seventh game, you lose, we should go home for the winter. You could use your whole pitching staff for the seventh. Tom Seaver is not short-rested. That's his regular day to pitch. He's pitched a lot of innings. He's struck out a lot of people. He's the best pitcher in baseball. So on the last day of the year, I do not want my third pitcher pitching, as opposed to my number one pitcher.

"George Stone was bypassed. And you tell me why?" Kranepool asks. "You come to your own conclusion. We should have won the World Series." A's manager Dick Williams agreed. "The Mets, having put our backs to the wall, could afford to blow off Game Six," Williams later wrote. "Yogi Berra could pitch a decent starter named George Stone—he was 12-3 that season— in Game Six. That would give their ace, Tom Seaver, an extra day's rest so that if there was a Game Seven, he'd probably be damn near unhittable, consider- ing he'd allowed just two runs in eight innings in Game Three. And if Seaver faltered, number-two pitcher Jon Matlack would be rested and in the bullpen to back him up. Either way, we figured, the Mets had us whipped."

No matter what anyone else thinks, however, it comes down to one man acting on experience. Yogi Berra's gut had helped the Mets go pretty far in 1973. Asked almost 40 years later if he regretted the decision to go with his ace on short rest, Berra didn't waver. "No. Seaver and Matlack—they were the best we had."

But the best weren't good enough.

⚾ ⚾ ⚾

In the Game Six rematch of future Hall of Famers, Catfish Hunter was as cool as ever. Whenever the World Series ended, he was hopping on the first plane back to North Carolina to go hunting—win or lose. Hunter didn't plan on losing, though.

This time he got through the first inning, getting two flyballs to center after putting two Mets on. As for the offense, Williams had benched Ray Fosse and inserted Deron Johnson at first base, with Gene Tenace catching—a wise decision considering the slow-footed Mets didn't attempt a steal in the series. The manager also made sure that his team understood that Tom Seaver wasn't throwing at full strength. "It was as if he'd decided to either win the series right there, with a pitcher working on three days' rest, or not win it at all," Williams said of Berra in *No More Mr. Nice Guy.* "Imagine my surprise to discover that we had it figured wrong. . . . Yogi played right into our hands. And the Swingin' A's were back."

To this point in the World Series, Reggie Jackson was hitting .238 with two runs batted in. His two extra-base hits resulted from a center fielder who could no longer catch and a right fielder who could no longer throw. Anxious to show the world he had what it took to be a superstar and break that $100,000 salary barrier, Jackson stepped up with a man on first and two out in the bottom of the first. Reggie roped a drive to left-center to score Joe Rudi from first. Seaver, who had set still-standing, single-game Mets records in 1973 for the NLCS (13 strikeouts) and World Series (12), only to have his team lose both times because they scored a total of just three runs for him, could see it was going to be a struggle.

"This wasn't Tom Seaver on ability; this was Tom Seaver on heart," said Jackson, who fanned against Seaver three times in their first meeting. In Game Six, Jackson's second double scored another runner from first—Sal Bando this time—to give Oakland a 2–0 lead in the third inning. Several A's mentioned after the game that Seaver hadn't thrown nearly as hard on three days' rest as he had on five.

Hunter was superb, taking a three-hitter into the eighth. Ken Boswell, who set a World Series mark by going 3 for 3 as a pinch hitter, singled to bring the tying run to the plate. In came lefty Darold Knowles to face the top of the order. Garrett and Millan both singled, cutting the lead to one and putting runners on the corners with one out. Rusty Staub, New York's offensive hero despite the shoulder injury with a sizzling .571 average in his first 21 at-bats against Oakland, could tie the game with a hit, a long fly, or a slow roller. Knowles knew he needed a strikeout or a double play, and by now he knew exactly what his manager would do.

"I had known Dick for a long time, way back even in my minor league days," says Knowles. The southpaw believes that once the Andrews incident occurred, Williams started managing more by the book than in the past. "I don't think he cared. . . . No, he cared, but I don't think it mattered that he knew that it didn't matter to me whether I threw every day or not. But the more I threw, it seemed the better I was."

Knowles struck out Staub on three pitches. Then, as if the manager stepped from the future where such bullpen moves became common, Williams walked to the mound and took the ball from the pitcher who had just gotten the biggest out of the game. Right-hander Rollie Fingers came in and got Cleon Jones to fly out to maintain the 2–1 lead.

Another hit by Jackson turned into three bases when Don Hahn let the ball get by him. McGraw, pitching in his fifth game of the series, finally looked fatigued, allowing a walk and a sacrifice fly to plate an insurance run that the Mets could ill afford. New York went quietly in the ninth, and the World Series was tied. The A's had turned it on when they needed to. Again. Facing the best pitcher in the National League, they found a way to win. The advantage was theirs. "Now that we've beaten Seaver," Williams recalled years later, "I thought we've won it all."

Time created the fable of what might have been, in an alternate universe, with George Stone on the mound, beginning with a long, cold, dark winter in the midst of an energy crisis. After the game ended and the crowd dispersed, neither the Mets contingent in Oakland nor the newspapers back in New York cried out, second-guessing Berra for not pitching Stone in Game Six and giving Seaver an extra day. Outrage of a completely different kind filled this particular Saturday night.

Elton John's single from the newly released *Goodbye Yellow Brick Road* intoned that "Saturday Night's Alright for Fighting," but this particular evening was a massacre. News reports just before 8:30 p.m., Eastern Time, announced that Attorney General Eliot Richardson resigned for refusing to fire Watergate special prosecutor Archibald Cox. President Nixon considered the information requested on the Watergate tapes to be privileged, so he met with Richardson to ask him to fire Cox and abolish the office of special prosecutor. Richardson had hired Cox, a respected Harvard law professor who had worked in the Kennedy justice department—his background all the better, Richardson had reasoned, to assure that Cox could resist accusations of being in Nixon's pocket. Now the president wanted to fire the special prosecutor for that very reason.

Richardson felt that complying with the president conflicted with the promise he had made to the Senate, so he resigned just 10 days after arranging to accept Vice President Spiro Agnew's resignation in exchange for not indicting him on tax evasion charges for accepting bribes as governor of Maryland. House minority leader Gerald Ford was nominated as vice president—the first time that the vice presidential vacancy clause of the Twenty-Fifth Amendment had been used—the same day that Nixon ordered Richardson to fire Cox. Ford's approval process in the House and Senate took until early December to complete.

With Richardson's resignation in hand, Nixon went down the line to Assistant Attorney General William Ruckelshaus to have him dismiss Cox. Ruckelhaus refused and was fired—though he claimed to have resigned. The president finally found a willing henchman in Solicitor General Robert Bork, who sent a two-paragraph letter dismissing Cox and signing it "acting attorney general." FBI agents then sealed Richardson's and Ruckelhaus's offices so that nothing could be taken out. Richardson, who had held several other posts in the Nixon administration, had taken the attorney general post on the same day in May that the televised Watergate hearings began. AG Richard Kleindienst had resigned as well because of his close association with people involved in the Watergate scandal.

"The country tonight is in the midst of what may be the most serious Constitutional crisis in its history," began NBC anchorman John Chancellor. After summing up the events, he reported, almost incredulously, "Nothing like this has ever happened before." More than 50,000 telegrams—Western Union still the fastest way for most Americans to communicate in writing in 1973—swarmed Capitol Hill. Most of the messages had a single word in common: "Impeach." Stop.

October 20, 1973, formed a breaking point for many who already had had enough of Nixon's bullying tactics, trail of deceit, and abuse of privilege. This Saturday nightmare quickly became known as the Saturday Night Massacre. The *Washington Post* called it "the most traumatic government upheaval of the Watergate crisis." Given all that had happened since the *Post* broke the Watergate story more than a year earlier, it was quite a statement. Calls for impeachment grew in Washington, even as Nixon tried to do damage control by appointing another special prosecutor. The public's suggestive response graced car bumpers all over the country: IMPEACH THE COX-SACKER.

With everything going on in Washington, the Middle East, Southeast Asia, and elsewhere, a ballgame may have lacked worldly importance, but, given the game's constancy in a sea of ever-changing turmoil, the game must go on—especially with the championship of the world to be decided.

Unlike the first game of the World Series, when several thousand seats went wanting, the Oakland Coliseum was packed for Game Seven. So was the A's bullpen, stuffed with seven mostly jacketed pitchers, both starters and relievers, waiting for the game to begin. The Watergate crisis would, alas, go on, but baseball was ending today.

The pitching matchup repeated Game One and Game Four: lefties Jon Matlack vs. Ken Holtzman. The teams had split the first two games against each other, with Matlack having the better of it. In fact, since losing a 1–0 game to the Cubs in his final start of the season, Matlack hadn't allowed an earned run in 25⅓ innings and only one earned run in his last 42. Broadcaster Monte Moore, perhaps echoing Chic Anderson's stirring call of Secretariat's record romp that spring at Belmont for the Triple Crown, said Matlack was "like a machine out there." The machine was about to throw a rod.

As was the case in Game One, Matlack's downfall began with the opposing pitcher at the plate. After pulling a ball just wide of the left field foul line, Ken Holtzman smacked the next pitch on the high side of the line for his second double of the series. In two official at-bats, he now had twice the number of two-base hits that American League pitchers combined for during the 1973 season—Milwaukee's Eduardo Rodriguez being the only AL pitcher to collect an extra-base hit in the first year of the designated hitter. With a runner on second, Bert Campaneris concentrated on hitting the ball to right field, where Rusty Staub was playing with that separated shoulder.

"I can get a base hit to right field [and] Ken Holtzman can score easily because Rusty Staub can hardly throw," explains Campaneris. "When I get to home plate, I said to myself *I'll hit this thing to right field*. I got lucky, he gave me a hanging curve, and . . . I hit the ball hard. As soon as I saw Rusty Staub's [back], I knew I hit it over his head, and when I got to first base I saw the ball land in the bleachers."

"I was definitely surprised," Matlack says of Campy's home run. "He hit a good pitch and took advantage of the elements and did what he had to do in that circumstance. I tip my cap to him. The ball that Reggie hit, on the other hand . . . When it came out of my hand, I said, 'Oh, shit.'" Every Mets fan said the same thing.

In a sequence of a dozen pitches, the A's scored four times and clubbed two home runs after going the first 61⅓ innings and 218 batters of the World

Series without one. Jackson's titanic blast—with Joe Rudi aboard—landed in the walkway between the stands in distant right-center. Admiring his blast and smiling as he circled the bases, Jackson landed with a stomp on home plate that not only signaled the A's as a dynasty but the birth of Mr. October.

"You knew right then, in the third inning, it was over," says Bob Heussler, removed from the Shea left field loge, and watching from his dorm room in Bridgeport. "You knew this was literally the crowning blow—as only Reggie could deliver. If someone else in that lineup hits that home run, like Sal Bando, it doesn't have the same flourish. Even if it makes the score 4–0, or whatever, it doesn't have the same feeling. But when Jackson did it and then stomped on home plate, you were like, 'Damnit, we're not going to do this.'"

At the Coliseum, a far different feeling prevailed. The outs clicked down. Dick Williams played it close to the vest by conventional 1970s standards, inserting center fielder Vic Davalillo into the lineup for defense in the third inning and moving Jackson to right field. Joe Rudi added an RBI-single to make it 5–0 in the fifth, but when Felix Millan and Rusty Staub collected back-to-back doubles in the top of the sixth, Williams bounded out of the dugout and brought in Fingers to extinguish the threat. George Stone finally entered the scene, pitching the last two innings of mop-up and—adding fuel to the fire of hindsight—fanned Rudi, Bando, and Jackson in a row. But it was just killing time until the ninth.

With Fingers still on the mound, Ray Fosse now catching, and Gene Tenace, who tied Babe Ruth's 1926 mark with 11 walks in a World Series, at first base, John Milner opened the ninth by drawing a walk. Don Hahn collected a one-out single. A slow grounder moved both runners up a base, and, with left-handed swinging Ed Kranepool up and one out to go, Williams resisted the urge to bring in lefty Darold Knowles, the manager not knowing—or caring—that it would have marked the first time a pitcher appeared in all seven games in a World Series.

But when Tenace booted Kranepool's grounder, a run scored, and the tying run came to the plate, Knowles was summoned. History would have been made either way since Fingers—who wound up getting the last out for the 1972 and 1974 world championships—would have been on the mound for three straight World Series clinchers, a feat subsequently accomplished only by Yankee Mariano Rivera (1998–2000). The Hall of Fame reliever dismisses the distinction as you would expect of any Swingin' A: "When you got a World Series ring, you don't want to complain about that."

There was a final out to get and a final second guess. With the southpaw in and the left-hitting Garrett due up as the tying run, some have hedged that the Say Hey Kid, with his 660 home runs, should have had a shot to tie the game with one swing or at least keep it going. Author, MLB historian, and Mets fan John Thorn was pulling for the kind of ending he'd read in dime store baseball fiction as a boy. "Everyone who watched it, including me, was thinking that very same thing—why not Mays? It's a storybook ending. He succeeds or he doesn't, but you want him there."

Yogi Berra didn't want him, though. His Baltimore chop and dribbler produced runs at fortunate times during October, but his stumbles in the outfield trumped memories of Mays the Giants superstar. It was Garrett, often platooned or passed over in pursuit of a "name" third baseman, who might cost an Amos Otis or a Nolan Ryan. But Garrett had as many home runs in the World Series as the whole Oakland roster. Besides, many of Mays's teammates considered the old man done and not worth the risk with the series on the line. Rusty Staub came up with Houston in the early 1960s, when Mays was at his peak. "Willie Mays was as good as there was," Staub says, but his 1973 teammate was a 24th man, not immortal number 24. "The end result was at that time, he was finished. His career was over." Garrett obviously agrees with his manager's decision. "I had played every inning of every game," he says. "He [Yogi] made a decision three months prior to that, and he lived with it through the whole season, even through the series. Again, if I had hit a home run, I would have tied the game. . . . I hit a couple of home runs prior to that in that Series, so who knows what could have happened? It's easy for people to second guess. I think Yogi made the right decision at the time."

Just as the World Series began with Garrett skying to the infield, it ended the same way. Campaneris, Oakland's sparkplug who'd seemingly played a part in every positive development for the A's in this series of sharp turns, squeezed it for the out. The terms "small market" and "big market" didn't exist in baseball speak in 1973; it was far simpler: The favored team had beaten the underdog, Oakland over NYC as expected. The A's were champions again, piling together near the mound as fans whizzed by and took positions on the field in search of mayhem. The field was theirs. For their part, the A's needed to return to the clubhouse stage so the drama's final scene could unfold.

⚾ ⚾ ⚾

It hadn't taken long for A's players to pass on anonymously that their manager was resigning. By Sunday, it was a known fact even though Williams, true to his word, denied the speculation. In the locker room, as champagne corks flew, details about Williams's dissatisfaction with his owner came to the fore. Williams had told Rudi, Bando, and Jackson in September that he was quitting, the manager admitting that originally he had made up his mind about the time of his emergency appendectomy just before the All-Star break. Unfortunately for him, that was after Charlie Finley had extended his contract through 1975.

Williams resigned in front of the TV cameras and even credited his boss for engineering the trades that helped the club repeat as champions, but, with the cameras still rolling, Finley said, "I told Dick two things: One, I'd like to keep you with me. Two, should you prefer to go to the Yankees if you're offered the Yankees job, I won't stand in your way."

After three years and three Octobers with Charlie Finley, Dick Williams well knew that promising and delivering often got lost before meeting.

Sport magazine named Reggie Jackson World Series MVP, a bit of a surprise given how Bert Campaneris collected the game-winning RBI in two games and scored the deciding run in another. Though Jackson's late surge pushed his average to .310 against the Mets—to Campy's .290—the shortstop scored a series-best six runs and stole the only three bases of the series. Some have said the MVP vote went to Jackson because he would draw a bigger crowd to the awards luncheon and be a better interview.

San Francisco Chronicle columnist Art Spander, in the press box but without a vote, has often wondered about the politics that resulted in Campy being bypassed. "I'm sure the TV people wanted somebody who would come across better," says Spander. "That's been one of the great complaints over the years by the Latin players . . . not as bad now because most of them are given English lessons before they come here, or they learn well enough. . . . I've read stories that they [Latinos] feel they get passed over in a lot of situations because they're not a good representative, or their English is poor. I did not vote, but knowing what I know in going back 40 years, 39 years, I'm sure that the country was a lot different."

Campy's recognition came later at the New York Baseball Writers Dinner over the winter, when the Babe Ruth Award—the original but overshadowed award for World Series excellence—was handed out. It wasn't the same. "In '73, I hoped to be the MVP," Campy concedes, though he admits that Jackson "hit really good, too." For someone who had received death threats and traveled around with a bodyguard during the World Series, Jackson looked happy indeed posing next to his new car from *Sport*. His MVP selection may not have seemed fair to all, but it did fall along party lines. As longtime National League home run champ turned Mets broadcaster Ralph Kiner liked to say: Singles hitters drive Fords, and home run hitters drive Cadillacs. Or in this case, a Dodge Charger.

There would be real fights in the A's locker room—in fact, Reggie Jackson and pitcher Blue Moon Odom got into one at a restaurant during a celebration the night they won the '73 title. Fighting, Finley, family—it went hand in hand for the A's. Some teams can't pull off wearing green and yellow with white shoes, but others look like world beaters in that ensemble.

Without 1973 the A's stand as one of several teams with two world championships in three years. Nice, but no dynasty. The '73 title formed the linchpin for the A's trifecta, an achievement few of the players involved go more than a day without thinking about—or being reminded of. Many of the now gray A's don't seem to mind being congratulated out of the blue for accomplishing something unique watched by millions, including—rare

AUTHOR PHOTO

today indeed—kids who saw it live on TV as the A's jumped up and down in the late day sun, becoming the first team in history to win the deciding game in four consecutive postseason series in 1972–73.

The kids would have to stay up later to catch number three in '74, but Fort Knox gold is easy to see at night. Now those kids themselves are graying, balding, and, yes, sometimes mustachioed, when they smile and shake the old ballplayers' hands at reunions, golf outings, business meetings, card shows, and even ballgames. As long as people are respectful, they usually get a smile back.

Wouldn't you smile, too?

Ralph Houk escaped New York for Detroit in managerial musical chairs. The Yankees were caught flat-footed when the music stopped. NATIONAL BASEBALL HALL OF FAME LIBRARY, COOPERSTOWN, NY

Epilogue

AFTERMATH

*H*e liked no part of being second banana—not in New York, not in Flushing.

The December 13 press reception to announce the next manager of the New York Yankees was first class all the way. And what a view! Looking northeast from the 120-foot-high perch of Feathers in the Park Restaurant in Flushing Meadows offered a splendid view of the World's Fair Grounds, the Unisphere, the US Open Tennis Center, and Shea Stadium, home of the National League champion Mets and the fourth-place Yankees.

George Steinbrenner was damned if he was going to let red tape get in the way of hiring his manager of choice, the man who could—*would*—lead his new club back to its previous glory. It so happened that this manager was the only one able to stop the 1973 Mets.

Some of the game's greatest managers had gone against the Mets in September and October 1973—Montreal's Gene Mauch, St. Louis's Red Schoendienst, Pittsburgh's Danny Murtaugh, and Cincinnati's Sparky Anderson—but only Oakland's Dick Williams had stopped them, and he had come from behind to do it.

Williams was the best available manager, and Steinbrenner was willing to pay him like it: $90,000 per year for three years, $20,000 more than he was getting in Oakland. Dick Williams said yes to the Yankees. Charlie Finley said no. As much as Commissioner Kuhn loved to overrule the A's owner, he couldn't do anything about it. Sure, Kuhn had fined Finley in the days after the World Series: $1,000 for violating rules and turning on the stadium lights prematurely; $1,000 for his P.A. announcement about Manny Trillo not being allowed on the World Series roster, a small incident that in retrospect became the opening salvo to the Andrews Affair; and that imbroglio, which cost Finley a $5,000 fine. But it wasn't Kuhn's place to rule on Williams. That task fell to the league president.

Joe Cronin knew about managerial compensation. When Cronin served as player-manager of the Washington Senators in 1933, his father-in-law,

Senators owner Clark Griffith, sold him to the Red Sox for $225,000 of Tom Yawkey's fortune. The money kept Griffith's Senators afloat during the Depression, and Yawkey kept Cronin as manager after he could no longer play, made him general manager when he tired of the bench, and then patted Cronin on the back when he became the first player elected to the league presidency in 1959.

Cronin, who turned 67 during the 1973 World Series, made two weighty decisions in his final days in office, and both went against the Yankees. He denied the Yankees' plea for compensation after the Tigers hired Ralph Houk; New York accepted the manager's resignation and didn't ask for compensation at the time he signed with Detroit. Since Charlie Finley didn't formally accept Dick Williams's resignation in writing (accepting on TV wasn't binding), the Yankees couldn't sign the former A's manager. The Yankees were shocked. Williams, in case he hadn't made himself clear earlier, reiterated his position: "There is no way I'm going back to manage in Oakland."

The Yankees offered Finley a choice of veterans the team wound up dumping, plus cash, up to $150,000, as compensation for letting his manager out of the last two years of his Oakland contract. When he scoffed at New York's offer, the Yankees switched to two minor leaguers instead, plus the money. As owner of the two-time world champs, Finley had no desire for players who didn't fit the A's current plans. He wanted New York's top prospects. The Yankees refused to part with the likes of Scott McGregor and Otto Velez. The two sides stood at a standstill.

So why had the Yankees persisted on hiring Williams, agreeing to a contract, arranging for such an elaborate introduction, and even bringing in shrimp at a dollar a pop? "They spent money to bring the press out to this fancy restaurant in Queens," explains Phil Pepe, who covered the Yankees for the *New York Daily News*. "They were convinced that this would go through. Everyone was surprised when it didn't go through. Oakland had nothing to gain by holding the Yankees up to get the players that they wanted. They would have been better off getting what they could and letting Williams leave. But because of the personalities, Finley being who he was and Steinbrenner being who he was, these two guys not liking one another [tried] to one up one another. . . . That caused that roadblock." Three strikes and you're out. Literally.

It made a humiliating end to a year that had begun with the fulfillment of Steinbrenner's dream of owning a big-time professional team. First his Yankees, picked by Las Vegas oddsmakers to win the AL East in

1973 and looking like a good bet to do so in July, fell from first place to fourth in August. In November, a month before the Dick Williams decision by the American League, two American Shipbuilding employees had testified to the Watergate Committee regarding sham bonuses directed to the Republican Party by Steinbrenner. (The Boss was indicted and finally entered a guilty plea in August 1974, the same month that Nixon resigned as president; Steinbrenner was later fined in US District Court, suspended from baseball, and, like Nixon, eventually pardoned.) After Steinbrenner lost Dick Williams in the tug-of-war with Finley, the Yankees settled for Bill Virdon, fired by the Pirates in September with his team in the thick of the NL East race. On January 3, 1974, the first anniversary of the press conference announcing the sale of the Yankees, Virdon's hiring was announced at the Yankees group sales office in Flushing, located in the nondescript Parks Administration Building—no view, no shrimp, no Feathers.

"He was a guy who was a fallback," Pepe says of Virdon. "Williams was the perfect guy for him [Steinbrenner] at the time. Billy Martin already was working [in Texas]. But he felt that Williams was available and had a good track record. He had won championships, he had that personality that Steinbrenner was attracted to, and he was the logical guy for him to hire. When he couldn't do that, he was stuck, and he had nowhere else to turn. He just let the baseball people suggest somebody, and he accepted Bill Virdon. . . . It was late in the game. All of the top-flight managers, all of the marquee guys were all taken by other teams."

On top of everything else, his team had to serve what seemed like two years of hard labor as second-class citizens in a ballpark that Steinbrenner didn't think worthy of the Yankees. Yet Steinbrenner was still operating in the biggest market in the country, and he learned how to get things done in baseball, even during his suspension, which began after the 1974 season. The shipbuilding owner became pals with another neophyte owner, who had a capacity for manufacturing compromises while working the system, a car salesman from Milwaukee named Bud Selig, who made the ultimate trade-in during the 1990s: the beat-up Brewers ownership for the commissioner package with plenty of horsepower.

It took suspensions by two different commissioners (neither an ex-owner)—sandwiched around Yankees world championships in 1977 and 1978—for Steinbrenner to emerge with a team ready to win *every* year, the expanded playoffs in the 1990s virtually assuring the team with the biggest payroll an annual date in October. A potential 19 extra nights of national prime time exposure pushed ticket sales, the brand, and the message. Even in years when the Yankees fell before reaching the World Series, announcers still talked about Steinbrenner's club more often than any of the other 28 teams that weren't playing. How's that for victory even in defeat?

The team drew three million people every year during its last decade at renovated Yankee Stadium, including four million each of the last four seasons. The club moved into a sparkling billion-dollar palace in 2009, the same year that the Mets got a new ballpark as well. The Yankees won the World Series that year, one more for the ailing old man in the owner's box, whose health made him as scarce and as quiet as he'd been in his 37 seasons as owner. The team was safe in the hands of the Steinbrenner offspring. George, 80, died the day of the All-Star Game the following year, the talk of the game and still the reigning world champion.

Seven world championships, 17 division titles, and even three Wild Cards—solely an NFL term in 1973—surpassed Steinbrenner's faults of ego, bombast, and mistreatment of employees (from firing Billy Martin five times to dismissing minions randomly for petty infractions). Many saw Steinbrenner's methods as what it took to win in New York. The markets, relatively even when he'd bought the team in 1973, now tilted heavily toward those with the largest revenue streams. It was good to be the Boss.

⚾ ⚾ ⚾

Charlie Finley allowed California Angels owner Gene Autry to hire Dick Williams just in time for the 1974 All-Star Game, managing the American League squad while wearing a different "A" on his cap. (Nolan Ryan, now his stud starter with the Angels, was left off the team, but six A's played in the game in Pittsburgh.) Alvin Dark, in his second stint managing the A's, guided Oakland to its third straight World Series title. Bill Virdon nearly captured a division title for the '74 Yankees, but the Orioles swept their final series of the year against Ralph Houk's last-place Tigers and won by two games. Virdon was named Manager of the Year by the *Sporting News*, the first Yankee so honored since Houk in his first year managing the team in 1961.

Yet the cerebral, quiet Virdon wasn't Steinbrenner's kind of manager, and his players weren't fond of him, either. The still-suspended Steinbrenner managed to manipulate the strings enough to bring in Billy Martin, finally introducing him to the public as manager at Old-Timers Day at Shea in

1975. Kuhn turned a blind eye to his orchestrations from exile, not questioning how the Yankees came up with the record sum of $3.75 million for Finley's prized pitcher, Catfish Hunter, made a free agent because of a missed insurance payment in 1974.

Kuhn continued to rein Finley in, though the coming of free agency declawed his baseball empire built from the ground up. After nine straight winning seasons, including five straight division titles, the A's averaged almost 100 losses per year and 5,500 fans per game from 1977 to '79. The commissioner refused to let Finley sell off his players before they all walked away as free agents, so by the end of the 1970s the team built for the decade had the worst record in the game. The 1979 A's drew just 306,763, far lower than even the worst season by the Kansas City A's and the lowest by any team since the soon-to-relocate Boston Braves of 1952. Their 108 losses were the most by an A's club since 1916, when the world champions had been broken up by manager and owner Connie Mack (who didn't have a commissioner to deal with then).

After a sudden resurgence by the A's, orchestrated by new manager Billy Martin, Finley sold the club in 1980. Living alone in the LaPorte house bought for his parents—the bigger LaPorte homestead had sold following his divorce—he lived out his days quietly. Well, quietly for Charlie Finley. He died in Indiana in 1996 and was buried on what would have been his 78th birthday. Reggie Jackson and Catfish Hunter, among others, spoke at his funeral.

⚾ ⚾ ⚾

The fall of the Mets came relatively quickly yet unmercifully. They made no major trade after the 1973 season, seeming to believe that lightning in a bottle was always on the menu rather than an exceptionally infrequent special. With the 1974 Mets in fifth place in late August, not many more games behind where they'd been at the same time in 1973, the team won 10 of 11 games and barely budged in the standings. The Pirates captured the division while the Mets finished with 91 losses. After sharing Shea for two years and outdrawing, though not outplaying, the Yankees both years, the Mets reached a level of irrelevance that had never existed for them previously. Even during their ongoing comedy routine for much of the early, mid, and late 1960s, the Mets had a level of panache that the New Breed and everyman found, at least for a while, somewhat invigorating. Now, in a sagging city, in post-Watergate America, in a dire economy, there wasn't much to believe in or even get excited about with the Mets.

The Yankees took the city back the week that the new Yankee Stadium opened in 1976, running away with the division title and claiming the first of three straight pennants. The Mets put together their second-best season in terms of wins in 1976. Their 86 victories were four more than the '73 pennant winners, but the Mets were old news in what was becoming an old stadium. Shea housed four teams in 1975—the tenant Mets and Jets, plus the Yankees and vagabond football Giants—and the ballpark seemed to age before its time.

A few Mets suffered that same fate, but the era ended irrevocably when the team's pitching core, the triumvirate of Seaver, Matlack, and Koosman, were all traded in an 18-month span starting in June 1977, joining exiled Tug McGraw and Rusty Staub, dispatched earlier. "Look at some of the deals they made. They were horrendous," says last original Met Ed Kranepool, spared the trade from his native city but left to finish his career on some of the most dispirited clubs in the team's—or his—tenure. "They unloaded everybody and didn't make a good deal."

The death of Joan Payson in 1975 left no one to check M. Donald Grant's power. Whitey Herzog had been right: Grant didn't know anything about baseball. As Herzog managed the Royals to three straight division titles (losing to the Yankees each time), the Mets sank deeper into the abyss. Grant forced the Seaver trade, and the men he'd advanced instead of Herzog in the front office ran the Mets into the ground. Grant was relieved of his duties as board chairman in 1978, but by then the damage had been done. The 1979 Mets had the lowest attendance in franchise history over a full season: 788,905, and their average crowd of 9,621 ranked worse than every team in the majors that year, except Oakland.

Kelly green and Fort Knox gold tops fell out of fashion. No 82-win team again reached the World Series (barring strikes), and two different men surpassed Babe Ruth's 714 home runs, but one constant that has remained in baseball since 1973 is the designated hitter. Avid supporters of the game—purists, and Mets broadcaster Howie Rose among their most vociferous devotees—still decry the DH and lobby for the rule's banishment. But four decades after its inception, the designated hitter has a better chance of becoming the rule in both leagues than it does of being eradicated. The DH is its own institution. It offers the slow of foot or lead of glove a chance to keep playing (to please the fans), pays far more than a utility player makes (to satisfy the Players Association), and keeps the game more offensively oriented (to please the owners).

Charlie Finley and George Steinbrenner are gone, as are Joan Payson and M. Donald Grant (since 1998), and many of the stars of the '70s—at least those still with us—are now at or approaching their 70s. AstroTurf has all but been eliminated in the major leagues, and cozy yet convoluted jewels harken back to the parks razed to make way for multi-sport stadiums in the first place. The Yankee Stadium of Babe Ruth and Mickey Mantle wasn't that of Reggie Jackson and Derek Jeter, nor is it the one housing C. C. Sabathia and Robinson Cano.

All things change—even in baseball, especially in baseball—yet teams that hover near the bottom of the pack can point to an October back in '73 when belief pushed crumbling New York to the brink of something miraculous at a time when most news tended toward the bad. But a bunch of guys from California with mustaches, bright shirts, and white shoes, who held a grudge against their boss, spoiled the fairytale ending—and made a dynasty in the process.

The A's crowd around their 1972 trophy 40 years later (from left): Joe Rudi, Mike Hegan, Gene Tenace, Vida Blue, Tim Cullen, Bert Campaneris, Bob Locker, and Darold Knowles. AUTHOR PHOTO

After '73

PLAYERS AND MANAGERS

NEW YORK METS

The coach who took **Lawrence Peter "Yogi" Berra**'s former spot on the staff in 1973, Roy McMillan, eventually took Berra's place as manager after he was fired in 1975 in the wake of a Cleon Jones standoff and a midsummer Mets malaise. Berra wound up back with the Yankees under former teammate Billy Martin. As he did with the Mets, Berra spent several years as coach before managing again. His time in the manager's chair under George Steinbrenner proved frustratingly short. His 87 wins in 1984 represented Berra's highest win total as a manager since his rookie year as a skipper in 1964, when he was dismissed after winning the pennant and losing a seven-game World Series. This time, he made it to his second year as manager, but Steinbrenner fired him after just 16 games in 1988, creating a split between Berra and the Yankees that lasted until a public healing with Steinbrenner in 1998 at the Yogi Berra Museum at Montclair State College in Yogi's adopted home state of New Jersey.

Lee William "Buzz" Capra picked up his nickname as a kid because the energy he expended swinging a bat was like a buzzsaw. Buzz's last action with the Mets was the Pete Rose–Bud Harrelson fight in the 1973 NLCS. Sold to the Braves the following spring training, he sat in the Atlanta bullpen next to Tom House, who caught Hank Aaron's record-breaking 715th home run that April. Nineteen seventy-four became the year of Buzz's life: He made the All-Star team and won the National League ERA crown. After arm injuries prematurely ended his career, Capra spent several years coaching in the minor leagues with the Braves, Phillies, and Mets. Though no longer in organized baseball, he still works with young pitchers outside his native Chicago, and he faithfully attends Mets fantasy camp.

The hat that Pedro Borbon tore with his teeth during the Rose-Harrelson fight? "I pinned it together with baby pins—just to keep it." He has turned down many offers for the hat and plans to give it to his grandson.

The third week of October 1973 was a tough one for **Ronald Wayne Garrett.** After making the last out of the World Series, he stopped in Tennessee to check out a housing development for a friend. While riding a horse on the unpaved roads, Garrett landed on his right shoulder after his mount slipped. "I didn't know it until a month before spring training when

I started working out and I couldn't throw," he says. Garrett worked through his sore shoulder, but the soreness lasted longer each year until he was with the Expos. Their staff helped rehab his whole body. His major league career ended in 1978 in St. Louis, and he spent three years in Japan. He went into real estate in his native Florida and then into business selling irrigation equipment to golf courses with his older brother Adrian, who also played in the majors.

Derrell McKinley "Bud" Harrelson is best remembered for taking on Pete Rose—and losing—during the 1973 NLCS. He hit .250 with a .379 on-base percentage against the A's in the World Series, the only postseason series in which he was on the losing side. Traded to the Phillies in 1978 after 13 years as a Met, he spent 1979 as a player beside Rose, though they had long ago patched up their differences. The pair has since done many card shows and signings together. Harrelson worked as a Mets announcer and then as a coach. He served on Davey Johnson's staff and replaced him as Mets manager in 1990. Harrelson remains in baseball as part owner of the independent Long Island Ducks.

The best moments of **Ron Hodges**'s career came as a rookie in 1973. Never again would he take part in a pennant race or play in the postseason, but he spent a dozen years in Flushing. Only Ed Kranepool, John Franco, and Bud Harrelson logged more seasons as Mets. The perennial backup catcher—"a Virginia gentleman" in the words of announcer Bob Murphy— went into real estate after leaving baseball in 1984. He is a member of the Salem-Roanoke Hall of Fame.

"Steady Eddie" Kranepool was a Mets fixture for the first 18 seasons of the team's existence. No Met has approached his length of service. He never accepted the bench player role of the latter part of his career and took it more as a challenge. "I would rather have guys like that who wanted to play every day, pushing the other guys, rather than the guys who are happy to sit on the bench every day and collect a paycheck," he says. Krane certainly pushed, batting .277 in his career as a pinch hitter—including an unequalled major league mark of .477 in 35 at bats in 1974. He collected 90 career hits off the bench, one of the many club records he still holds.

Though signed by the fledgling Mets out of Manhattan's James Monroe High School at age 16, Kranepool had an acumen for finance and business and worked in that field while a player. He even belonged to a group seeking to purchase the Mets, making a presentation near the time he was taking his final at-bat in 1979. His group didn't get the bid, but Kranepool's status as a born-and-bred New Yorker—and New York Met—has resulted in countless appearances, both official and unofficial. Like 1973 Mets teammates Jerry Grote, Bud Harrelson, Cleon Jones, Jerry Koosman, Tug McGraw, Tom Seaver, and Rusty Staub, he is a member of the Mets Hall of Fame.

Though overshadowed by Tom Seaver early in his career and by fellow southpaw Jon Matlack in the mid-1970s, **Jerry Koosman** holds the title as the best left-hander in Mets history and owns most of the club records by a southpaw. Even on a team with a pitching-rich history, no Mets triumvirate has ever come close to Seaver-Matlack-Koosman. While the other two were traded, Kooz stayed around—unfortunately for him. In 1977, he became the last major league pitcher to lose 20 after winning 20 the previous season. He was stiffed with the unfortunate franchise record for most losses (137). Kooz threatened to quit if he wasn't traded to his native Minnesota, where he won 20 in 1979. He retired as a Phillie at 40 with 222 major league wins, and served as a Mets pitching coach in the minors. He went into machine design, but failure to pay income taxes resulted in a six-month prison term in 2010. The genial lefty came to Citi Field in 2012 to congratulate R. A. Dickey after he broke Kooz's 1973 mark for consecutive scoreless innings.

"Imagine having the future of this kid," NBC broadcaster Curt Gowdy wondered with 23-year-old **Jon Matlack** on the mound early in Game Seven of the 1973 World Series. Despite a long and meritorious pitching career, that day marked the big lefty's last appearance in the postseason. Matlack led the National League in shutouts as a Met in 1974 and again two years later. Wins Above Replacement, a rating stat, was totally unheard of in Matlack's day, but his "WAR" in '74 translates as the league's best among pitchers. The numbers that counted in his time, however, read 14-16, a losing record on a losing club. The 1976 Mets won 85 games but never contended despite the lowest team ERA (2.94) on a staff that *Sports Illustrated* called "decidedly the best in the majors." He voiced his frustration over the team's failure to upgrade the offense or defense.

After the worst year of his career and the worst season by the Mets in a decade, he was traded with John Milner in a four-team trade in December 1977. Matlack experienced the same tough luck with the Texas Rangers as he had in New York, and the best of his six years in Texas was just a 15-13 record despite a career-low 2.27 ERA. Matlack plied the pitching craft he knew so well after his playing days ended. He served as a pitching coach, scout, and supervisor in various capacities for the Padres, White Sox, and Tigers. In late 2011 the Astros hired him as minor league pitching coordinator.

Willie Mays, the Say Hey Kid, remained in a Mets uniform through the end of the 1970s as a coach, as the club had promised Horace Stoneham. Commissioner Bowie Kuhn ended this arrangement, insisting that Mays either relinquish his position with the Mets or as a greeter at Bally's Casino in Atlantic City. Mays, inducted into the Hall of Fame that year, decided on the former. Commissioner Peter Ueberroth later reinstated him, as he did Mickey Mantle, also in the same boat. Mays got back into baseball in the employ of the Giants, helping godson Barry Bonds. Though Mays's time with the Mets was too short to justify putting him in the team's Hall of Fame, issuing his number 24 in 1990 created such rancor among fans that no Met has worn it since, except Rickey Henderson, who received Mays's blessing.

Frank Edwin "Tug" McGraw earned his nickname as an infant for the effort he put into breastfeeding. His iconoclast older brother Hank was a catcher in the Mets system, but he never made it to New York. Tug only lasted with the Mets one year after he pushed the club from the abyss into October. In 1974, neither Tug nor the Mets had a late-season rebound in them, and the front office, skeptical as to the condition of McGraw's left shoulder, traded him, along with Dave Schneck and '73 teammate Don Hahn, to the Phillies for John Stearns, Mac Scarce, and Del Unser. The Phillies, who didn't even know about McGraw's balky shoulder at the time of the trade, had McGraw undergo a simple surgery, and he again became one of the game's top relievers.

A 1973-esque finish for McGraw led the Phillies to their first world championship in 1980. McGraw retired four years later and did everything from sportscasting to creating a syndicated cartoon, *Scroogie*, named after his signature pitch. He reluctantly accepted Tim McGraw, the result of a premarital affair, and helped him get the record contract that launched the country music legend. Tug and Tim became very close, and the father died in the son's Tennessee cabin after succumbing to a brain tumor at age 59 in January 2004. The sleeve of the Mets uniform that year featured Tug's name and three simple words: "Ya Gotta Believe."

John "The Hammer" Milner was one of the few power hitters developed by the Mets between the late 1960s and mid-1980s. Milner's legacy, however, wasn't his power or even for starting the double play that resulted in the 1973 Pete Rose–Bud Harrelson fight. It was in Pittsburgh, where he'd been sent in a December 1977 trade and won his only World Series two years later. While testifying at the Pittsburgh Drug Trials in 1985, Milner stated that he received amphetamines from Willie Mays as a Met, an assertion Mays denied. As *Willie Mays* author Paul Hirsch wrote, "It would be naive to think that Mays never took amphetamines." The same goes for many players from that era. Let it be said that in the 1970s drugs were experimented with in society and in the locker room, whether to help players "get up" for a game or to relax afterward. An unfortunate casualty of the era, Milner died of cancer at age 50 in 2000.

George Thomas Seaver claimed his second Cy Young Award in 1973, his third in 1975, and his fifth and final strikeout title in 1976, the year he extended his own record with eight straight years of 200 strikeouts. A contract extension that year set in motion ill feelings between Seaver and board chairman M. Donald Grant. When *New York Daily News* columnist Dick Young, a Grant supporter, claimed that good friend Nolan Ryan's contract with the Angels made Nancy Seaver jealous, Seaver called off a contract in the works and demanded a trade. He was sent to Cincinnati on June 15, 1977, for four marginal players—not as bad a deal as the Ryan trade in 1971 but far more devastating.

The Mets didn't emerge from the malaise until 1984. By then, Seaver had been back for a one-year encore in '83 only to be lost to the White Sox in a free agent compensation claim. He won his 300th game for Chicago at renovated Yankee Stadium, of all places. Seaver's last appearance in a major league uniform was at Shea Stadium in the 1986 World Series in the visiting dugout of the Red Sox. "The Franchise" was the first Mets player to have his number retired and be inducted into the National Baseball Hall of Fame with a Mets insignia on his plaque. His percentage of the vote for Cooperstown, 98.84, remains the highest ever. He is a vintner in his native California.

Daniel Joseph "Rusty" Staub was the heart of the Mets lineup, becoming the first Met to drive in 100 runs in a season. He was dealt to Detroit in December 1975 before the newly minted status of 10 years in the majors and five with one team allowed him to veto a trade. The New Orleans–born chef still had a restaurant in New York, and he returned to the Mets as a pinch hitter extraordinaire in 1981. Le Grand Orange retired with 2,716 hits in 1985, working as an announcer and later as a team ambassador. He founded the New York Police and Fire Widows and Children's Benefit Fund in 1986.

George "The Stork" Theodore spent just two years in the majors, but he lives on in Mets lore as one of the team's great characters. Remembered in

New York for slamming into Don Hahn in a horrific collision in 1973 and for his stated fondness for marshmallow milkshakes, he remains a legend in his native Salt Lake City for his work as a school counselor for three decades.

NEW YORK YANKEES

Ron Blomberg didn't know much about the designated hitter rule before he became the first DH in history, achieving lasting fame for being in the right place at the right time. "I screwed up the game," he says jokingly. He batted a career-best .329 in 1973 and was a lifetime .293 hitter, though managers rarely played the lefty-swinger against southpaws—despite hitting .267 against left-handed starters. Injuries kept him from being part of the Yankees when everything turned around in the mid-1970s. The former number one draft pick remains committed to the game, the Yankees, and his Jewish heritage. He plays a key role in the New Jersey YM-YWHA Camp, the largest Jewish sleep-away camp in the country, in Milford, Pennsylvania. He wrote a book with Dan Schlossberg, *Designated Hebrew*, and managed in the Israel Baseball League. A member of the Jewish Hall of Fame, "Boomer" lives in his native Atlanta, where he scouts for the Yankees.

After the 1973 season, **Ralph Houk** took over the retooling Tigers. He managed All-Star starters Mark "The Bird" Fidrych and Rusty Staub in 1976, and two years later he guided the Tigers to their first winning season since '73. Houk retired, soon replaced by Sparky Anderson. The Major returned to manage in Boston in 1981, with three winning seasons out of four, before retiring for good at 65 in '84. A rare feat in the managing trade, Houk was never fired in 21 seasons on the job, leaving each time of his own volition. He worked for the Twins as special assistant to general manager Andy MacPhail, son of his former Yankees GM, Lee MacPhail. Minnesota's 1987 World Series victory provided Houk his first championship association since he won pennants his first three years as manager (1961–63). He died at age 90 in July 2010, a week after George Steinbrenner.

Injured during his ill-fated 1973 season, **Mike Kekich** came back to the majors briefly in 1975 and resurfaced in 1977 with a winning record for the expansion Mariners. He returned to the minors and then pitched in Mexico. He has gone out of his way to stay out of the spotlight, taking a new identity and a new wife—*not* the former Mrs. Peterson—in New Mexico.

Gene "Stick" Michael came from the same part of Ohio as Thurman Munson and, like the Yankees catcher, also attended Kent State. Michael's career as a shortstop ended in 1976, and he joined the Yankees as a coach. He served two brief tenures as Yankees manager—and later spent two years managing the Cubs—but his greatest contribution was to help rebuild the Yankees as general manager and vice president of scouting, developing the team's core of Derek Jeter, Andy Pettitte, Jorge Posada, Bernie Williams, and Mariano Rivera.

Thurman Munson was a great teammate but a tough opponent. A three-time Gold Glove winner and seven-time All-Star, he always raged at the adulation of Boston's Carlton Fisk. He turned his fury on the Big Red Machine during the 1976 World Series, hitting .529, angry that all the attention went to catcher Johnny Bench of the victorious Reds. The Yankees captain was the American League MVP that year. After quarterbacking world champion pitching staffs the next two years, he was filling in at other positions due to his bad knees. He even contemplated one day playing in Cleveland, closer to his family in Ohio. To see them more easily on his days off, he became a pilot. Munson died in a plane crash in 1979. He was 32.

Bobby Murcer, Michael Burke's $100,000 ballplayer with the perfect Yankee Stadium swing, faltered after the team relocated to Shea. He was traded to San Francisco for Bobby Bonds after the 1974 season. While the Yankees went on to win three straight pennants, Murcer struggled as a Giant and Cub. Finally reunited with the Yankees in 1979, he arrived shortly before the tragic death of friend Thurman Munson. Murcer knocked in all five runs in a comeback win over Baltimore on national TV after the team had spent the day at Munson's funeral in Ohio. Murcer finally reached the postseason as a reserve, with one hit over four series in 1980 and 1981. He became a George Steinbrenner favorite, serving as a broadcaster for almost 25 years. He died of a brain tumor at age 62 in 2008.

Fred Ingles "Fritz" Peterson was a workman pitcher masquerading as a flaky lefty until he achieved fame by swapping wives with teammate Mike Kekich. Arm troubles dogged him after a trade to Cleveland in 1974, but his marriage to the former Susanne Kekich remained on firm ground as he moved on to business life after baseball and became a devout Christian. Peterson wrote a memoir with both an athletic and religious bent, *Mickey Mantle Is Going to Heaven.* He is a consultant for a proposed film about the 1973 swap.

The lefty-hitting catcher spent just a week as a 1973 Yankee, but **Duane "Duke" Sims** remains forever in the record books for hitting the last home run at the original Yankee Stadium. He was in such a hurry to get on the bus to the airport and pick up his car at Tiger Stadium in Detroit, though, that he learned well after the fact that Ralph Houk had resigned as Yankees manager following the last game in New York. Sims began 1974 as a Yankee, but his former Tigers manager Billy Martin needed a veteran catcher to help break in young catcher Jim Sundberg in Texas. Sims finished his career as a Ranger and ended up working for owner Brad Corbett, selling plastic water piping during the building boom on the West Coast. He also helped develop an updated version of the early video game, *Pong*, and later worked in financial planning. Sims has lived all over the country but now resides in Las Vegas.

OAKLAND A'S

Released two weeks after his battle with Charlie Finley in the 1973 World Series, **Mike Andrews** played in Japan in 1975. He joined Mass Mutual Life Insurance but left to work full-time for the Jimmy Fund, the Massachusetts-based charity that supports adult and pediatric cancer care. He served as the fund's executive director from 1984 to 2010.

Named captain of the A's by Hank Bauer in 1969 at age 25, **Sal Bando** led Oakland from its rise to power to the exodus of its stars—including himself—after the 1976 season. He went to Milwaukee and later spent eight years as Brewers general manager. He also took over a Wisconsin company that makes collectible dolls. He knew from lifeless entities. "I gave the ballpark the nickname of the Oakland Mausoleum because that's what it looked like," Bando says. "Gray concrete in the outfield, empty seats, big—a lot of foul territory. Not many fans."

Some of Charlie Finley's biggest contract feuds involved **Vida Blue,** yet he stuck around longer than any of the A's All-Stars—by order of Commissioner Bowie Kuhn. Finley tried to sell him to the Yankees for $1.5 million in 1976 only for Kuhn to put the kibosh on the deal. The following year Finley worked out a trade with the Reds for $1.75 million and minor leaguer Dave Revering, and Kuhn killed it again. The third deal finally stuck, sending Blue across the Bay to the Giants for seven players and $300,000 in 1978. That year he became the first pitcher to start the All-Star Game for both leagues. Blue had also started the game in 1971, the year he won the MVP and Cy Young for the A's.

He won 209 games over 17 seasons, but involvement with cocaine in Kansas City resulted in prison time and a year's suspension. After a comeback with San Francisco, he signed with the A's but failed a urine test and chose to retire. Blue turned around by helping turn around the lives of others as commissioner of the "Junior Giants." The program, run by the Giants, provided equipment and accommodations for a youth baseball league for disadvantaged Bay Area children. "For a kid not to have a baseball mitt," Blue said in 2004, "is like not owning a bicycle. It's about being an American."

Dagoberto Campaneris never liked being called Bert, but most opponents called him a pest. Always getting on base and causing havoc, he had 649 career steals. Quiet off the field, the shortstop was loyal—some say too loyal—to Charlie Finley, but he joined everyone else in abandoning ship after the 1976 season. His best years behind him, Campy showed the same tenacity for which he was famous with the A's. He convinced Billy Martin, who wanted to kill him after he threw the bat against Detroit in 1972, to take a chance on him with the Yankees at age 41 in 1983. Campy responded by hitting .322 in part-time work. He remains active in the game in alumni and charity events.

"I'm not just a guy with a crazy mustache, I'm a Hall of Famer with a crazy mustache," pronounced **Roland Glen Fingers** during a 2003 *Late Show with David Letterman* "Top 10" bit. His handlebar mustache is indeed Hall of Fame–caliber facial hair, but Fingers made it to Cooperstown because he dominated like few relievers before or since. In 16 World Series games with Oakland, he had two wins, six saves, and a 1.36 ERA in 33⅓ innings—13⅔ of those innings during the 1973 World Series, when he had a 0.66 ERA. Fingers was MVP of the 1974 World Series. He was an All-Star seven times, including each of his last four seasons with the A's.

He spent four years with the Padres and four more with the Brewers. In 1981, his first year with Milwaukee, Fingers led the team to its first-ever postseason berth and claimed the league's Cy Young and MVP, the first reliever to win both. After he was released at age 38 in 1985, Pete Rose asked Fingers to join the Reds, who had a no facial hair policy. He retired rather than shave. His 341 career saves set the record until Jeff Reardon broke it in 1992, the same year Fingers was inducted into the Hall of Fame. A near scratch golfer, he spent almost a decade on the Celebrity Players Tour. Both the A's and Brewers retired his number 34.

Ken Holtzman passed Sandy Koufax for most wins by a Jewish pitcher with 174, with 77 of those wins, plus four division titles, and three World Series rings, coming during just four years with the A's. He also had as many World Series wins as Koufax (four). Holtzman and Reggie Jackson were both dispatched to Baltimore in 1976, an early version of the popular practice of dumping players before they become free agents. Holtzman was passed on to the Yankees. Holtzman wound up back where he started, at Wrigley Field, playing under Herman Franks and finishing his career as a Cub. The St. Louis native stayed in the Chicago area, working as a stockbroker and in the commercial insurance business. He never pitched on a High Holy Day, and he keeps Kosher.

Charlie Finley's failure to pay an insurance premium as stipulated in **Jim "Catfish" Hunter**'s 1974 contract cost the A's not only the Cy Young winner but the linchpin of their vaunted pitching staff. Nancy Finley, cousin of the A's owner and a front office employee, says of the insurance payment snafu, "Charlie was the kind who would sit on a bill until it was like the due date. . . . I can really see how that happened. I know Jim Hunter did not want to leave." But leave he did. With half of the major league teams coming to his little corner of North Carolina, Hunter decided on the Yankees mainly because their representative, Clyde Kluttz, had scouted him in high school for the A's.

Hunter's five-year, $3.75 million contract was the first free agent contract of its kind. Between the two teams, he had five straight 20-win seasons, five World Series wins, and five rings before retiring in 1979. Unwilling to choose between Finley and Steinbrenner, Hunter chose to have no insignia on his Hall of Fame plaque when inducted in 1987. Suffering from amyotrophic lateral sclerosis (Lou Gehrig's disease), he died after a fall in his home in 1999. He was 53. Since 2004, Oakland has given the Catfish Hunter Award to the A's player who best displays the "competitive and inspirational spirit" exemplified by Hunter. Jonny Gomes won the award in 2012.

Oakland's number 9 appeared on the cover of *Sports Illustrated* nine times (four in an A's uniform). **Reginald Martinez Jackson** was the first of Charlie Finley's K.C. kids to become a star and the first to leave. Sent to Baltimore before he could become a free agent, he signed with New York and hit five home runs in the 1977 World Series to become the first player to be Series MVP with two different teams. Both clubs retired his uniform number (44 with the Yankees). Jackson finished his career with the A's in 1987, retiring the year before Oakland won the first of three more consecutive pennants. Though he spent almost half of his long career with the A's, his Hall of Fame plaque depicts him as a Yankee. Four decades later, the 1973 AL MVP can still make news as he did in a 2012 *Sports Illustrated* article in which he criticized fellow Hall of Famers and current Yankees—for whom he served as special advisor. Jackson has never been afraid to praise himself or criticize others. As '73 teammate Darold Knowles once put it: "There's not enough mustard in the whole world to cover that hot dog."

The 1971 acquisition of **Darold Knowles** and Mike Epstein from the Washington Senators provided new manager Dick Williams with a first baseman as well as a lefty to pair with Rollie Fingers in the bullpen. Ironically, Knowles pitched just one postseason game for the A's other than the 1973 World Series. Williams used him all seven games against the Mets in '73, a feat not duplicated before or since. He struggled the next year and was traded to the Cubs with Bob Locker and Manny Trillo for Billy Williams. After reuniting with Dick Williams in Montreal in 1978, Knowles finished his career with the Cardinals in 1980. The former schoolteacher has been a major and minor league pitching coach and got his own bobblehead day in his seventh year with the Dunedin Blue Jays in 2012.

Bill North lit a fire under the A's already potent lineup and locker room. Losing him to injury nearly sidetracked the A's in October 1973, but they pulled off another world championship. With North atop the lineup in 1974, leading the league in steals—and getting into a memorable confrontation with Reggie Jackson—the A's rolled to another title. He remained with Oakland after all the other October alums. He was traded to the Dodgers in 1978 and then joined Vida Blue in San Francisco the next year. He ended his career with 395 steals and later went into financial planning.

Joe DiMaggio's lessons went a long way toward forging the best left fielder of the day. **Joe Rudi** rebounded from illness and injury in 1973 to become runner-up in the AL MVP voting for the second time in three years in 1974.

An All-Star and Gold Glove winner three times apiece, Rudi was sold to the Red Sox by Charlie Finley in 1976, along with teammate Rollie Fingers, only to be sent back to Oakland by Commissioner Bowie Kuhn. Rudi went to the Angels as a free agent, but injuries limited him to just one more season with 500 plate appearances. He finally played in Boston in 1981 and finished his career with Oakland a year later. An accomplished ham radio operator, "Gentleman Joe" often brought his equipment with him on road trips. He served as an A's batting coach under old friend Tony LaRussa but gave it up after 1987 because he had four kids and a ranch in Oregon. He is a Realtor in Baker City, Oregon.

Dick Williams guided the Red Sox (1967), A's (1972–73), and Padres (1984) to pennants—Bill McKechnie is the only other manager to take three different teams to the World Series. Williams also managed the Angels, Expos, and Mariners. His teams had a record of 1,571-1,451 (.520) over 21 seasons. Old school manager all the way, Williams said that the A's were 25 versions of himself, not caring "about anything but winning." High praise indeed. Williams was inducted into the Hall of Fame in 2008, three years before his death at age 82.

OTHER TEAMS

Henry "Hammerin' Hank" Aaron finished 1973 with 713 home runs. He planned to sit out the opening series of 1974 in Cincinnati and try to break Babe Ruth's record when the Braves returned to Atlanta. Commissioner Kuhn forced Atlanta to play Aaron at least two games in Cincinnati, and he homered his first time up to tie Ruth. He broke the mark in the home opener in Atlanta, with the commissioner conspicuously absent. Death threats and racism dogged him throughout his chase of Ruth.

After the year, he was traded to Milwaukee, where he had spent the first dozen years of his career before the Braves relocated (and where he'd been cheered wildly during a charity game in 1973). Aaron finished his career as designated hitter for the Brewers, adding to numerous records he already held, including home runs, with 755. He returned to the Braves as a vice president and was inducted into the Hall of Fame in 1982. When Barry Bonds broke his home run record under a cloud of controversy regarding steroid use, Aaron, not present, surprisingly taped a congratulatory message that ran on the video board.

A tough-minded kid who became batboy for USC after returning a found baseball to legendary coach Rod Dedeaux, **George Lee "Sparky" Anderson** spent one year in the majors and ten in the minors as a player, plus five more managing in the bushes before getting the call to manage the Reds in 1970. He won a pennant that year, the first of five postseason appearances in seven seasons. The only time he lost in the NLCS was against the 1973 Mets. The Reds won back-to-back World Series in 1975 and 1976. After winning 92 games and finishing 2½ games behind the Dodgers in 1978, Anderson was inexplicably fired despite a .596 career winning per-centage. "Captain Hook" landed in Detroit and guided the Tigers to the 1984 world championship, the first manager to win a World Series in both leagues. He remained in Detroit through 1995, finishing with a career mark of 2,194-1,834 (.545), at the time the third-highest win total in history. He was inducted into the Hall of Fame in 2000. He died in 2010.

Pedro Borbon, one of the most durable and effective relievers for Cincinnati, pitched in 255 games for the Reds, plus 20 more times in the postseason. His lone postseason win came in the opener of the 1973 NLCS, and his first October save came the day after he cold-cocked Mets reliever Buzz Capra and then bit his hat. Borbon listed "rooster fighting" as a favorite activity—legal in his native Dominican Republic—and earned his "Dracula" nickname after biting Pittsburgh's Daryl Patterson in the side during a 1974 brawl. Apparently he had a taste for obscure pitchers.

Pedro Borbon Jr., a lefty, unlike his dad, pitched in more games but was not as effective as his namesake. He also didn't have his father's biting sense of humor. Pedro Sr. died of cancer in 2012, two years after being inducted into the Reds Hall of Fame.

While Thurman Munson took two teams to world championships, **Carlton Fisk** is still remembered for the home run he hit in October 1975— in a World Series his team lost. Fisk never got back to the World Series, but he did play in 11 All-Star Games and stuck around to catch more games (surpassed by Ivan Rodriguez) and homer more often than any backstop (surpassed by Mike Piazza). Fisk was elected to the Hall of Fame in 2000.

Joe Morgan was MVP in 1975–76. As free agency ate away at the core of the Reds, Little Joe left the club in 1980 to rejoin Houston, which had sent him to the Reds in a one-sided deal in 1971 that had gassed up the Big Red Machine for their awesome 1970s run. The five-time Gold Glover spent time with the Giants and Phillies before retiring with his hometown Oakland A's in 1984. He ranked third all-time in walks (1,865), eighth in steals (689), and had the most home runs (268) by a second baseman at the time of his retirement. He has since moved down those lists. Morgan was inducted into the Hall of Fame in 1990. Never afraid to share his views, he became an announcer for several teams, plus NBC, ABC, and ESPN.

Pete Rose's reign as baseball's most controversial personality was just getting started when his takeout slide touched off the Shea Stadium brawl during the 1973 NLCS. Rose and his Reds dominated the National League in the 1970s. He accumulated 2,000 hits during the decade, reaching hit number 3,000 in 1978, the same year he tied Willie Keeler's National League record with a 44-game hit streak. He surpassed Tommy Holmes's post-1900 NL mark of 37 at Shea Stadium in 1978, and, for one of the only times in his post-brawl career, was cheered in Flushing.

Rose played with the Phillies and Expos before returning to the Reds as player-manager in 1984, breaking Ty Cobb's career record for hits the following year. An All-Star at five different positions, Rose is now best known for being declared ineligible by Commissioner A. Bartlett Giamatti for gambling on baseball in 1989. His name hasn't appeared on the Hall of Fame ballot, and he denied betting on baseball until his 2004 book said he lied about that as well. In 2007, he admitted that he bet on the Reds every night—to win—while managing the team.

Lynn Nolan Ryan set the modern strikeout mark in 1973 with 383. Ryan set the mark for most 10-K games (148), most 15-K games (23), and most career Ks (5,714). He also threw the most career no-hitters (7). The Ryan Express was just getting started in '73 and chugged all the way to the Hall of Fame and the team president's box in Texas.

WRITERS AND BROADCASTERS

Marty Appel quit his dream job at age 28, resigning as Yankees PR director following the 1976 season and the team's first pennant since he was in high school. "Every year working with Steinbrenner was like seven years anywhere else," he admits. Appel later worked with the team as executive producer of Yankees telecasts on WPIX. He also worked for Major League Baseball, World Team Tennis, the Atlanta Committee for the 1996 Olympics, and the Topps Company. He has his own PR firm and has written and ghostwritten numerous books, including *Pinstripe Empire* in 2012.

Nancy Finley remained in the Bay Area after her A's playoff ticket processing days ended. She and her husband, attorney Morgan King, created a website devoted to the baseball legacy of her late father, Carl, and her cousin Charlie, www.morganking.com/Athletics/charlieofinley.html. She frequently appears in media reports concerning the 1970s Swingin' A's. She is writing a book about the team from the family's perspective.

During his extended stay in the Shea loge in October 1973, **Bob Heussler** ended up convincing his friend Tom Hassan, who'd waited all night for tickets, to transfer from Seton Hall to the University of Bridgeport, where he became the Mets-centric roommate Bob needed. Heussler settled not far from where he went to college and served as broadcaster for University of Connecticut football and basketball, calling Tate George's miraculous last-second shot in the 1990 NCAA tournament. He later handled Fairfield University basketball and the Connecticut Sun of the WNBA.

He is best known for providing regular updates on New York's WFAN, fittingly being referred to as "Mr. Met" by afternoon host Mike Francesa for his never-wavering optimism for the club. Among Heussler's biggest

Mets disappointments was attending a game in July 1978 when fans at Shea cheered '73 villain Pete Rose during his 44-game hitting streak. "Never got caught up in that stuff," he says. "I never forgot."

Steve Jacobson covered the Mets from their humble beginnings in 1962 through the Miracle of 1969 and their near-miraculous run at another title in 1973. After 45 seasons covering sports for *Newsday*, he authored the 2007 book *Carrying Jackie's Torch*. He served as a technical advisor for the ESPN miniseries *The Bronx Is Burning*, portrayed in the show by Alan Ruck from *Ferris Bueller's Day Off* and the TV show *Spin City*. Jacobson still lives in Long Island and spends winters skiing in Vermont.

Sal Marchiano worked all over the dial on New York TV newscasts during a 40-year career, retiring in 2008. He spent after-hours time with the men he covered, carpooling with Tug McGraw and watching the 1973 NLCS fight at Shea standing with Joe Namath. He came to prominence at ABC, filling in for Howard Cosell on TV and radio. He worked many major fights, including the fabled "Thrilla in Manilla" in 1975, only to fly back with the tape from the Philippines and have Cosell record his part for the delayed broadcast as if he'd been there. "There was no scrutiny back then," Marchiano says. There wasn't much in the early days of ESPN, either. He helped the network garner much-needed ratings with boxing twice per week in the early 1980s. He disliked ESPN's remote location in Bristol, Connecticut—settling closer to the shoreline—and titled his memoir, *Happiness Is Bristol in My Rearview Mirror*. His daughter, Sam, later worked for ESPN.

Phil Pepe's first year on the Yankees beat was with the *New York World Telegram and Sun* in 1961, the year Roger Maris broke Babe Ruth's home run mark and the Yankees won the World Series. He moved over to the *New York Daily News* and covered the Yankees from 1971 to 1984, taking over as the paper's lead sports columnist. A former president of the Baseball Writers Association as well as the New York chapter, he was also sports director at WCBS-FM. Pepe has written approximately 50 books. Actor Josh Pais portrayed him in the ESPN miniseries *The Bronx Is Burning*.

Howie Rose was one of the voices of Sportsphone, which gave callers the day's sports events in 59 seconds. Hired at WHN in the spring of 1977, one of his first big radio moments was a LaGuardia Airport interview with the just-traded Tom Seaver all the way to the airplane that carried him away from New York. Rose stayed local, working for several years at WHN and returning to the station in 1987 as host of the pregame show *Mets Extra* through 1995, interacting with players, managers, and callers for the station into which WHN evolved: WFAN. He did hockey play-by-play for the New York Rangers and TV for the Islanders. He served as a Mets TV broadcaster until he returned to WFAN to take the place of retiring Bob Murphy in the Mets radio booth in 2004.

Art Spander joined the *San Francisco Chronicle* in 1965 and became lead sports columnist for the *San Francisco Examiner* in 1979. He has worked for many other publications, including the *Oakland Tribune*. In 1999 he received the McCann Award at the Pro Football Hall of Fame and in 2009 earned the PGA of America Lifetime Achievement Award. In 2012, he was still hustling from the US Open in San Francisco to England for Wimbledon and the British Open and then to South Carolina for the PGA Championship, with plenty of Giants and A's games sprinkled in.

John Thorn thought he would be a lifelong editor. Hart Publishing handed him, at age 26 in 1973, anecdotes worked over years earlier by Joe Reichler, Ben Olan, and Maury Allen, asking him to make it into a book. He had six weeks. The finished product, *A Century of Baseball Lore*, became the first of 70-plus books in which Thorn has served as author or editor. These include two landmark efforts with Pete Palmer: *The Hidden Game of Baseball* and *Total Baseball*, concepts that he later expanded to football. These books spawned a revolution in information still felt from the grandstand to the owner's box.

He served as senior creative consultant to the Ken Burns documentary *Baseball* and as publisher of Total Sports Publishing, a cross-platform sports-information company that produced many titles, including the official encyclopedias for Major League Baseball and the National Football League. The foremost authority on the origins of baseball, Thorn spent almost three decades on *Baseball in the Garden of Eden*, which came out in 2011. That same year he was named MLB's official historian, the second person to hold the title. "I've got footprints in the snow. . . . There are plenty of books, some are better than others," Thorn says. "A couple of them have enduring value. On balance, everything is OK—it all works together. Even the books that are not so great."

Acknowledgments

When someone whose name I can't remember told me that I needed to come up with better material, it took one day to come up with the concept for a book on the 1973 season. It took three and a half years, however, to come up with the right publisher and the manuscript. Anne Marie O'Farrell took over as my literary agent and shepherded the process from concept to cover. We worked on almost a dozen versions of the proposal before we both agreed. When Lyons Press concurred with our appraisal, we had a happy and hard-working family. Editor James Jayo worked diligently and patiently on every aspect of the book while I played perfectionist and procrastinator both. Like a 1970s bullpen "fireman," Ellen Urban logged the innings needed to finish the job. Sara Baker, Shana Capozza, and Laurie Kenney formed a solid PR staff.

Picking the three main subjects was easy and fun: The "Ya Gotta Believe" Mets, the first-year Steinbrenner/last-year Yankee Stadium Bronx Bombers, and the big, bad Oakland A's. I've followed the Charlie Finley order, which threatened punishment or at least up-close bluster for anyone referring to the team by a name other than the A's. He may no longer be with us, but it was never a good idea to get on Charlie Finley's bad side.

A special thank you goes to those who helped me get in touch with the participants in the tale that give the book its voice. (The subjects are included in the Sources section and the interview dates in the Notes section.) I am indebted to Debbie Gallas and Bob Rose of the Oakland A's, who were also great hosts; Steve Grande and M. J. Trahan with the Houston Astros; David Newman, Jay Horwitz, Lorraine Hamilton, and Shannon Forde of the New York Mets; and Dave Kaplan, director at the Yogi Berra Museum and Learning Center on the campus of Montclair State University. Thanks also go to Fox Valley Sports Academy in Elgin, Illinois, for acting as intermediary for my talk with Buzz Capra and to Bob Heussler for doing the same at WFAN in New York. Also thanks to Sharon Chapman, Spencer Gale, Paul Hirsch, Ray Martel, Matt Merola, John Noto, Bill Nowlin, Dan Schlossberg, Jon Springer, and Saul Wisnia for their efforts. Special thanks to Blair Rafuse, who keeps my website, metsilverman.com, functional and as the place for continuing discussion on this subject, and to Alan Silverman, whose computer skills are as reassuring as Oakland's 1973 rotation.

Libraries played a big role in this effort: The Oakland Public Library's main branch, plus the Oakland History Room, the Macdonald DeWitt Library at the State University of New York at Ulster, and the National Baseball Hall of Fame Library all went out of their way to aid my research. My local Stone Ridge Library is staffed with All-Stars every day.

Hall of Famers Freddy Berowski, John Horne, Pat Kelly, and Tim Wiles helped gather the photos of 1970s New York baseball for the book. Ron Riesterer, clicking away when the A's were Swingin' away, provided the wonderful images from the Oakland Coliseum. Diana Nuhn created the fantastic cover that pulls back the corner of time.

As a general note, the majority of statistics, records, numbers, and fact-checking done for this book was handled via baseball-reference.com, unless otherwise noted.

Jeffrey Marcus transcribed many of the interviews used in this book. No mere typist, he is a sports and publishing expert who acted as editor in the process and read chapters in rough form. I could no sooner have completed this book without his help than the A's could have won it all in 1973 without a durable and terrific bullpen. Bruce Markusen, already an old friend of mine by 1973, has trod this soil before. He was helpful both with suggestions and the work he left behind in an award-winning book by two different names, *Baseball's Last Dynasty* and *A Baseball Dynasty*, as well as his work with the *Hardball Times* and other dispatches from Cooperstown.

I must thank my family for putting up with a lot over the years. Jan and Tyler were patient and listened to my coaching and coaxing. Debbie acted as professionally as possible, taking messages and handing me the receiver with a casual "Sal Bando for you." Even our dog, Cleo, helped keep me company during the innumerable hours of interviewing and writing. My father, Syd, showed me how to be both a good dad and a competent writer. My elder siblings, Marie, Mark, and Michael, all shared a capital letter with me and spent '73 driving me around in our beat-up Country Squire. Words cannot express the contributions of two people no longer with us: my mother, Jan M. Silverman, not a writer but who thought like one, and Michael Gershman, who was a writer and got me started in this business, teaching me to be thorough and to look at the big picture.

Two colleagues died during the writing of this book. When I mentioned to Dana Brand that I was frustrated in finding representation, he put me in touch with his agent at Marcil-O'Farrell Literary, and Anne Marie became my agent. It deeply saddens me that I never got to talk at length about 1973 with Dana, a writer and Hofstra University English professor with a PhD from Yale—and Shea Stadium. But the event that he founded and that colleagues Richard Puerzer and Paula Uruburu (plus Jeannine Rinaldi, Allison Denicola, Natalie Datloff, and many others) put together at Hofstra for the 50th anniversary Mets conference in 2012 helped me meet many people who recalled 1973 as if Watergate were still going on.

Greg Spira and I collaborated on more projects than I can count, and even in the last month of his life he helped me locate broadcasts of the 1973 World Series and a hard-to-find documentary on Swingin' Oakland. I miss his friendly yet critical ear and those late-night phone calls that started as business discussions and digressed into long, amusing talks about nothing— and everything.

Of the many people involved in this story unable to see 1973 turn 40, the missing link is Frank Edwin "Tug" McGraw. Even with a Mustache Gang plus a truckload of colorful characters from 1973—quotable Yogi, unmatchable Tom Terrific, cunning Catfish, bombastic George, braggart Reggie, audacious Charlie O., and the many others who formed part of this absorbing tale—my mind returns to Tug and his thigh-slapping glove, putting the Mets on his back in the last month of '73 and taking the team from the basement to the edge of the moon. A Falstaffian character with an unhittable screwball, mid-'70s mojo, and a motto that lives on in the underdog in each of us, Tug inspired this story.

"Ya Gotta Believe!" he said.

He never said when to stop.

Notes

PROLOGUE: REUNION

ix "You have to be at least 50": Interview with Art Spander, June 22, 2012.

ix "I have tried to impart": Interview with Bob Rose, April 21, 2012.

x officially became O.co Coliseum: Beth Snyder Bulik, "O, No! Overstock Backs Off O.co Name Change," *Advertising Age*, November 14, 2011.

xi A group of fans calling themselves Let's Go Oakland!: *Oakland Tribune* advertisement, May 8, 2012. (Note: The number of titles was changed to reflect the amount as of the end of 2012.)

xii "Gave me chills": Monte Moore, Oakland A's broadcast, Comcast Sports Net California, April 21, 2012.

1. A WALK INTO HISTORY

1 Sherm Feller, the gravelly, invisible voice: David Kruh, "Of Changes, Choices, and a Day of Infamy," shermfeller.com.

1 "The times in '67": Interview with Ron Blomberg, July 27, 2012.

2 "You're basically pinch-hitting": Blomberg and Schlossberg, *Designated Hebrew*, 4.

2 "I said absolutely": Blomberg interview. (Note: Wally Pipp, the first Yankee to win a home run crown, spent a decade as the team's first baseman before his headache afforded Lou Gehrig a spot in the lineup in 1925. Pipp never started another game for the Yankees.)

2 "It was 55 degrees at game time": Interview with Dick Bresciani, February 22, 2012.

3 these new duds: Morris Levin, "Even the Yankees Change Their Stripes." www.proleagueauthentics.com/blogs/news/6016864-even-the-yankees-change-their-stripes.

3 "You're not playing first base today": Blomberg and Schlossberg, *Designated Hebrew*, 6.

3 "A gift double": Yankees Opening Day radio broadcast, April 6, 1973.

3 "I'll probably go back": Jim Ogle, "Blomberg's First DH Bat Earns Cooperstown Niche," *Newark Star-Ledger*, April 28, 1973.

3 "You smoke cigarette after cigarette": Roy Blount, Jr., "Swinging In His Own Groove," *Sports Illustrated*, September 10, 1973.

4 "Blomberg would have been more forgotten": Bresciani interview.

5 the first manager plucked directly: William Leggett, "The Lights Go On Again," *Sports Illustrated*, April 9, 1973.

6 "No one ever called": Ron Fimrite, "A Hero Finds There's No One for Tenace," *Sports Illustrated*, April 2, 1973.

6   Rudi admits: Interview with Joe Rudi, June 12, 2012.

6   Bando's ghostwriter: Interview with Steve Somers, March 9, 2012.

7   with all eyes trained on him: Interview with Bert Campaneris, April 20, 2012.

7   "So the reality was": Interview with Duke Sims, July 31, 2012.

8   "Be my guest": Kuhn and Appel, *Hardball*, 138.

9   and soon was: Al Harvin, "Berra's Pain in the Side Not Caused by 2-0 Mets," *New York Times*, April 9, 1973.

10 While the middle class tuned: Peter Kihss, "Poor and Rich, Not Middle Class, The Key to Lindsay Re-election," *New York Times*, November 8, 1969.

10 but Procaccino siphoned: Richard Reeves, "Lindsay, Garelik and Beame Victors," *New York Times*, November 5, 1969.

10 Lindsay's predecessor: Richard Severo, "Wagner Casts Vote for Lindsay as 'the Least of Three Evils'," *New York Times*, November 5, 1969.

10 His goals, not to mention: "The Nation: Out in a Rowboat with Mayor Lindsay," *Time*, June 1, 1971.

11 "The Comfort Shirt from Sears": www.tias.com/11382/PictPage/1922715146.html.

12 "Even Napoleon": www.polishsportshof.com/inductees/baseball/danny-ozark/.

13 Maybe the guy operating: Steve Cady, "Seaver-Carlton Better Than Grant and Lee," *New York Times*, April 7, 1973.

2. "MATTER OF FACT, IT'S ALL DARK"

15 Elvis Presley, in his own orbit: About the King: Film & TV, www.elvis.com/about-the-king/film_and_tv.aspx

16 the Floydian trance concludes: "Everything Else You Ever Needed to Know About *The Dark Side of the Moon*," *Pink Floyd*, 61.

17 On the first night of the American: Neill and Kent, *Anyway, Anyhow, Anywhere*, 239.

17 stepped out of the audience: Mike Leonard, "Who Are You? The Guy Who Played with the Who, That's Who," *Hoosier Times*, Bloomington, Indiana, February 19, 2006.

18 became the first coach to bristle: "McLendon Resigns as Coach," *Milwaukee Journal Sentinel*, January 30, 1962.

18 He asked his father: Stuart Miller, "Where Steinbrenner and 3-Pointers Started," *New York Times*, December 25, 2011.

18 "I won't be pressured": Madden, *Steinbrenner*, 7.

20 Steinbrenner's controlling 11 percent: Ibid., 9.

20 buying the Yankees: Ibid., 15.

21 Burke later wrote: Burke, *Outrageous Good Fortune*, 315–16.

21 "We plan absentee ownership": "From the Boss's Mouth and Back," *New York Times*, July 13, 2010.

21 sent teammates letters from Gulden's: Peterson, *Mickey Mantle*, 64–65.

22 Kekich still: "Ex-Yanks Fight Wife-Swap Film," *New York Post*, February 24, 2011.

22 "I encouraged Mike": Interview with Fritz Peterson, June 22, 2012.

23 "Nobody knew": Ibid.

23 he explained that: Peterson, *Mickey Mantle*, 69–71.

23 he was never caught so off guard: Marty Appel interview, June 8, 2012.

23 "Back then the writers": Ibid.

24 arrived in Mets camp: Interview with Sal Marchiano, June 30, 2012.

25 It wasn't the same: Malcolm W. Browne, "Vietnam Reporting: Three Years of Crisis," *Columbia Journalism Review*, Fall 1964, www.cjr.org/fiftieth _anniversary/viet_nam_reporting_three_years.php?page=all.

25 "When I got back I was": Marchiano interview.

25 "I was astounded": Ibid.

26 After receiving more mail: Joseph Durso, "Kuhn Says He's Appalled by Kekich-Peterson Case," *New York Times*, March 20, 1973.

26 "I thought it was a closed": Ibid.

26 couldn't help but blast: Ibid.

26 that was part of: Phil Pepe, "CBS Sells Yanks to Burke, 11 Others, Group Pays $10M," *New York Daily News*, January 4, 1973.

3. RING OF TRUTH

27 Finley boasted that: Green and Launius, *Charlie Finley*, 180–81.

27 later noted: Interview with Sal Bando, September 14, 2011.

27 Finley's own ring: Robert Edwards Auctions, 1972 Charlie Finley A's World Series ring, www.robertedwardauctions.com/auction/2009/1155.html#photos.

27 His father, Oscar: Interview with Nancy Finley, April 13, 2012.

27 rose to division head: Green and Launius, 21.

27 The Marines judged him: Ibid., 17–25.

29 Never one to be deterred: Ibid., 27–33.

29 Yet it was only after: Ibid., 34.

29 Finley ultimately bought: Ibid., 37.

29 Finley trumped the club's past: Peterson, *The Kansas City Athletics*, 136.

30 When the Dallas Texans: Green and Launius, 69–70.

30 become the de facto: Ibid., 42.

30 One of the incentives: Interview with Joe Rudi, June 12, 2012.

31 Biographers: Green and Launius, 85.27272727

31 "You had to give credit": Bando interview.

31 he used his own peculiar: Finley interview.

31 With the end of his: Green and Launius, 73.

32 plus a five-year: Ibid., 124–25.

32 Half the size: Population of the 100 Largest Urban Places: 1970, www.census .gov/population/www/documentation/twps0027/tab20.txt.

32 The 20-year lease: Green and Launius, 122.

32 In the winning locker room: Ibid., 181.

33 Finley also tried: Ibid., 176.

33 At a time when the average: National Average Wage index, Social Security Online, www.ssa.gov/oact/COLA/AWI.html.

33 and the average major league: Biz of Baseball, 1973–1975, www.bizof baseball.com/index.php?option=com_content&view=article&id=682:1973-1975&catid=45:cba-summaries&Itemid=76.

33 Finley told Hendrick: Markusen, *Baseball's Last Dynasty*, 189.

34 "A Vida Blue or": Ibid., 190.

34 "You've got to be kidding": Ron Bergman, *Sporting News*, April 14, 1973.

34 "It was an artfully": Interview with John Thorn, March 16, 2012.

34 "a dime-store creation": Hunter and Keteyian, *Catfish*, 4.

35 the Second City pushed: John Schmeltzer, "Sears Tower Opens," *Chicago Tribune*, www.chicagotribune.com/news/politics/chi-chicagodays-searstower-story,0,5053776.story.

35 Architect Bruce Graham: Willis Tower, History & Milestones, www.willis tower.com/media/news/Historical%20Fact%20Sheet.pdf.

36 Realizing that baseball's: www.bizofbaseball.com, 1973–1975.

37 American League average: Thorn, et al., *Total Baseball*, seventh edition, 77.

38 When Bowie Kuhn addressed: G. Richard McKelvey, *All Bat, No Glove*, 24.

38 The idea had arisen: Thorn, *Baseball in the Garden of Eden*, 239.

38 In 1906, Connie Mack: McKelvey, 24.

38 "Whenever the game": Thorn interview.

39 The league's hitting spiked: League by League Totals for Batting Average, www.baseball-almanac.com/hitting/hibavg4.shtml.

39 "because it enables": Interview with Ken Holtzman, May 3, 2012.

4. THE PLAYERS' MARCH

41 Zippo lighters to thatched roofs: Morley Safer, "The Burning of Cam Ne," *Reporting America at War*, a film by Steve Ives, www.pbs.org/weta/reporting americaatwar/reporters/safer/camne.html.

41 went to Vietnam: Guy Raz (host), *All Things Considered*, "Final Words: Cronkite's Vietnam Commentary," National Public Radio, July 17, 2009, www.npr.org/templates/story/story.php?storyId=106775685.

42 More than 58,000: *The Veterans Hour*, "Vietnam War Statistics," www.veterans hour.com/vietnam_war_statistics.htm.

42 The Selective Service had inducted: Selective Service System Induction Statistics, www.sss.gov/induct.htm.

43 Before becoming the 1973: Bruce Markusen, "Baseball and Vietnam," Cooperstown Confidential, *The Hardball Times*, September 17, 2010, www.hardballtimes.com/main/article/cooperstown-confidential-baseball-and-vietnam/.

43 White Sox rookie outfielder Carlos May: Ibid.

43 Jerry Koosman, one of the stalwarts: Irv Goldfarb, "Jerry Koosman," *The Miracle Has Landed*, 136.

44 "I did have to worry about it": Interview with Jon Matlack, March 14, 2012.

45 "We lost a lot of friends": Rudi interview.

45 Under the rules of the day: Rory Costello, "Joe Rudi," SABR Bio Project, http://sabr.org/bioproj/person/59c2abe2.

46 "The A's put me in the Marine Corps Reserves": Rudi interview.

46 "I was one of the few guys": Interview with Bud Harrelson, August 10, 2011.

47 Mets infielder Wayne Garrett caught a break: Interview with Wayne Garrett, June 22, 2012.

47 Ryan's Army Reserve unit: Wendel, *Summer of '68*, 11.

47 Detroit's Mickey Lolich: Ibid., 11–12.

47 "It was a very stressful, trying time": Matlack interview.

48 The first game Fritz Peterson pitched: Peterson interview.

48 But the wear and tear of the race: James S. Hirsch, *Willie Mays*, 501.

49 He had signed a two-year, $330,000 contract: Ibid., 506–7.

49 Stoneham hoped to get: Ibid., 508.

50 was ultimately an "unhappy experience": Interview with Stan Isaacs, June 21, 2012.

50 never much of a disciplinarian: Shirley Povich, "A Collision Course," *Stamford Advocate* (syndicated column), March 16, 1973.

50 observed Mays in March 1973: Rosengren, *Hammerin' Hank*, 96–97.

5. THE CUTTING

53 On October 4, 1955: Appel, *Now Pitching for the Yankees*, 11.

53 Ten years later: Ibid., 32–33. (Note: Marty Appel attended the State University of New York [SUNY] at Oneonta.)

54 The juggernaut began promptly: Prime Time TV Schedule—1973, www.superseventies.com/primetime_73.html.

55 had decided in 1970 to retire: Berkowitz, *Something Happened*, 205–6.

55 the two-part episode: "Maude's Dilemma," *Maude*, www.youtube.com/watch?v=zxy0DTMXhwY.

55 one of four states: Abortion Timeline, www.nrlc.org/abortion/facts/abortiontimeline.html.

56 Another landmark program: *60 Minutes*, The Museum of Broadcast Communications, www.museum.tv/archives/etv/S/htmlS/60minutes/60minutes.htm.

57 had spoken casually: Burke, 236.

57 Former co-owner Del Webb: Ibid., 236–38.

57 His fellow team executives: Kuhn, *Hardball*, 31–33.

57 "a long lilting holiday": Burke, 284.

57 had called Burke "Mr. Yankee": Madden, 11.

57 "I'll make that long-haired": Ibid., 16.

58 saying that Steinbrenner looked: Burke, 318–19.

58 "Burke, at that time": Interview with Steve Jacobson, February 16, 2012.

58 "I couldn't believe Mike still didn't get it": Madden, 18.

59 At the January 10 press conference: Burke, 316–17.

60 a more festive birthday offering: Michael Wagner, "Babe's Place," www
    .ultimateyankees.com/babesplace.htm.

60 When he wrote his memoirs: Burke, 320.

61 where "The Major" had been decorated: Dave Anderson, "Sports of the Times:
    Lucky to Be a Yankee and Lucky to Be Alive," *New York Times*, July 24, 2010.

61 "I was on the list": Peterson interview.

61 "In college football": Interview with Paul Lukas, September 16, 2010.

61 "Do your duty as you see it": Goodreads, "George Patton Quotes," www
    .goodreads.com/author/quotes/370054.George_S_Patton_Jr_.

62 "It made no sense for us": Burke, 320.

62 Burke's letter of resignation: Madden, 47.

62 When the players heard: Bashe, *Dog Days*, 244.

62 "Any time ownership changes": Appel interview.

63 It wasn't the same: Burke, 321.

63 Among these was a photograph: Ibid., 318–19.

6. NOT YOUR AVERAGE JOE

65 in the words of his thorough: Cramer, *Joe DiMaggio: The Hero's Life*, 425.

66 and recalls playing left field in Yankee Stadium: Rudi interview.

66 Yogi Berra said of his former Yankee teammate: Joe DiMaggio Quotes, www
    .baseball-almanac.com/quotes/quodimg.shtml.

67 "He had a great sense of humor": Rudi interview.

67 "We changed our thinking on the DH": Markusen, *Baseball's Last Dynasty*,
    200.

67 "In April and May all of us struggled": Rudi interview.

69 Valentine was supposed to fill in for Berry: *Studio 42 with Bob Costas*, MLB
    Network. Guest: Bobby Valentine. Air date: February 13, 2012.

69 "I thought I could catch anything": Ibid.

69 "Instead of it healing straight": Ibid.

70 Due to antigambling legislation: Larry Schwartz, "Man o' War Came Close to
    Perfection." ESPN.com. www.espn.go.com/sportscentury/features/00016132.
    html.

70 Named after a stable secretary: "Ask Penny," Secretariat.com. www.secretariat
    .com/fan-club/archive/ask-penny/.

70 "Secretariat is alone": Secretariat Belmont Stakes 1973 & Extended Post Race
    Coverage. www.youtube.com/watch?v=cS4f6wiQJh4.

71 manager Billy Martin, angrier than anyone: Markusen, *Baseball's Last Dynasty*, 204.

72 Williams preferred California's Jim Singer: Eric Aron, "1973: The Last Time the Royals Hosted an All-Star Game," www.throughthefencebaseball.com/1973-the-last-time-kc-hosted-the-all-star-game/23892/.

73 The fans rained cheers: Rosengren, 147.

73 "So here I was": Williams and Plaschke, *No More Mr. Nice Guy*, 159.

74 When asked before the game: Rosengren, 147–48.

74 Hunter made his own rubber insole: Hunter and Keteyian, 28.

74 Finley then sent him: Ibid., 35.

75 "Do you have a nickname?": Ibid., 3.

75 (Finley briefly tried: Markusen, *Baseball's Last Dynasty*, 206.

75 "Heck, it might help me": Ibid., 214.

7. WOUNDED KNEE, FRACTURED SKULL

77 The standoff finally ended: "Wounded Knee: We Shall Remain," *The American Experience*, PBS, 2009, www.youtube.com/watch?v=5yFr5groCJg.

77 The bizarre appearance: Beth Pinsker, "An Offer He Could Refuse," *Entertainment Weekly*, July 2, 2004.

78 "I'm trying to nail down this game": Matlack interview.

79 shaking his head at the memory: Interview with Rusty Staub, June 22, 2010.

79 "They're messing with me": Matlack interview.

79 "You think about Herb Score": Interview with Ed Kranepool, January 27, 2012.

79 "That's the first I hear his name": Matlack interview.

80 Disabled List Table: Provided by Jon Springer, metsbythenumbers.com.

81 "There's the Krane": Interview with George Theodore, February 27, 2012.

81 "I am imbedded in boredom": *1974 New York Mets Official Program and Scorecard*.

81 "They got a kick out of things like that": Theodore interview.

84 "The performance rocked me": McGraw and Yaeger, *Ya Gotta Believe*, 108–9.

85 "That was their choice": Garrett interview.

85 "I can't speak for him": Ibid.

85 and Grant got into a shouting match: Lang and Simon, *The New York Mets: Twenty-Five Years of Baseball Magic*, 126–27.

85 "unless forced to by public opinion": Joseph Durso, "Mets Say Berra's Job Is Safe—Unless Fans Say Otherwise." *New York Times*, July 6, 1973.

85 Only 611 of the 4,000-plus: Lang and Simon, 127.

85 looks philosophically at his close call: Interview with Yogi Berra, January 30, 2012.

8. THE WINNING DIET

87 A beef shortage: Bruce Watson, "Another '70s Flashback: The Meat Crisis," *Daily Finance*, www.dailyfinance.com/2008/10/15/another-70s-flashback-the-meat-crisis/.

87 In a 1973 Gallup poll: Lydia Sonnenberg, "What about 'Dr. Atkins' Diet Revolution'?," *Ministry Magazine*, November 1974, www.ministrymagazine.org/archive/1974/November/what-about-dr.-atkins-diet-revolution.

89 But Atkins, who tried the diet on himself: Douglas Martin, "Dr. Robert Atkins, 72, Author of Controversial Diet Book, Dies," *New York Times*, April 18, 2003, www.nytimes.com/2003/04/18/obituaries/18ATKI.html?pagewanted=all.

89 Ever the epicurean: Green and Launius, 81–82.

89 the A's logo emblazoned on his barn: Ibid., 150–52.

89 He made a rare exception for the farm itself: Ibid., 29.

90 On August 7, 1973: Ibid., 184.

90 "Maybe there was a little rivalry": Rudi interview.

91 was thinking about the Iron Horse: National Public Radio, *Mickey Mantle: America's Last Boy*, by Jane Levy, hosted by Neal Cohan, November 24, 2010, www.npr.org/2010/11/24/131569913/mickey-mantle-america-s-last-boy.

92 with Allen encouraging him: Clip of Mickey Mantle Old-Timers Day Home Run, www.youtube.com/watch?v=I9fNcMLaW_A.

92 "It was fun": Appel interview.

92 Joe Rudi was watching: Rudi interview.

92 Reggie Jackson, who had a superb weekend: Clark, *Champagne and Baloney*, 159.

92 Williams was ready to empty the Oakland bench: Rosengren, 204.

93 the popular lefty had been the first reliever: Appel, *Now Pitching for the Yankees*, 101.

93 "When you have that many guys": Interview with Rollie Fingers, April 20, 2012.

94 In May in Kansas City: Rosengren, 110–11.

95 After Epstein and North traded insults: Clark, *Champagne and Baloney*, 161–62.

96 Jackson pulled a hamstring: Rosengren, 208–9.

96 "Finley loved this": Williams and Plaschke, 158–61.

97 Four decades later: Holtzman interview.

9. COMING DOWN

99 A contact hitter who rarely struck out: Anthony McCarron, "Where Are They Now? Former New York Yankee Second Baseman Horace Clarke Fondly Recalls His 'Era'," *New York Daily News*, April 17, 2010, www.nydailynews.com/sports/baseball/yankees/new-york-yankee-baseman-horace-clarke-fondly-recalls-era-article-1.167587.

99   "Horace Clarke was a very good second baseman": Blomberg interview.

99   The Yankees had lost a game that week: Rosengren, 158–60.

100   Munson, from a blue collar upbringing: Appel, *Munson*, 12–13.

100   "the hatred each catcher had": Peterson interview.

100   "Munson genuinely hated Fisk": Appel, *Munson*, 61.

100   Munson came charging homeward: Ibid., 88.

100   "You trace the rivalry of the teams to today": Appel interview.

100   "In those days a lot of the players didn't like each other": Bresciani interview.

101   When Callison's misplay turned a probable loss: Bashe, 261.

102   "Guys were thinking more of George Steinbrenner": Ibid., 262.

102   "We misread him": Interview with Phil Pepe, July 31, 2012.

103   Other shows had been based on authentic: Charles B. Slocum, "The Real History of Reality TV, or How Alan Funt Won the Cold War," Writers Guild of America, West, www.wga.org/organizesub.asp?id+1099.

104   Even Archie Bunker: *All in the Family*, episode 2, "The Man in the Street" (1971), www.imdb.com/character/ch0021603/quotes.

104   On the Republican side: Madden, 63.

105   Steinbrenner tried to get the employees: Rosengren, 163.

105   "We knew we had a problem": Appel interview.

106   As a precaution during football Sundays: Burke, 300.

107   but Michael Burke, according to his memoir: Ibid., 301–2.

108   "Simply put, we are asking the city": Ibid., 302.

108   Robert Moses, the city builder: Killen, *1973 Nervous Breakdown*, 195.

109   "It would be extremely embarrassing": Burke, 311.

109   The original copper was sold and melted down: Oren Yaniv, "Iconic Façade Comes Down from Old Yankee Stadium as Part of Demolition," *New York Daily News*, September 4, 2009, http://articles.nydailynews .com/2009-09-04/news/17940069_1_yankee-stadium-frieze-new-stadium.

109   "That *was* the stadium": Peterson interview.

110   NFL Films, which captured the game for posterity: Giants vs. Eagles, September 23, 1973, www.youtube.com/watch?v=l1P9uhHOR7I.

111   but he went to see Bouton: Allan Barra, "Pitching Deep and Inside," *Wall Street Journal*, April 7, 2010.

111   "The city was generally down on Ralph Houk": Appel interview.

112   "We didn't know that Thurman had gone home": Sims interview.

112   Something else was going on: Peterson interview.

113   "It was the worst thing I ever saw": Ibid.

113   "It was very hurtful to everybody": Appel interview.

114   "We really thought we had a winner": Sam Goldaper, "Houk Out as Yankees Manager," *New York Times*, October 1, 1973.

114   Asked four decades later about his feelings: Peterson interview.

114   It was the culmination of a season in which he had toured: Cohen, *The Man in the Crowd*, 238.

114   "There are, in the end, only two guides to remembrance": Ibid., 230–31.

115 And he joined the throng by grabbing his piece of history: Ibid., 234.

115 Many of those mementos ended up in the hands: Frank J. Priel, "At Lunch With: Bert Sugar; Attention, Fans: Amazing Facts! Fun Fictions!" *New York Times*, March 29, 1995.

115 "Baseball hadn't yet embraced the whole marketing plan": Appel interview.

116 Among the booty he hauled: Priel, *New York Times*, March 29, 1995.

116 Sugar sold most of them to the chain discount store Korvettes: 1974 advertisement, http://yankeestadiumseats.com/id2.html.

116 for the ceremony at the empty stadium: Murray Schumbach, "$27 Million Face-Lifting of Yankee Stadium," *New York Times*, October 2, 1973.

10. BELIEVE IT IF YOU NEED IT

117 "My teams were my teams": Interview with Howie Rose, March 14, 2012.

117 "That year sports was on the front page": Marchiano interview.

117 "one of the sorriest NHL teams ever": E. M. Swift, "Who'd Have Thunk It," *Sports Illustrated*, October 11, 1982, http://sportsillustrated.cnn.com/vault/article/magazine/MAG1126003/1/index.htm.

119 "Yeah, that was an extraordinary year": Marchiano interview.

119 In *Mets Fan*, his book about the psyche of rooting for the team: Brand, *Mets Fan*, 33.

120 Grant had an athlete's background: Rob Edelman, "M. Donald Grant," *The Miracle Has Landed*, 303–7.

121 Lou Niss, hired as the publicity director: Lang and Simon, 21.

121 "He was a big windbag": Jacobson interview.

121 "The guy who really should have managed the Mets in '72": Rose interview.

122 McGraw spent a lot of time talking with Joe Badamo: McGraw and Yaeger, 110–12.

122 "He was probably making fun of him": Harrelson interview.

122 "I think he mocked him a little bit": Garrett interview.

122 Grant said he was offended: McGraw and Yaeger, 110–12.

122 refers to how the players initially felt: Interview with Buzz Capra, March 23, 1973.

123 Pitcher Jon Matlack recalls how McGraw adamantly screamed: Matlack interview.

123 "The Mets remain on the fringes": Leonard Koppett, "Dodgers' Osteen Evens a 1-0 Score with Mets," *New York Times*, August 9, 1973.

123 "I had been hit in May by Ramon Hernandez": Staub interview.

127 The 1973 *Monday Night* opener took no prisoners: "TV Listings," *New York Times*, September 17, 1973.

128 Met-turned-Yankee Ron Swoboda had taken a swipe: "Mets Like the Yankees and Vice Versa," Special to the *New York Times*, April 8, 1973.

128 Even frantically reaching into their Mets library: 1973 Official Yearbook, New York Mets.

129 "I don't know how much faith Yogi had in me, actually": Capra interview.

129 "He's one of the best bad ball hitters": Ibid. (Note: Players received $50 for appearing on the Mets postgame show, *Kiner's Korner*.)

130 King, already in Houston playing the Virginia Slims tournament: "Mrs. King Defeats Riggs," *New York Times*, September 21, 1973.

130 Congress approved: The Equal Rights Amendment, www.equalrights amendment.org.

132 "I grew up in a garden apartment development": Rose interview.

132 "Cleon got it and threw it to me": Garrett interview.

132 "He made a perfect throw to me": Interview with Ron Hodges, July 26, 2012.

132 "Once he was tagged out": Rose interview.

132 Even Cleon Jones, who manned left field: 1973 World Series Preview, Interview by Lindsey Nelson, www.youtube.com/watch?v=ys8atAUSkaw&fe ature=related.

133 "That play there and the game-winning hit": Hodges interview.

133 "The wisecrack around the league": Jacobson interview.

134 The Mets promoted Willie Mays Night: Koppett, *The New York Mets*, 303.

134 Most of the planning of the event: Hirsch, 520.

135 Dabbing his eyes and speaking without notes: Ibid., 523.

135 "They gave Willie all sorts of trinkets": Jacobson interview.

135 later noted that as a result of this comment: Lang and Simon, 131.

135 "I find Willie always a far cry": Jacobson interview.

135 "Absolutely, it was special": Matlack interview.

136 Mays, who a week earlier: "'Maybe I'll Cry Tomorrow,' Says Mays," *New York Times*, September 21, 1973.

136 but quoth Yogi: Rosengren, 223. (Original Berra quote: "We're the only club that hasn't had a hot streak. Maybe we're gonna have one now. It's never over until it's over.")

136 "The Mets were in a strangely relaxed mood": Koppett, *The New York Mets*, 304.

139 "The batting of glove on the leg": Matlack interview.

139 "I just remember him having told Ralph Kiner": Rose interview.

139 "That was my eleventh year": Staub interview.

11. "AND A FIGHT BREAKS OUT!"

143 "For some reason": Joseph Durso, "Mets Open Playoffs Today, Banking on Pitching to Foil Reds," *New York Times*, October 6, 1973.

143 "If my shoulder is tender": Joseph Durso, "Seaver Is Doubtful on Starting Playoffs," *New York Times*, October 3, 1973.

143 A couple of days later: Rosengren, 243.

143 "Once we get in the shadows": Arthur Daley, "Shadows and Substance," *New York Times*, "Sports of the Times," October 7, 1973.

144 "It was a masterful job of pitching": Matlack interview.

144 "It wasn't like you're trying to pitch a shutout": Ibid.

144 received some promising intel: Ibid.

145 a less-than-neighborly meeting: Harrelson interview.

145 "He and Tommy Helms": Ibid.

146 "I got the ball and threw it": Ibid.

146 Ringside announcer Bob Murphy: 1973 National League Championship Series Highlights, www.youtube.com/watch?v=Xk7Ma8eDn5U.

146 "The crowd screamed, obviously": Staub interview.

146 "I don't think I had seen it start instantly": Interview with Jerry Koosman, July 10, 2011.

146 "I saw Pete hit him [Harrelson] pretty good": Garrett interview.

147 "Yeah, I like seeing replays of that": Theodore interview.

147 "We opened the gates there at Shea": Hodges interview.

147 "Buddy and I are probably the two smallest guys": Capra interview.

148 "Truth be known, I wasn't even there": Matlack interview.

148 "It was like a parachute coming down on the three of us": Interview with Bob Heussler, March 26, 2012.

149 Sparky Anderson said he wasn't going to let his team: Joseph Durso, "Mets Win, 9 to 2, As Fight Erupts; Lead Playoff, 2-1," *New York Times*, October 9, 1973.

149 "I didn't pick it up, but there was a Jack Daniels bottle": Interview with Pete Flynn, August 23, 2009.

150 "We'd been talking about Willie and Yogi": Red Smith, "Feeney's Peace Party Calms Left-Field Stands," *New York Times*, October 9, 1973.

150 "The players went out there and talked to them": Flynn interview.

150 "I can remember holding up the peace sign": Heussler interview.

151 "Rose is doing long toss in the bullpen": Ibid.

151 "We couldn't believe it": Ibid.

152 After the game, Seaver effusively praised his catcher: WOR-TV Postgame 1973 NLCS audio, www.youtube.com/watch?v=DxzoEUeA7QA&feature=related.

152 "Vice President Spiro Agnew resigned today": ABC News Video, October 10, 1973, http://abcnews.go.com/Archives/video/oct-10-1973-vp-agnew-resigns-11095879.

153 In the midst of hearing oral arguments: Brad Snyder, *A Well-Paid Slave*, 288.

153 "the Harry Parker of Jewish holidays": Prince, *Faith and Fear in Flushing*, 49–50.

154 Half of his mind focused on Bob Murphy's voice: Interview with Greg Prince, July 24, 2012.

154 the throng on Fifth Avenue and 56th Street: Fred Ferreth, "Met City Explodes With Joy," *New York Times*, October 11, 1973.

154 and Payson, who'd brought him back to New York: Hirsch, 524.

154 "Spiro Agnew resigns as Vice President": Einstein, *Willie's Time*, 338.

155 "I'm very emotional about a lot of things": 1973 World Series Preview, Interview by Lindsey Nelson.

155 Even Seaver yelled at the crowd: Murray Chass, "For the Fans, Game Was Over Before the Last Out," *New York Times*, October 11, 1973.

155 His mind wasn't on the bases-loaded, one-out jam: 1973 World Series Preview, Interview by Lindsey Nelson.

156 "It's the only cap I have right now": Chass, "For the Fans, Game Was Over Before the Last Out."

157 Sirens sounded on Fifth Avenue: Ferreth, "Met City Explodes With Joy," October 11, 1973.

157 The Reds tore apart the visiting clubhouse: Rosengren, 253.

157 "It was unsettling, it was disturbing": Heussler interview.

12. THE PLAYOFF VAULT

159 At 4:00 a.m., the alarm clock sounded: Finley interview.

159 hiring and firing the volatile "Trader" Jack Lane: Green and Launius, 59–60.

160 but their families went in different directions: Finley interview.

160 Charlie had talked—that is, bribed: The Pop History Dig, "Charlie O. & the Beatles," September 17, 1964, www.pophistorydig .com/?tag=beatles-american-concert-tour-1964.

160 With the pipeline of quality ballplayers finally showing results: Finley interview.

161 "Carl was wonderful": Spander interview.

161 While working the night desk: Ibid.

161 managed the feat: Somers interview.

161 A color scheme that even the Beatles: The Beatles Ultimate Experience, Beatles Press Conference: Kansas City 9/17/1964, www.beatlesinterviews .org/db1964.0917.beatles.html.

162 the Greatest Sports Mustache of All Time: "Keith Hernandez May Lose Sports Mustache Title," September 7, 2012, www.americanmustache institute.org/blog/2012/09/keith-hernandez-may-lose-sports-mustache-title/.

162 three relocations and a merger later: The Uniform History Project: Introduction, June 9, 2009, http://theother6seconds.blogspot .com/2009/06/uniform-history-project.html.

162 There, in the vault of a relocated bank: Finley interview.

163 Despite all the care and the hush-hush nature: Ibid.

163 TV and radio color man Bill Rigney: Markusen, *Baseball's Last Dynasty*, 232.

164 The A's owner fumed: Ibid., 235.

164 Saturday, October 6, was Yom Kippur: *Our World*, "Fall 1973," ABC, Originally aired December 11, 1986, www.youtube.com/watch?v=gyUXJ4E xlh8&feature=relmfu.

164 Consumers who'd paid 38 cents per gallon. "Oct. 17, 1973: OPEC States Declare Oil Embargo," www.history.com/this-day-in-history/opec-states-declare-oil-embargo.

165 "In '71 we blew everybody away during the season": Fingers interview.

166 "Mike Cuellar seemed to have their number": Jacobson interview.

166 After the tragic killing of 11 Israeli athletes: Dan Epstein, *J Living Magazine*, "Sports," January 2012, http://trendmag2.trendoffset.com/display_article.php?id=935108.

167 "Dick Williams had complete trust and faith": Holtzman interview.

167 Campaneris was short on pithy quotes: Clark, *Champagne and Baloney*, 170.

168 "That got our attention": Bando interview.

169 "We saw it as a compliment": Finley interview.

13. SCAPEGOAT BY THE THROAT

171 "Will the real New York Mets stand up": ESPN Classic—NBC Broadcast of World Series: Game One, October 13, 1973.

171 "Yes, we're better": Ibid.

171 "Anybody who says they worked in the big leagues": Interview with Monte Moore, April 20, 2012.

171 Because the A's said the marauding fans: Ron Fimrite, "Bufoonery Rampant," *Sports Illustrated*, October 22, 1973.

171 The biggest hand in the pregame introductions: Broadcast of Game One.

173 "He fooled me": interview with Bert Campaneris.

173 Joe Rudi, considered in the Mets scouting reports: Broadcast of Game One.

173 After the game, Williams said: Ibid.

173 a "bullpen in himself": Ron Bergman, *Oakland Tribune*, October 22, 1972.

173 "You don't see guys going out there, today": Fingers interview.

174 the fewest by a team since: Broadcast of Game One.

174 the uniform greeted the players: Bando interview.

175 the Northern Californian term: ESPN Classic—NBC Broadcast of World Series: Game Two, October 14, 1972.

175 "Boy, Curt, this is the thing": Ibid.

175 The former minor league infielder had started umpiring: "Augie Donatelli—A Major League Umpire at War," Baseball in Wartime Blog, http://baseballinwartime.blogspot.com/2010/01/augie-donatelli-major-league-umpire-at.html.

176 Harrelson got in the best insult: 1973 World Series (Highlight) Film: Mets vs. A's, MLB Properties.

176 After taking a slider, Mays commented to Fosse: Hirsch, 529.

176 was jumping for joy: Rose interview.

177 The manager later claimed: Williams and Plaschke, 166.

177 "It was clearly Tenace's fault": Ibid.

177   "the greatest center fielder who ever played": Ron Bergman, "Game 2 Belonged to Willie." *Oakland Tribune*, October 15, 1973.

177   finally end the longest: Broadcast of Game Two.

177   "Are you tired?": McGraw and Durso, *Screwball*, 172.

177   "Dick, we're putting Andrews on the disabled list": Williams and Plaschke, 166.

178   John Claiborne, then A's farm director: Green and Launius, 7.

178   "I should have walked out": Ibid., 9.

178   When Williams next saw Andrews: Williams and Plaschke, 167–68.

178   "At the moment I grabbed Mike's limp hand": Ibid., 168.

178   The film scheduled for the A's flight: Clark, *Champagne and Baloney*, 178.

179   but that was exactly the language used: *Oakland Tribune*, October 15, 1973.

179   "He's a professional player, and he made an error": Kranepool interview.

179   "To embarrass a guy like that for making an error": Garrett interview.

179   "One of our own was getting shafted": Bando interview.

179   "We were going to strike unless": Rudi interview.

180   Esteemed *New York Times* columnist: Red Smith, "Charlie I and His Subjects," *New York Times*, October 17, 1973.

180   Before Game Three, Dick Williams held a closed-door meeting: Williams and Plaschke, 170.

180   "We were a little shocked because nobody expected it": Interview with Darold Knowles, April 20, 2012.

180   "Maybe I tried to smoke": Hunter and Keteyian, 120–21.

181   and cheering when "Sign Man": ESPN Classic—NBC Broadcast of World Series: Game Three, October 16, 1973.

181   No one had told Hahn that the warning track: William Leggett, "Mutiny and a Bounty," *Sports Illustrated*, October 29, 1973.

181   sympathizes with Hahn: Rudi interview.

181   "McGraw might not be able to shave": Broadcast of Game Three.

182   "The Mike Andrews stuff was actually good for us": Markusen, *Baseball's Last Dynasty*, 250.

182   "Never in my wildest dreams did I think": Staub interview.

182   "I haven't played in two, three months": Theodore interview.

183   "The most amazing thing wasn't that these tough New Yorkers": Williams and Plaschke, 171.

183   "It was the coldest I had ever been at a ballpark": Rose interview.

183   Just a few nights earlier: McGraw and Durso, 177.

184   "About the only thing the A's averted": Ron Bergman, "A's Down to Last Stand," *Oakland Tribune*, October 19, 1973.

184   Already the question: Rose interview

185   While the sun: Markusen, *Baseball's Last Dynasty*, 256.

185   stenciled across the front page: *Oakland Tribune*, October 20, 1973.

185   "That's what second guessing is all about": Staub interview.

185 "Stone was funky, but he wasn't our best pitcher": Harrelson interview.

185 "I think Yogi made the right decision at the time": Garrett interview.

185 "That question has been debated for 40 years": Matlack interview.

186 on the club before any other '73 Met: Kranepool interview.

186 A's manager Dick Williams agreed: Williams and Plaschke, 171–72.

186 Asked almost 40 years later: Berra interview.

187 "It was as if he'd decided to either win": Williams and Plaschke, 172.

188 "This wasn't Tom Seaver on ability": 1973 World Series (Highlight) Film.

188 "I had known Dick for a long time": Knowles interview.

188 "Now that we've beaten Seaver": Williams and Plaschke, 172.

189 Nixon considered the information requested: Berkowitz, *Something Happened*, 23–27.

189 "The country tonight is in the midst": *The American Experience*, "The Saturday Night Massacre," PBS, www.youtube.com/watch?v=Yfnhuf-piq4&feature=related.

190 "the most traumatic government upheaval": Carroll Kilpatrick, "Nixon Forces Firing of Cox; Richardson, Ruckelhaus Quit," *Washington Post*, October 21, 1973.

190 perhaps echoing Chic Anderson's stirring call: ESPN Classic—NBC Broadcast of World Series: Game Seven, October 20, 1973.

191 With a runner on second: Campaneris interview.

191 "I was definitely surprised": Matlack interview.

191 "You knew right then": Heussler interview.

192 was pulling for the kind of ending: Thorn interview.

192 came up with Houston in the early 1960s: Staub interview.

192 "I had played every inning of every game": Garrett interview.

193 Williams had told Rudi, Bando, and Jackson: Ron Bergman, "Williams Kisses It Goodbye," *Oakland Tribune*, October 22, 1973.

193 "I told Dick two things": Green and Launius, 12.

194 in the press box but without a vote: Spander interview.

194 "In '73, I hoped to be the MVP": Campaneris interview.

194 As longtime National League home run champ: Kiner and Peary, *Baseball Forever*, 207. (Note: Ralph Kiner borrowed the saying from old Pirates teammate Fritz Ostermueller.)

EPILOGUE: AFTERMATH

197 the 120-foot-high perch: Joseph Berger, "Flushing Meadows Journal: Towers With Babel's Diversity, but a Much Happier History," *New York Times*, June 17, 2011.

197 $90,000 per year for three years: Madden, 55.

197 $20,000 more than he was getting: Ron Bergman, "Williams Kisses It Goodbye," *Oakland Tribune*, October 22, 1973.

198 in case he hadn't made himself clear: Leonard Koppett, "League Ruling Bars Yank-Williams Pact," *New York Times*, December 21, 1973.

198 The Yankees offered Findley: Markusen, *Baseball's Last Dynasty*, 264–65.

198 and even bringing in shrimp at a dollar a pop? Appel, *Pinstripe Empire*, 398–99.

198 "They spent money to bring the press out": Pepe interview.

199 (The Boss was indicted and finally entered: Madden, 63.

199 "He was a guy who was a fallback": Pepe interview.

202 "Look at some of the deals they made": Kranepool interview.

AFTER '73

205 The hat that Pedro Borbon tore with his teeth: Capra interview.

205 landed on his right shoulder after his mount slipped: Garrett interview.

206 "I would rather have guys like that who wanted to play": Kranepool interview.

207 "Imagine having the future of this kid": Broadcast of Game Seven.

207 "decidedly the best in the majors": Kent Hannon, "The Throes of Frustration," *Sports Illustrated*, September 13, 1976.

208–9 Milner stated that he received amphetamines: Hirsch, 540.

210 "I screwed up the game": Blomberg interview.

211 He was in such a hurry to get on the bus: Sims interview.

212 "I gave the ballpark the nickname of the Oakland Mausoleum": Bando interview.

213 "For a kid not to have a baseball mitt": Dennis Chanin, "Where Are They Now: Vida Blue," www.baseballsavvy.com/archive/w_vidaBlue.html.

213 "I'm not just a guy with a crazy mustache": *Late Show with David Letterman*, Top 10 Perks of Being a National Baseball Hall of Fame Member, Originally aired July 23, 2003, www.youtube.com/watch?v=2txIsLDiFeY.

214 "Charlie was the kind who would sit on a bill": Finley interview.

214 "There's not enough mustard": Reggie Jackson Quotes, www.baseball-almanac.com/quotes/quojackr.shtml.

215-16 the A's were 25 versions of himself: Williams and Plaschke, 120.

216 where he'd been cheered wildly: Rosengren, 186-87.

218 "Every year working with Steinbrenner": Appel interview.

219 "Never got caught up in that stuff": Heussler interview.

219 "There was no scrutiny back then": Marchiano interview.

220 "I've got footprints in the snow": Thorn interview.

Sources

INTERVIEWS

Marty Appel, Sal Bando, Yogi Berra, Vida Blue, Dick Bresciani, Buzz Capra, Bert Campaneris, Stanley Cohen, Dan Epstein, Rollie Fingers, Nancy Finley, Pete Flynn, Wayne Garrett, Bud Harrelson, Keith Hernandez, Bob Heussler, Paul Hirsch, Ron Hodges, Stan Isaacs, Steve Jacobson, Tommy John, Ralph Kiner, Darold Knowles, Jerry Koosman, Ed Kranepool, Sal Marchiano, Jon Matlack, Monte Moore, Phil Pepe, Fritz Peterson, Greg Prince, Bob Rose, Howie Rose, Joe Rudi, Duke Sims, Steve Somers, Art Spander, Rusty Staub, John Stearns, George Theodore, John Thorn, and Luis Torres.

BOOKS

Appel, Marty. *Munson: The Life and Death of a Yankee Captain.* New York: Doubleday, 2009.

Appel, Marty. *Now Pitching for the Yankees: Spinning the News for Mickey, Billy, and George.* Kingston, NY: Total Sports Illustrated, 2001.

Appel, Marty. *Pinstripe Empire: The New York Yankees from before the Babe to after the Boss.* New York: Bloomsbury, 2012.

Bashe, Philip. *Dog Days: The New York Yankees' Fall from Grace and Return to Glory, 1964–1976.* New York: Random House, 1994.

Berkowitz, Edward. *Something Happened: A Political and Cultural Overview of the Seventies.* New York: Columbia University Press, 2006.

Blomberg, Ron and Dan Schlossberg. *Designated Hebrew.* Champaign, IL: Sports Publishing, 2006.

Bock, Duncan and John Jordan. *The Complete Year-by-Year N.Y. Mets Fan's Almanac.* New York: Crown Publishing, 1992.

Bouton, Jim, and Leonard Schecter (ed.). *Ball Four: My Life and Hard Times Throwing the Knuckleball in the Major Leagues.* New York: World Pub. Co., 1970.

Brand, Dana. *Mets Fan.* Jefferson, NC: McFarland & Company, 2007.

Burke, Michael. *Outrageous Good Fortune.* Boston: Little, Brown and Company, 1984.

Castle, George. *When the Game Changed: An Oral History of Baseball's True Golden Age: 1969–1979.* Guilford, CT: Lyons Press, 2011.

Clark, Tom. *Champagne and Baloney: The Rise and Fall of Finley's A's.* New York: Harper & Row, 1976.

Cohen, Stanley. *A Magic Summer: The '69 Mets.* San Diego: Harcourt Brace Jovanovich Publishers, 1988.

Cohen, Stanley. *The Man in the Crowd: Confessions of a Sports Addict.* New York: Random House, 1981.

Cramer, Richard Ben. *Joe DiMaggio: The Hero's Life.* New York: Simon & Schuster, 2001.

Edelman, Rob. "M. Donald Grant." In *The Miracle Has Landed: The Amazin' Story of How the 1969 Mets Shocked the World,* ed. Matthew Silverman and Ken Samuelson. Hanover, MA: Maple Street Press, 2009.

Einstein, Charles. *Willie's Time: Baseball's Golden Age.* Carbondale, IL: Southern Illinois University Press, 2004.

Epstein, Dan. *Big Hair and Plastic Grass: A Funky Ride Through Baseball and America in the Swingin' 70s.* New York: Thomas Dunne Books, 2010.

Goldfarb, Irv. "Jerry Koosman." In *The Miracle Has Landed: The Amazin' Story of How the 1969 Mets Shocked the World,* ed. Matthew Silverman and Ken Samuelson. Hanover, MA: Maple Street Press, 2009.

Green, G. Michael and Roger D. Launius. *Charlie Finley: The Outrageous Story of Baseball's Super Showman.* New York: Walker and Company, 2010.

Hirsch, James S. *Willie Mays: The Life, The Legend.* New York: Scribner, 2010.

Hunter, Jim "Catfish" and Armen Keteyian. *Catfish: My Life in Baseball.* New York: McGraw-Hill Book Company, 1988.

Kanarek, Jacob. *From First to Worst: The New York Mets, 1973–1977.* Jefferson, NC: McFarland & Company, 2008.

Killen, Andreas. *1973 Nervous Breakdown: Watergate, Warhol, and the Birth of Post-Sixties America.* New York: Bloomsbury, 2006.

Kiner, Ralph, and Danny Peary. *Baseball Forever: Reflections of 60 Years in the Game.* Chicago: Triumph Books, 2004.

Koppett, Leonard. *The New York Mets* (revised edition). New York: Collier Books, 1974.

Kuhn, Bowie, and Marty Appel (Editorial Assistant). *Hardball: The Education of a Baseball Commissioner.* New York: McGraw-Hill Book Company, 1988.

Lang, Jack and Peter Simon. *The New York Mets: Twenty-Five Years of Baseball Magic.* New York: Henry Holt and Company, 1986.

Lockwood, Kathleen. *Major League Bride: An Inside Look at Life Outside the Ballpark.* Jefferson, NC: McFarland & Company, 2010.

MacCambridge, Michael. *America's Game: The Epic Story of How Pro Football Captured the Nation.* New York: Anchor Books, 2005.

Madden, Bill. *Steinbrenner: The Last Lion of Baseball.* New York: Harper, 2010.

Markusen, Bruce. *Baseball's Last Dynasty: Charlie Finley's Oakland A's.* Indianapolis: Masters Press, 1998.

McGraw, Tug, and Joseph Durso. *Screwball.* Boston: Houghton Mifflin Company, 1974.

McGraw, Tug, and Don Yaeger. *Ya Gotta Believe!* New York: New American Library, 2004.

McKelvey, G. Richard. *All Bat, No Glove: A History of the Designated Hitter.* Jefferson, NC: McFarland & Company, 2004.

Neill, Andy and Robert Kent. *Anyway, Anyhow, Anywhere: The Complete Chronicle of the Who, 1958–1978.* New York: Friedman/Fairfax Publishers, 2002.

Okrent, Daniel. "Remembering the Deal of the Century: When Yankees Pitchers Swapped Wives." In *Damn Yankees: Twenty-Four Major League Writers on the World's Most Loved (and Hated) Team.* Edited by Rob Fleder. New York: Ecco, 2012.

Palmer, Pete, et al. *The ESPN Pro Football Encyclopedia* (second edition). New York: Sterling, 2007.

Perry, Gaylord, and Bob Sudyk. *Me & The Spitter: An Autobiographical Confession.* New York: Signet, 1974.

Peterson, Fritz. *Mickey Mantle Is Going to Heaven.* Denver: Outskirts Press, 2009.

Peterson, John E. *The Kansas City Athletics: A Baseball History, 1954–1967.* Jefferson, NC: McFarland & Company, 2003.

Prince, Greg. *Faith and Fear in Flushing: An Intense Personal History of the New York Mets.* New York: Skyhorse Publishing, 2009.

Rosengren, John. *Hammerin' Hank, George Almighty and the Say Hey Kid: The Year That Changed Baseball Forever.* Naperville, IL: Sourcebooks, 2008.

Snyder, Brad. *A Well-Paid Slave: Curt Flood's Fight for Free Agency in Professional Sports.* New York, Plume, 2006.

Thorn, John. *Baseball in the Garden of Eden: The Secret History of the Early Game.* New York: Simon & Schuster, 2011.

Thorn, John, Pete Palmer, and Michael Gershman. *Total Baseball* (seventh edition). Kingston, NY: Total Sports Publishing, 2001.

Wendel, Tim. *Summer of '68: The Season That Changed Baseball and America Forever.* Boston: DaCapo Press, 2012.

Williams, Dick, and Bill Plaschke. *No More Mr. Nice Guy: A Life of Hardball.* San Diego: Harcourt Brace Jovanovich Publishers, 1990.

Woolum, Janet. *Outstanding Women Athletes: Who They Are and How They Influenced Sports in America,* 2nd ed. Phoenix: The Oryx Press, 1998.

PERIODICALS

1973 Official Program and Scorecard, New York Mets
1973 Official Yearbook, New York Mets
1973 World Series Souvenir Program & Scorecard
1974 New York Yankees Yearbook
1974 Official Program and Scorecard, New York Mets
1974 Scorecard and Souvenir Yearbook, Oakland A's
2010 Maple Street Press Mets Annual
Advertising Age
Baseball Digest
Boston University Law Review, Volume 90
Chicago Tribune
Columbia Journalism Review

Daily Finance
Entertainment Weekly
Hoosier Times
J Living Magazine
Milwaukee Sentinel
Ministry
Newark Star-Ledger
Newsweek
New York Daily News
New York Magazine
New York Post
New York Times
Oakland Tribune
Pink Floyd, London: Mojo Special Editions, 2004
San Francisco Chronicle
Sporting News
Sports Illustrated
Stamford Advocate
Time
Wall Street Journal
Washington Post

WEBSITES

americanmustacheinstitute.org
baseball-almanac.com
baseball-reference.com
baseballinwartime.blogspot.com
baseballlibrary.com
baseballsavvy.com
beatlesinterviews.org
bizofbaseball.com
dailyfinance.com
elvis.com
equalrightsamendment.org
espn.com
goodreads.com
hardballtimes.com
hawes.com
history.com
imdb.com
m.kitsapsun.com
metsbythenumbers.com
momsteam.com

museum.tv
nba.com
npr.org
pbs.org
polishsportshof.com
pophistorydig.com
proleagueauthentics.com
retrosheet.org
sabr.org
secretariat.com
shermfeller.com
sss.gov
stuffnobodycaresabout.com
superseventies.com
theother6seconds.com
throughthefencebaseball.com
tias.com
timelines.ws
ultimatemets.com
ultimateyankees.com
uni-watch.com
utahutes.cstv.com
veteranshow.com
wga.org
willistower.com
worldtimeline.info
yankeestadiumseats.com

COMPACT DISCS AND DVDS

1973 Mets (Highlight) Film. Rebroadcast by SportsNet New York as *Mets Yearbook.*
1973 World Series (Highlight) Film: Mets vs. A's. MLB Properties.
ESPN Classic—NBC Broadcast of World Series: Game One, October 13, 1973.
ESPN Classic—NBC Broadcast of World Series: Game Two, October 14, 1973.
ESPN Classic—NBC Broadcast of World Series: Game Three, October 16, 1973.
ESPN Classic—NBC Broadcast of World Series: Game Seven, October 21, 1973.
The Miley Collection: Radio Broadcast, Yankees-Red Sox, April 6, 1973.
Rebels of Oakland: The A's, the Raiders, the '70s. HBO Sports Documentary, 2003.

VIDEO

1973 National League Championship Series Highlights. www.youtube.com/watch?v=Xk7Ma8eDn5U.

1973 World Series Preview, interviews with Lindsey Nelson. www.youtube.com/watch?v=ys8atAUSkaw&feature=related.

The American Experience, "The Saturday Night Massacre," PBS, 1990. www.youtube.com/watch?v=Yfnhuf-piq4&feature=related>F.

The American Experience, "Wounded Knee: We Shall Remain," PBS, 2009. www.youtube.com/watch?v=5yFr5groCJg.

Jim "Catfish" Hunter's perfect game ninth inning radio broadcast, May 6, 1968. www.youtube.com/watch?v=uKEs3EjGcOM.

Late Show with David Letterman, "Top 10 Perks of Being a National Baseball Hall of Fame Member." Originally aired, July 23, 2003. www.youtube.com/watch?v=2txIsLDiFeY.

Mickey Mantle home run in 1973 Old-Timers Game. www.youtube.com/watch?v=I9fNcMLaW_A.

"Maude's Dilemma," *Maude.* www.youtube.com/watch?v=zxy0DTMXhwY.

Don Meredith—A Legend RIP—NY Jets vs. Green Bay Packers *Monday Night Football* Intro (September 17, 1973). www.youtube.com/watch?v=6F0I6YFcDkc.

Keith Moon collapses at the Cow Palace during Who concert, 1973. www.youtube.com/watch?v=h8qm1i2f_FA.

NFL Films, Week 2, 1973, Eagles at Giants. www.youtube.com/watch?v=l1P9uhHOR7I.

Oakland A's broadcast, Comcast Sports Net California, April 21, 2012.

Our World on ABC, hosted by Linda Ellerbee and Ray Gandolf; aired December 11, 1986. www.youtube.com/watch?v=gyUXJ4Exlh8.

Morley Safer, "The Burning of Cam Ne," *Reporting America at War,* a film by Steve Ives. www.pbs.org/weta/reportingamericaatwar/reporters/safer/camne.html.

Secretariat Belmont Stakes 1973 & Extended Post Race Coverage. www.youtube.com/watch?v=cS4f6wiQJh4.

Studio 42 with Bob Costas, on MLB Network. Guest Bobby Valentine. Air date: February 13, 2012.

WOR-TV Postgame 1973 NLCS audio from YouTube. www.youtube.com/watch?v=DxzoEUeA7QA&feature=related.

Index